Stauffenberg

Claus Schenk Graf von Stauffenberg

Joachim Kramarz

Stauffenberg

The Architect of the Famous July 20th Conspiracy
to Assassinate Hitler

*Translated from the German
by R. H. Barry*

Introduction by Professor H. R. Trevor-Roper

THE MACMILLAN COMPANY, NEW YORK

First American Edition

Originally published in Germany
under the title *Claus Graf Stauffenberg*
15 November 1907-20 Juli 1944 Das Leben Eines Offiziers
© Bernard & Graefe Verlag Für Wehrwesen
Frankfurt Am Main 1965

The Macmillan Company, New York
Collier-Macmillan Canada Ltd., Toronto, Ontario

Printed in the United States of America

Contents

Introduction

H. R. TREVOR-ROPER

The history of the German resistance to Hitler is now a familiar topic. It is a tragic history of individuals who had no party behind them, and little agreement among themselves, and who yet knew that they must challenge an entrenched dictatorship, solidly based on mass support and armed for the prosecution of war. Almost all those individuals have by now received recognition. The few survivors have given their personal accounts; the papers of some of the leading figures have been published; and numerous historical studies and biographies have been written. But one man has never received the full justice that is due to him, and that man was, I believe, the most interesting, as well as the most resolute and effective, of them all. He was Claus Schenk von Stauffenberg, the Swabian aristocrat who, in the end, brought the long story to its climax: the hero (I think it can be said) of the bomb-plot of 20th July 1944.

In the long, fluctuating history of opposition, Stauffenberg is a late arrival. He only appears, it seems, for the last act. But when he appears, he instantly takes command, and with every month his command becomes more obvious. When the old opposition was broken by the arrest of its leaders, it was he who reanimated it with new courage, new ideas. When purpose flagged, it was he who overcame the prudent hesitations of some, the moral scruples of others. He was the link between the idealists of the Kreisau circle and the activists of Army Group Centre, between the social radicalism of Julius Leber and the military force of the Army General Staff. Above all, he insisted on action. There was to be no compromise, no delay: Hitler must be assassinated. On the fatal day, it was he who flew with the time-bomb to Hitler's headquarters at Rastenburg in East Prussia; he who carried the bomb in his brief-case, already ticking, into the conference-room; he who placed it under the table. Then he slipped out of the room, bluffed his way past successive guards, and flew to Berlin to take effective command of the next stage of the conspiracy: the seizure of power in the Reich. In both centres of action, at Rastenburg and in Berlin, he was the motive force: the head and the hand of the whole venture.

Of course, the venture failed, and Stauffenberg's life failed with it. But how narrowly it failed! But for a series of small accidents, it might well have succeeded, and then how different the course of history might have been! Had the conference taken place in the usual underground bunker instead of in a fragile hut above ground, the blast of the explosion would have found no escape and all present would have perished. Even as it was, had Colonel Brandt not casually shoved Stauffenberg's brief-case further under the table, against the upright support, thus accidentally shielding him from the blast, Hitler himself would probably have been killed. And even if Hitler had survived, the political conspiracy might still have succeeded had the telephone communications from Rastenburg been effectively stopped. A military junta might then have seized the initiative, overthrown the Nazi regime, and offered peace before the Russians had crossed the Vistula or the Western Allies had advanced beyond Normandy. Such a change had already been carried out in Italy. Who can tell what might have happened had it been repeated in Germany? Incalculable destruction would have been avoided. The map of Europe might well look very different today.

In view of the huge consequences which hung on the events of that day, it may amaze us that so much was allowed to depend on one man. Stauffenberg it seems, had to be everywhere at once: in Berlin, to direct the conspiracy; in Rastenburg, to kill Hitler; in Berlin again, to direct the military *coup*. This personal indispensability is even more extraordinary when we think of his personal handicap. For Stauffenberg, by that time, was terribly crippled. Badly wounded in Africa in 1943, he had lost his left eye, his whole right hand, and three fingers of his left. If he was both the head and the hand of the venture, he was a head with only one eye and a left hand with only two fingers. In spite of this, he remained essential. Partly it was an unfortunate accident: he alone of the conspirators, thanks to his position as chief of staff of the Replacement Army, had direct access to Hitler's conference. But there was also another reason. He was essential because of his extraordinary personality.

At every point that personality comes through to us. We only have to read the diaries and papers of the other conspirators to see it. Whenever Stauffenberg appears in them, an electric impulse is felt, new positions are taken up. Many of the older conspirators disliked him, and he them. He would have nothing to do with tainted figures like Johannes Popitz, the former finance minister. Carl Goerdeler, who regarded himself as the only politician among the conspirators, their future Chancellor, saw Stauffenberg only as 'a cranky obstinate fellow who wanted to play politics' – i.e. to infringe his own monopoly. Goerdeler would have spared Hitler's life, compromised with his crimes, and saved as much as possible of his work. Stauffenberg would have none of this: his Chancellor would have been the socialist Leber. Another whom Stauffenberg refused to trust, and who therefore hated him with a neurotic, personal hatred, was Hans Bernd Gisevius, a former police official who joined the conspirators. Surviving, Gisevius was the first to publish a widely translated account of the German opposition, and was thus able to avenge his exclusion by belittling a far bigger man. However, Gisevius' spite is self-correcting: his caricature of Stauffenberg has been universally rejected by historians.

But if some feared and distrusted this radical new leader, others were inspired by him. They saw in him the man of action in whom the native hue of resolution was not sicklied o'er by the pale cast of thought. We see this in the moving account of the Tresckow circle in Fabian von Schlabrendorff's *Offiziere gegen Hitler*, as published in 1946. We see it, against its contrasting background of indecision, in that faithful mirror of the long agony of the German Opposition, the Diary of Ulrich von Hassell. It was in November 1943 after years of disappointment and disillusion with Goerdeler, Schacht and Popitz, Brauchitsch and Halder, that Hassell first met Stauffenberg and was deeply impressed by him. To Hassell, Stauffenberg represented "the younger generals", "the younger group", absolutely opposed to the old compromising figures: he was the man of decision who would at last cut through the glutinous web of their recurrent second thoughts. Even the Nazis recognized the character of the man as they blackened it. One of the most interesting documents on the events of the 20th July is an account afterwards drawn up by an SS officer, Georg Kiessel. Kiessel described Stauffenberg as "a spirit of fire, fascinating and inspiring all who came in touch with him", "a truly universal man", a revolutionary aristo- crat, careless of himself, without a trace of vanity or ambition – that is perhaps somewhat excessive – who sought to unite "ethical socialism with Christian tradition". The same picture of relentless energy and irresistible persuasive power emerges from the long series of reports submitted regularly by the Gestapo to Bormann and Hitler. Even in the fragmentary record of the grim People's Court we sense a note of involuntary respect when the voice of the infamous prosecutor, Roland Freisler, rises to cast the customary abuse on that hated name.

What lay at the base of Stauffenberg's compulsive personality? Such a question is never easy to answer. Though everyone who met him recognized its force, there was no agreement on its real motivation. Some said that he was an ex-Nazi. He was captivated by Hitler's social views, says Kiessel, and often known ironically as "the Nazi count". Undoubtedly, like many of his class, he gave at least a qualified approval to the movement at first. Herr Kramarz admits that he welcomed the harmony of classes which it seemed to offer and even the purge of 30 June 1934 which can now be seen as a fatal surrender. But he disposes – effectively it seems – of the story that Stauffenberg, in uniform, headed a crowd demonstrating in favour of the Nazi "seizure of power". Others saw him as a romantic reactionary. The resentful Gisevius portrayed him as a mere *condottiere*, a radical, ambitious adventurer who looked eastwards, towards Bolshevism, for his last inspiration. Only Schlabrendorff, among the early post-war writers, found a more positive intellectual quality. Stauffenberg, he wrote, fitted into no easy category. He stood apart from his contemporaries. Military life, for all his brilliance as a soldier, never satisfied him. In his younger days, says Schlabrendorff, "his spiritual quest had led him into the circle of the poet Stefan George" and to that master he remained always true. "The intellectual and spiritual world of Stefan George dominated him. He knew many of his poems by heart." It is Schlabrendorff who tells us how Stauffenberg would win his friends over to conspiracy by reciting Stefan George's famous poem "Antichrist".' Herr Kramarz completes the evidence. To me some of the most interesting passages in his book are those which describe Stauffenberg's relations with Stefan George and his "circle".

Stauffenberg was in fact not merely an able officer and a resourceful conspirator. He was an intellectual in action. The clarity of purpose which he showed, and which he imposed upon the other opponents of Hitler, sprang from a positive philosophy, spiritually generated, intellectually tested. When he had once decided that Hitler was not merely leading Germany to defeat but was the Antichrist who must be destroyed, no prudential consideration could modify that conviction or change its logical consequence. It was not Alamein or Stalingrad but the fundamental immorality of Nazism, as shown especially by German policy in Russia during the year of victory, in 1941–2, that had decided him. Therefore he had nothing but contempt for those fair-weather military conspirators whose opposition varied with time and circumstance. Already by 1942 his mind was made up. To those who said that the Führer must be warned first, his reply was clear: "the point is not to tell him but to put an end to him, and I am prepared to do that." "Is there no officer in the Führer's headquarters," he cried one day in Russia, "capable of taking his revolver to the brute?" When he returned from Africa, mutilated by his wounds, he believed that Providence had saved him for the act and he resolved to do it. Some fellow-conspirators feared the popular verdict. Would not such an act be represented as treachery, a stab in the back? Stauffenberg rejected such egotism. "It is now time that something was done," he replied. "He who has the courage to do something must do so in the knowledge that he will go down to history as a traitor. But if he does not do it, he will be a traitor to his own conscience."

Philosophy in action, the fusion of thought and action in one man, is always an exhilarating spectacle. No one in the German opposition showed it so completely as Stauffenberg. On one hand we see a gallery of admirable men who had the courage to oppose but lacked the temperament, or the opportunity, to act. Such were the men of the "Kreisau circle" of Count Helmut von Moltke and many others who suffered for their thoughts alone. On the other hand we see the generals who had the opportunity but hesitated to use it, because the moral basis of action was lacking. Always they interposed political or tactical objections: the way was not clear or the time was not ripe. Between these two stood "the younger generals" – or, more often, colonels – who knew what to do and were ready to do it. Among them Stauffenberg was unique in unity of purpose. Because of this quality, he ended as the hero, and one of the first victims, of 20th July.

Had the plot succeeded, he would be remembered as the man who destroyed Hitler and perhaps brought the war to an end. Whether he would even then have succeeded in controlling the events he had launched is, of course, another matter. Perhaps, like so many other idealists, he would have been swept aside by the torrent. But in fact he was never put to that test. Before 20th July was out, the news of Hitler's survival came through. The fair-weather conspirators veered round and sought hastily to bury the evidence of their own complicity. On the orders of his own commanding officer, General Fromm, Stauffenberg and his three immediate supporters were shot in the courtyard of the German War Ministry. Thus Fromm secured a respite for himself. It did not last long. A few weeks later he too would be shot in Hitler's prison.

After the failure of the Plot and its fearful aftermath, many worthy Germans cast the blame for the disaster on Stauffenberg. If only those intemperate young men had not rushed in, they said, they themselves, the real, responsible opponents of Hitler, would have matured their slower, more prudent plans for a more successful transfer of power. I confess that when I heard this argument – and I heard it often in and after 1945, from Germans who could produce very little evidence of other than retrospective disloyalty – I was roused to contempt, and my interest in Stauffenberg, as the man who was not afraid to think and speak and act clearly, was proportionately increased. I wished to discover more about him. But it was not easy. Documentary evidence seemed not to exist. Since Stauffenberg was killed before the Gestapo could secure him, he was neither questioned nor tried. His own papers were seized and have never been seen again. One day in 1947 I went to Überlingen, on Lake Constance, to visit Stauffenberg's surviving brother Alexander (for his other brother, Berthold, was executed in the great purge which followed 20th July). There I met also Professor

Rudolf Fahrner, the friend and counsellor of Claus von Stauffenberg – "one of the few survivors", as Herr Kramarz says, "who could give some account of political discussions with Stauffenberg". From them I heard much about Stauffenberg's political plans, his faith in Julius Leber, his social philosophy. But the missing papers have not been found, or released, and in the twenty years since 1944 no documented biography has appeared. The gap was noted by the ablest English historian of the military opposition to Hitler. "A properly documented biographical study of Claus von Stauffenberg," wrote Sir John Wheeler-Bennett in 1953, "would provide both a valuable contribution to history and a most repaying undertaking". One day, perhaps, the material will be complete. Meanwhile we must be grateful to Herr Kramarz who has supplied the gap and given us a clear personal portrait of the man who, in our century, had both the conviction and the courage of the great tyrannicides of the past.

Foreword

In his book on Carl Goerdeler, Gerhard Ritter was able to say that Goerdeler's voluminous writings had been available to him. Stauffenberg's biographer is, however, in an exactly opposite situation, for Stauffenberg, as the principal actor in the events of 20 July 1944, was an immediate target for the Gestapo. Both his Berlin apartment and his family home in Bamberg were searched at once, and even the smallest scrap of written evidence was confiscated.

The confiscated material has never reappeared. Possibly, it still exists in the archives of some Iron Curtain power. But Iron Curtain publications on the German resistance in general—and Stauffenberg in particular—give no evidence of any sources so far unknown to the western historian, and enquiries made of the occupation authorities in the Soviet zone were unsuccessful. Research in the West German archives—the Bundesarchiv (Military Section) in Koblenz and the Institut für Zeitgeschichte in Munich—was equally fruitless. There was no material on Stauffenberg in either place.

The only documents of a personal nature which I could find are one or two letters, one postcard, a logistics order of the French campaign period, a typewritten Staff College essay with notes and corrections in manuscript, and a copy of a lecture on "Home Defense against Enemy Parachute Troops".

At the National Archives in Alexandria, Virginia, U.S.A., I was able to study valuable material from captured files stored there on microfilm. Among the most important documents was the 1942 war diary of the General Staff organization section, which gave much information both on Stauffenberg's activities and on the background to the Russian campaign. And from the Military Research Office in Freiburg, I obtained photostatic copies of orders drafted by Stauffenberg when head of Group II in the organization section. No other original sources were available.

Naturally the documents I did find give little information about Stauffenberg's connection with the resistance. It was hardly to be expected that written material on this subject by Stauffenberg would be found. His contribution to the conspiracy consisted primarily of the military planning of the coup d'état, the written results of which were the "Valkyrie" orders and the supplementary instructions. His contribution to the political planning of the resistance was primarily oral, and almost all the participants in the conversations concerned are now dead. One of the few survivors who could give some account of political discussions with Stauffenberg is Prof. Rudolf Fahrner. Other information has been gleaned from the literature already available concerning the resistance, and in particular, from Stauffenberg's friends and relatives.

There are, of course, the Gestapo reports prepared for Hitler after 20 July 1944, initially daily, and subsequently at greater intervals. There are also records of the results of the interrogations. As source material these are highly problematical. They can not be discarded, but they have to be cross-checked with care.

Verbatim extracts from the interrogations are given only on very rare occasions, and then usually only in the form of individual sentences. But one can never be sure that the sense of a sentence taken in isolation is its true one. In addition, the Gestapo reports are coloured by their authors, who in many instances were clearly trying to present the accused in the most unfavourable possible light, and to produce proof of their moral degradation. It is comparatively easy to see through this layer of denigration and vilification. It is far less easy to establish the truth about the thinking and the motives of those concerned. Memoranda or statements concerning the political intentions of the conspirators are not in general given textually in the reports, but are merely summarized by Gestapo officials. Finally, the reports contain definite untruths originating from the accused themselves, many of whom were trying to protect either themselves or their friends by false statements. The Gestapo reports can therefore only be used with considerable caution, and in particular, they have to be carefully checked insofar as the political thinking of the accused is concerned.

The most valuable sources of information for this biography were Stauffenberg's friends and those who served with him. In most cases they were prepared to put their recollections on paper. In other instances I was able to arrange interviews, of which I kept notes.

Utilization of sources of this nature, however, presents difficulties. Twenty and in some cases thirty years have now gone by since the events with which we are concerned. Frequently, therefore, all that people could remember was a general picture of Stauffenberg's personality. Concrete supporting detail was lacking. A second problem was posed by the danger that now that Stauffenberg has become an historical figure, the picture of him remaining in people's minds may have become unconsciously idealized. I have accordingly not reproduced statements which amounted only to vague and exaggerated praise. One impression, however, stands out from all the statements of those who knew Stauffenberg, and the unanimity of the statements is such that there can be no question of panegyrics based on hindsight: Stauffenberg was a man whose personality continuously excited admiration and who won the confidence both of his fellow officers and his superiors.

Because the material I have collected has in most cases been written specifically for the purposes of this book, I have made considerable use of direct quotations, to preserve the full effect of the statements concerned, and to give the reader the advantage of my sources in the original.

The assembly of the material took several years, and although by no means all those questioned are included in the list at the end of the book, there may still be people who knew Stauffenberg but whom I did not come across during my researches. Any new suggestions or any further assistance will be gratefully accepted.

My thanks are due to all those whose contributions have made the publication of this biography possible. First, I would thank Frau Gräfin von Stauffenberg, without whose generous assistance this book could not have been written. Then I would like to thank Dr. Eberhard

Zeller for his help in reading the manuscript. Finally, all my thanks to my colleague Dr. Helmuth Rönnefarth; his profound knowledge of the military material, his help in discovering important sources, and his readiness to check my drafts contributed greatly to the completion of this book.

Joachim Kramarz
Berlin-Wilmersdorf, August 1965

Preface

"A very small clique of ambitious, unscrupulous, criminal, and stupid officers has forged a plot to eliminate me, and at the same time, exterminate the highest level staff of the German Wehrmacht."

This sentence from the speech broadcast by Adolf Hitler over all German radio networks during the night 20–21 July 1944 set the tone for all National Socialist references to the members of the German resistance. Hitler's disciples were only too ready to follow his lead. Martin Bormann spoke of Stauffenberg as "the meanest of worms"; the foreign minister, von Ribbentrop, called him "an intellectually subnormal creature in colonel's uniform"; and Göring declared he was part of "a miserable clique." In a speech by the Reichsführer SS, Himmler, the world at large was told that the bodies of those executed would be burned and their ashes scattered to the four winds. Himmler added that Göring's reaction had been: "Ordinary land is too good for them; scatter them in some sewage farm."[1]

Through this crude but effective form of vilification the National Socialist leaders succeeded in suppressing any psychological reaction the attempted coup might have provoked. Who was to know that just before 20 July Himmler himself had thought Stauffenberg suitable for the post of head of the General Staff operations section? Who was to know that in the Gestapo reports on the 26 August interrogations Stauffenberg was described as having "a remarkable gift of oratory and a fascinating ability to captivate others"?[2]

The National Socialist leaders concentrated their venom around the fact that the central figure in the attempted revolt was an aristocrat and that the circle of followers he had gathered around him was

equally composed of aristocrats. It is true that on 24 July 1944 Bormann
warned against any temptation to attack or insult the aristocracy as
such. But this was a mere tactical manoeuvre to avoid an internal
political crisis. The National Socialists were determined that one day
they would sweep away the entire aristocracy.[3]

A pointer to National Socialist intentions was the reaction of Bormann, the "Führer's secretary," to a letter dated 22 July 1944. The
writer was one of the regime's more pedestrian ideologists, and the
letter requested Bormann to allocate paper for a new edition of the
Gothaischen Genealogischen Taschenbuch, the *Who's Who* of the German
nobility. Bormann answered the letter by telling the writer to "reflect
upon the basic issues." For, Bormann said, "at this terrible, shattering
moment, when all are beset by anxiety for our one and only Führer,"
his (Bormann's) own thought was that the only use for such a *Who's
Who* in National Socialist "political personality work" was as a register
of criminals. The aristocracy, he went on, had shown itself to be a
cancer in the body of the nation. "This obsolete stratum of society, this
class of pseudo-leaders which over the last three centuries has repeatedly
proved itself a genealogical abortion, this sort of aristocrat rash or
intellectual eczema from which the nation suffers, still in large measure
governs society and exerts considerable influence over numerous factors
and conditions governing the implementation of the will of the
nation."[4]

There is little doubt of the reason for this National Socialist hatred
of the German aristocracy. The Nazi leaders knew that they could not
change the traditional outlook of the aristocracy and that the aristocracy would not submit without a struggle to the Führer's totalitarian
state.

And they were right. The motive behind Stauffenberg's resolve to
undertake a coup d'état against Hitler and his regime and to make the
assassination attempt himself was neither ambition nor self-interest[5]—
had he been a conformist, he could have satisfied both. At the root of
his decision was that which has always animated the best of the German
aristocracy: a sense of special responsibility for the welfare of the nation
as a whole.

I

Family and Early Years

Claus Philipp Maria Schenk Graf (Count) von Stauffenberg was born at Jettingen in Bavaria on 15 November 1907, the third son of Graf Alfred Schenk von Stauffenberg. His brothers, Berthold and Alexander, were twins, two years older than Claus.[1]

The family belonged to the old Swabian nobility. Stauffenberg Castle, from which the name originated is now a ruin. It lies not far from Hechingen. The earliest known member of the family is Hugo von Stophenberg, referred to in a document dated 21 August 1262. From 1382, starting with Hans Schenk von Stoffenberg, the line can be traced unbroken.[2]

Claus's great-grandfather Freiherr Franz Ludwig von Stauffenberg was made hereditary counsellor to the King of Bavaria and created Graf (Count) by Ludwig II in 1874. This honour was not, however, granted by the King with any good will nor accepted with any gratitude. Freiherr von Stauffenberg was far too self-willed for the King's liking. When Stauffenberg's seventieth birthday came and some mark of royal favour was obviously due, the chancellery enquired what form of recognition he would prefer. He replied, "Anything you like—except an additional title." This gave the King the opportunity to signify his esteem in the manner least acceptable to the recipient—whom he at once made a count.[3]

Claus's father, Graf Alfred Schenk von Stauffenberg, spent many years in a high official position—senior marshal of the court to the King of Württemberg. In 1918 the monarchy ended, and this office lapsed. However, after his abdication King Wilhelm II of

Württemberg appointed Graf Stauffenberg his general plenipotentiary and president of his Chamber of Revenues. Duke Philipp of Württemberg,[4] son of the last pretender to the throne paid this tribute to Graf Alfred von Stauffenberg:

> He was an outstanding marshal of the court and a most faithful servant of the King. In the sad days of November 1918 he was the only man who did not lose his head like everybody else; he supervised the move of the King and Queen to Bebenhausen; he thought of everything and, more important still, of the future. During the violent revolutionary period he put himself selflessly and whole-heartedly at the service of his master; he risked his own life and future and that of his family; he was a true nobleman. . . . On the death of the King on 2 October 1921 my father confirmed him in his office as president of the Court Chamber and also as his plenipotentiary. He remained in these offices until the spring of 1928, when, for reasons of age, he went into honourable retirement, not, however, before completing the difficult settlement negotiations between the House and the Republic of Württemberg initiated during the King's lifetime and on the King's instructions.[5]

Theodor Pfizer, an old family friend who was at school and college with the Stauffenberg brothers, described Graf Alfred as follows:

> He was a devout but not political Catholic; he looked and was a conservative aristocrat; he was an expert on the protocol of official functions and on court ceremonial, adept at the arrangement of festivities but equally efficient in the day-to-day practicalities of life. He would have nothing to do with sentimentality, which drew from him good-humoured sarcasm. He was a first-class handyman who could repaper a room, rewire a house, and repair furniture. He loved the garden of his estate at Lautlingen and would weed the paths, cultivate his roses, and prune his fruit trees; in spite of the severe Alpine weather, he even managed to grow artichokes.[6]

When she first joined the family, Claus's mother was taken aback by the habits of her husband and his brothers. Instead of normal conversation, they used a series of short growling noises, a peculiar method of communication for which the family expression was "signalling."[7] To some extent Claus von Stauffenberg inherited these uncouth and unconventional ways. One of his later divisional commanders said that he bothered little about haircuts, shaving, or even the correct fit of his uniform. A fellow staff officer stated that he "did not care what other people looked like."[8]

Claus's mother, Caroline Gräfin von Stauffenberg (nee Üxküll), had none of the practical ability or energy of her husband. Theodor Pfizer, now mayor of Ulm and a frequent visitor to Lautlingen until the Countess's death, describes her thus:

> She was the exact opposite of the Count in that she remained entirely divorced from the practicalities of life; she would deal with day-to-day matters with such charming naïveté that the resulting situations were frequently excruciatingly comic. Whenever possible she would escape from the constraints of court life and take refuge in her own world of Goethe, Shakespeare, and the contemporary poets. When, after 20 July 1944, she was kept in solitary confinement for several months and initially was not allowed books, she would repeat from memory long passages from Goethe lyrics, Hamlet and Faust. Although for years she was lady-in-waiting to the Queen, and therefore fully *au fait* with court ritual, she herself admitted that she never overcame a certain shyness; although always self-possessed even in the most awkward situations, she was never entirely at ease.[9]

The Stauffenberg sons had the artistic abilities which ran in the Üxküll family. Up to the time he left school Claus von Stauffenberg was proposing to study architecture and from time to time dabbled with the idea of becoming a musician. He played the cello and would practice with his brothers, Berthold on the piano and Alexander on the violin. They even gave little public concerts with some of their schoolfellows. He gave up the idea of studying music, however, when he came to realize that he would never get beyond a certain level. Later he gave up his music altogether; even his wife, Nina Gräfin von Stauffenberg, never heard him play. His view was that it was no good dabbling in music; if anyone wanted to play an instrument, he should either do it well or give it up altogether; so, since he had not the time to devote himself intensively to music, he gave it up.[10]

Claus von Stauffenberg spent his childhood and adolescence in Stuttgart. While his father was still marshal of the court the family lived in the "old castle," the fortress of the counts and dukes of Württemberg, a massive, towered Renaissance building where the family had a roomy apartment on the second floor. Claus went to the Eberhard-Ludwigs School in Stuttgart, a school with hundreds of years of tradition behind it.[11] The tone of the school was humanist, and Stauffenberg developed a special leaning towards the classics. Even after joining the army he would often read classical works, and he took a great interest in problems of translation.

A number of questions need to be answered at this point: What was the effect upon Stauffenberg of the society in which he grew up? of his family? and of the atmosphere of the Württemberg court? What influence did the traditional surroundings of his early years exert upon him? How much store did he set by the social milieu into which he was born?

According to Nina von Stauffenberg, both "the times and their mode of life" were calculated to reinforce the parents' sense of membership in the aristocracy.[12] Their conservative class-consciousness was not, however, inherited by their sons, though the latters' outlook on life was naturally influenced by the fact that they were of noble birth. The parents insisted upon proper recognition of their rank and position; the sons, however, considered the state into which they had been born as laying upon them a special responsibility rather than conferring upon them any particularly exalted social status. Stauffenberg did feel that he was a member of an elite class, but for that very reason, he considered himself called upon to carry responsibility. His birth and upbringing were no doubt at the root of this trait in his character, but to those around him his self-confidence and powers of decision gave the impression of a personality at peace with itself rather than of any consciousness of rank.

Colonel General Halder, the future chief of staff of the army, referred to Stauffenberg as a "natural commander," and many others, both superiors and fellow officers, thought likewise. To select a single appreciation from many: "Stauffenberg was a born leader who from his earliest years had been accustomed to make up his own mind, to get his views accepted, and to take the lead (or rather to be under an obligation to do so, which in his eyes came to the same thing). This capacity for leadership was a function neither of rank, position nor birth; he had not 'acquired' it during his service; it was basic to his nature and a natural attribute of his character."[13]

A friend of Stauffenberg's recalled a conversation in which the question of property, and particularly of old, inherited family estates, came up. Although a great country lover, Stauffenberg gave it as his view that possession of land was only a means to an end—to ensure to the family a sufficient standard of living to enable them to give their sons a good training in the services, the civil service, or civilian life. There were more important duties, he went on, than looking after an inherited family estate. For him the most worthy task was service to the community.[14]

The Württemberg monarchy was overthrown in 1918 and a republic proclaimed. For the Stauffenberg family this entailed moving from the "old castle" to a smaller official residence belonging to the Royal Chamber of Revenues.

During the next few years the youth of Germany went through a kind of spiritual breakdown. With the collapse of the conservative order of society, the new-fangled artistic and political ideas which had been developing prior to the war took the young by storm. From time to time there were disagreements within the Stauffenberg family; the father clung to his traditional notions, whereas for the sons new prospects were opening up. The old man carried his conservatism so far that he refused to go to the Royal Theatre, now in the possession of the republican government, in spite of the fact that the Stuttgart theatre of the twenties maintained a remarkably high artistic level and Fritz Busch was director of the opera.

The old man did not, however, compel his sons to follow his line. They were fully at liberty to go to the local theatre, and this they did very frequently, for at this particular period they had a theatre craze. They took part in school amateur theatricals—Claus von Stauffenberg took the part of Stauffacher in *William Tell*; and in the Stauffenberg home they played the fourth act of Shakespeare's *Julius Caesar* with Berthold as Caesar's ghost, Alexander as Brutus, and Claus as Lucius.[15]

The disappearance of social barriers in the post-war world led to a revival of the youth movement which had developed in pre-war years as a kind of protest by the young against the constraints of the adult world. Berthold and Claus, the latter frequently hampered by bad health, joined a group of these new pioneers.[16]

They would "go out into the local mountains and woods, throw spears, read Stefan George's *Stern des Bundes* by the light of their campfire, and sing folksongs." Theodor Pfizer records that at Christmas 1922, "We decorated our very ordinary schoolroom ourselves. By the light of the Christmas tree we read the passage on faith, hope, and charity from the Epistle to the Corinthians, together with some poems by Hölderlin; we sang round the Christmas tree hand in hand with our teachers."[17]

The sons' adherence to the youth movement led to considerable differences of opinion between them and their father. The old Count had no use for such goings-on; the exaggeratedly emotional tone of these groups drew from him nothing but scorn. The sons, however, refused to be influenced by their father. On one occasion, for instance, they invited to the house one of the more senior youth leaders, although they knew that their father disliked having anything to do with such people. Nevertheless the old man gave orders that he should be received like any other guest. However much he may have disliked the man, the old Count was a stickler for the proprieties: a guest of his sons was a guest of the house.[18]

Stauffenberg was a home and country lover from childhood. The fact that he spent much of his time in Lautlingen no doubt had something to do with it. Lautlingen is a village in the southwest Swabian Alps, the site of the family mansion. The house was right in the middle of the village, with peasants' cottages next door. The family and the villagers formed a close-knit community. The Countess would visit the old and the sick in the village, and when, in 1933, "popular togetherness" (*Volksgemeinschaft*) became the official cry, she said that there was no need to proclaim that sort of thing in Lautlingen, since they had all been one family for ages. The sons would help with the harvest when necessary; Claus was particularly proud of the fact that he could scythe hay not only on level ground but on a slope as well. The close connection between the family and the villagers lasted long after the boys were grown up. Even today many of the people of Lautlingen are named after the Stauffenberg sons with whom their parents had played and worked.[19]

From Lautlingen the brothers would frequently hike long distances, alone or with friends. Theodor Pfizer remembers going out one day early in the morning with Claus von Stauffenberg through the sleeping village "to the Felsentor, his favourite spot, a prominent Alpine peak surrounded by the green of the beech forests, whence there was a magnificent view over the sleeping valleys below. We talked of the future, of the birth pangs of the new Germany, of the tasks of the state and the possibilities of working in it, of our hopes and desires for a career."[20]

Stauffenberg never lost his love of his home district. As soon as he entered Swabia he would at once fall back into Swabian dialect. During the war the Swabians clung together even in the most outlandish places, and Stauffenberg once remarked, "The only freemasonry Hitler has been unable to break up is that of the Swabians."[21]

The family tradition was Roman Catholic. Although the mother belonged to the evangelical church she brought up her sons as Catholics. Claus von Stauffenberg was always a faithful member of the Catholic church and clung to his religion even though he did not always follow all the church rules. He insisted that his children be brought up as Catholics, and after the National Socialists came to power, would make a point of taking them to church in his uniform.[22]

General Halder says that his "sense of responsibility towards God was a deep-rooted trait" of Stauffenberg's character. One of his friends on the General Staff said that "every now and again one would find a striking sign of Stauffenberg's religious convictions, a book or a cross for instance; he hardly ever spoke about religion, but never denied his Christianity." Another who worked with him about the same time, an evangelical, tells us that "Stauffenberg's religious convictions were strong but metaphysical; he was never dogmatic."[23] As the times changed, Stauffenberg's attitude to religion developed. Initially he was probably somewhat influenced by Stefan George, who considered Christianity out of date, but as he saw a state-inspired atheism growing up around him, his Christian convictions hardened. The more involved he became in the resistance to Hitler the more he reverted to strict churchmanship. There is a report, not altogether confirmed, that in July 1944 he went once more both to confession and communion. He laid it upon his wife to ensure that whatever happened he should not die without receiving the last sacrament.[24]

II

The Influence of Stefan George

In 1923, through Prof. Albrecht von Blumenthal, Berthold and Claus von Stauffenberg made the acquaintance of the poet Stefan George and were accepted into George's circle. The third brother, Alexander, followed them later.[1]

Stauffenberg once remarked to his wife that he had had the greatest poet of the age as his master, and indeed George considered himself not only a poet but a teacher, even going so far as to compare himself with Socrates. When asked what was his most important work, he would sometimes reply, "My friends."[2]

George exerted a powerful influence on Stauffenberg, which the latter communicated to his collaborators in the resistance. The group found their aims clarified and their actions justified through the medium of George's poems; one of these poems was the foundation of the friendship between Henning von Tresckow and Stauffenberg.[3] Talking to someone early in 1944, Stauffenberg merely quoted the poem "Anti-Christ" and then left it to the poetry to win his companion over to the plans of the resistance.[4] The idea of naming the resistance movement "Secret" or "Hidden" Germany was Stauffenberg's—and "Geheimes Deutschland" (Secret Germany) was the title of a poem in George's anthology *Das neue Reich* (*The New Reich*).[5]

George strove to teach his friends a sense of form acquired in and through poetry and regarded as a mental discipline and guide to relationships with others. At a time when spiritual, social, political, and artistic standards were collapsing, George offered "form" as an ideal, maintaining that poetry was the air which the intellectual

movement in Germany must breathe if it was to live.[6] George was a
revolutionary; he loathed the bourgeois mentality, the strict con-
ventional code of morals, and the antiquated rites of the church. But
in his eyes liberation from all this was no invitation to lawlessness and
anarchy, but carried with it the obligation to set up a new, nobler
standard of values.[7]

Stefan George's circle was often suspected of holding extraordinary
secret ceremonies and building up a somewhat unattractive cult around
him. It is true that the habits of the so-called Cosmics—a circle formed
prior to 1900 and including Karl Wolfskehl, Ludwig Klages, and
Alfred Schuler in addition to George—were distinctly peculiar. Their
object was to destroy decayed Europe and "break through to a
glowing life," and they looked to George's magic for the act of
liberation. George broke with Schuler and Klages, but the new friends
whom he gathered around him idolized him with almost religious
fervour. Among them were Friedrich Wolters and the well-known
German philologist Friedrich Gundolf. Between 1910 and 1912 these
two produced the *Jahrbuch für die geistige Bewegung* (Yearbook of the
Intellectual Movement), in which Gundolf wrote that one had to be
either pro- or anti-George and that George must be recognized as an
outstanding intellectual figure. He was extolled as a "royal priest";
both he and his work were labelled divine; Wolters referred to him as
the "creator of an intellectual empire".

These extravagances were never indulged in by George himself and
were confined solely to his friends. As time went on they disappeared,
and when, after the First World War, a new circle of young men
gathered around George, hardly a trace of them remained. There were
certain conventions which every member of the circle was expected to
observe;[8] otherwise, however, the atmosphere of this later George
circle was perfectly normal. In a lecture given some years ago
Alexander von Stauffenberg said: "Previously there was talk of a
kind of 'ritual,'—of gorgeous robes, incense, and secret ceremonies.
Whatever substance there may have been in these rumours at the
time (and they were undoubtedly exaggerated), we never detected
a trace of anything of the sort. Life went on very normally—meals,
walks in the country, discussions in the evening—all completely
simple. . . . Only for the major poetry readings was there a special

atmosphere of solemnity, and that was quite understandable."⁹

George had the misfortune to be claimed by the National Socialists as one of their intellectual elder statesmen, although in fact he never had anything whatsoever in common with them.

Prussianism was George's pet aversion, a target for his biting scorn; there was nothing he loathed more than the overbearing manners and false patriotism of those he referred to as the "censorious Prussian and his embryo, the member of a students' fraternity."¹⁰ By Prussianism, however, George did not mean some localized social order; for him Prussianism was a disease affecting the entire civilized world, but showing its most virulent symptoms—the race for "broad acres" and the worship of technical progress¹¹—in Germany.

When the First World War broke out George refused to be carried away by the blind patriotism to which even his followers succumbed. He feared that a German victory won too quickly and too easily would sap the moral virtues for which he was striving.¹² He considered the loss of the war an advantage, since it carried with it the collapse of the empty Wilhelmian façade, which in his eyes was both ripe and meet for destruction.¹³ But this gain was Germany's alone. The spirit of Prussianism which he had opposed, though temporarily exorcised in Germany, raised its head among Germany's former enemies. Paradoxically, in his view external defeat thus brought internal victory, since Germany was forced onto a path which gave her a decisive lead over the victors in the race towards a new standard of moral values. George considered Germany's defeat not as a disgrace but as a penance which must be paid in order to open the door to the emergence of a new type of German manhood. Though he had little liking for the men of the republican government, he respected them for having swept away the old, stratified social order; for him they were bigger men than the generals who carried out their putsches against the republic. Since his own daily life was the essence of simplicity, he was prepared to give credit to these new men, who were similarly simple and unpretentious, and who had at least been prepared to assume the responsibility which the former upper class had evaded when their self-inflicted catastrophe came upon them.¹⁴

A number of the symbols and expressions later used by National Socialism originated from the ideas current in George's circle—the

"Thousand-Year Reich," for instance, the "fire of the blood," and possibly even the swastika.[15] Nevertheless George's concept of nationhood
had nothing in common with the racial theories of National Socialism
and its crude nationalism. Theories of racial superiority and supermen
were abhorrent to him. "All this chatter about the superman," he said,
"will merely act as a challenge to the oppressed to rise. Is it not better
quietly to ensure that man is capable of meeting the highest demands
which can be made upon him? A racial policy is no new thing; it is
no more than an evil legacy from the nineteenth century. Only the
spirit, not some breeding establishment, is capable of producing a good
new race of men."[16] Although George would sometimes refer to the
"white man's way of life," he meant thereby the cultural heritage of
Greece and Rome. He rejected the east European and Slav-Mongolian
cultures; equally, however, he rejected the pure Nordics, whom he
found akin to the Slavs in their tendency to gloomy and confused
thinking.[17]

George hoped to build his pupils up into an elite, not only to point
the way in the artistic field but also to give a new sanctity to life through
their manner of living; they were to be an order of nobility founded
not upon the claims of birth but upon those of the mind. The hallmarks of this new elite, this new order of nobility, were to be a straight
piercing eye, readiness to serve and to assume responsibility, and a
capacity for devotion and self-sacrifice.[18] George laid down a new code
of rules for his pupils; in it, shame, revenge, and execration—standard
reactions at the time—had no place. He who was called to service
should "rejoice in deeds which, in the perverted view of the people,
cried to high heaven."[19]

George's philosophy was a philosophy of action; action was to him
a necessity of life. George did not say what was to be done. He would
speak of new obligations, but did not indicate clearly what they were,
for in his view anyone called to serve would himself perceive what his
duty was. Every man had an obligation laid upon him which no one
but he could fulfill and which he could not evade; he had set his foot
upon the ladder of duty and achievement. His individuality would
determine his position on the ladder and equally ensure that he was
more than just a cog in the machine.[20]

This philosophy found a character ideally suited in Claus von

Stauffenberg, who was basically predisposed to action. The sculptor Ludwig Thormaehlen has described the impression made by the seventeen-year-old Stauffenberg when he was accepted into the circle: "Young though he was, his radiant energy, which he was ready to turn to everything around him, produced an impression of absolute reliability. He would intervene in a manner which showed his intelligence—frank and honest in opposition, good humoured in criticism, but equally vigorous in agreement or in support of any justified demands by others."[21]

A central tenet of George's philosophy was the monistic concept, inherited from Greek literature, that body and soul were inseparable. The Greek notion that "the body was God" was, he said, "the most creative and irrefutable, the greatest, most daring, and most noble conception, superior to all others, including even the Christian ideal."[22] As a result of this exaggerated value attributed to the body, George believed that the outward appearance of a man could be taken to indicate his inherent worth and could serve as a criterion for his qualifications for acceptance into the circle of poetry lovers.[23]

In 1929, a young sculptor, Frank Mehnert, made a bust of Stauffenberg. The two had known each other in the Eberhard-Ludwigs School, Mehnert having matriculated a year later than Stauffenberg. Both joined George's circle, where they formed a close and profitable friendship. Mehnert's bust is still in existence and is now in the possession of Gräfin Nina von Stauffenberg; it bears out the description of the young Stauffenberg's face in Thormaehlen's memoirs, a description which exemplifies the monistic background of the George circle:

> The eyes were the most striking feature of Stauffenberg's face; in them could be seen all his good humour and high-mindedness, his intelligence and good will. They were of a dark metallic blue. He probably resembled his father, whereas Berthold took more after his mother. Though the face gave no striking impression of breadth, it was wide and symmetrical, with broad cheek bones— a sign of strength. The chin was strong and slightly cleft. The forehead firm and determined, with slightly protruding temples above the eyebrows, a sign of alertness, power of observation, strength of will, and pertinacity. In addition, there was the bold

curve of the nose and a well-formed, shapely mouth. The cheeks
were the only feature which might be called sensitive. Later they
showed signs of the hardships of military life. The hair was dark,
shining, and slightly wavy; he wore it close cropped.[24]

In conclusion, Thormaehlen summarizes Stauffenberg as follows:
"Quickness of intellect, rapidity of action, determination to do fully
and at once whatever his emotions, his brain, or the circumstances
indicated should be done—all this Claus had in full measure. With him
there was neither differentiation nor interval of time between thinking
and doing, between realization and action."[24]

Stauffenberg's natural predisposition to action was no doubt shar-
pened by George, but there was no necessity for education in the strict
sense of the word; Thormaehlen has told us that George never found
it necessary to instill anything into Stauffenberg; he never had to train
him; he hardly had to teach him anything. George merely confirmed
and reinforced the characteristics Stauffenberg already possessed. To
the majority of the members of the circle their master gave a
pseudonym, some title summarizing and describing their characteristics. It is significant that George never found it necessary to give
Stauffenberg a name; he remained just Claus. Even as a teenager his
character was so obviously fully formed that no symbolic name was
necessary to describe it.[25]

When the Stauffenberg sons first joined Stefan George's circle, their
mother was most disturbed. She probably knew the current rumours
about the poet, some of which even accused him of homosexuality.
She accordingly drove over to Heidelberg to get to know George
herself and to discover what were the bonds which held this circle
together.[26] Her visit entirely reassured her regarding George's motives,
and from then on she placed no obstacles in the way of her sons having
as much to do with George as they pleased.

In later life Stauffenberg's military duties kept him from maintaining
sufficiently close contact with the poet to be counted as one of the
innermost circle. On Stauffenberg's occasional visits, however, George
always received him with the greatest pleasure. During the winter of
1927–8, for instance, Stauffenberg had the opportunity to visit the poet
in Berlin on many occasions while on a course at the infantry school in

Dresden; equally, in 1930, while on a course at Döberitz, he was a frequent visitor.

It is reasonably certain that Stauffenberg was present for the great poetry reading which brought George's life work to an end. His last volume of poems, *Das neue Reich*, appeared in October 1928; the reading took place in November. George himself read the two great hymns "Burg Falkenstein" (Falkenstein Castle) and "Geheimes Deutschland" (Secret Germany).[27]

George's sixty-fifth birthday fell on 12 July 1933. He was afraid that the Nazi leaders, who had recently come to power, might try to appropriate his authority for their movement by giving him some public recognition; Goebbels, who had attended Gundolf's lectures at Heidelberg University, had already made use of George's name for propaganda purposes. Earlier than usual, therefore, George departed for Minusio in Switzerland, where he usually spent the winter.

George died on 4 December 1933 and was buried very early in the morning of 6 December. His friends were afraid that some official German representative might appear. Following the Tessin custom, the Stauffenberg brothers, with twelve of their friends, kept watch day and night around the deathbed of their great master; the roster was arranged by Claus von Stauffenberg himself.

III

Initial Military Training

Claus von Stauffenberg matriculated on 5 March 1926. He had been a delicate child, prone to illness, and had been absent from school on several occasions for extended periods, during which he had therefore been taught privately in Lautlingen. As a result, he could only sit for the final examinations as an "external candidate." His gradings were "good" for French, history, and mathematics; "satisfactory" for other subjects, except Latin, in which he was only "adequate"; in judging these classifications, however, account must be taken of the fact that he only sat the examination as an external candidate.[1]

Until shortly before leaving school he had intended to become an architect. It is not clear what caused him to give up this long-standing intention and become an officer; his change of mind must have been a very sudden one, for it came as a complete surprise to his friends.[2] Stauffenberg's bent for architecture stemmed perhaps from his capacity to plan and direct complicated organizations, the gift for which he later proved brilliantly as a General Staff officer; but as time went on an architect's work seemed to him to be too exclusively concerned with things rather than people. It may be that Stefan George played some part in the decision—a decision which was to have such far-reaching consequences in German history. It may be that his master's example as a trainer of men, his philosophy of action, and his hopes for a rebirth of Germany influenced Stauffenberg to turn to a profession in which he could give full rein to all his natural qualities and capabilities: planning, man management, assumption of responsibility, and service to the community.[3]

In 1926 Stauffenberg joined the family regiment, the Seventeenth Cavalry, stationed in Bamberg.[4] In accordance with the current regulations for the training of officers, he had first to serve in the ranks. A year later, as a candidate for a commission, he was sent to the infantry school in Dresden. Having completed this course, which lasted a year, he went to the cavalry school in Hannover.[5]

In Hannover he first met Freiherr Von Loeper, then a major and later his divisional commander. His reports were so good that he was nominated course leader, and Loeper says that from the outset he was clearly the leading personality. Having the confidence not only of his superiors but also of those on the course, he was able to smooth out difficulties on a number of occasions, in spite of the fact that his course included men of very different backgrounds.[6]

According to Loeper, Stauffenberg was at first by no means physically cut out to be an officer. When applying to join the army as a cadet he had in fact been afraid that he might be rejected on physical grounds. With remarkable determination, however, he eventually made himself capable of outstanding achievements in sports and outdoor pursuits. He was able to force himself to an athletic standard at which he could rival and frequently outstrip his more physically robust contemporaries.[7]

After finishing at Hannover, Stauffenberg returned to his regiment in Bamberg. On 1 January 1930 he was commissioned second lieutenant. From November 1930 to February 1931 he was sent on another course at Döberitz, this time for regimental close-support gun platoon commanders; the course was attended by a lieutenant or second lieutenant from each of the eighteen cavalry regiments.[8]

Stauffenberg was promoted to lieutenant on 1 May 1933. Four months later, on 26 September, he married Freiin Nina von Lerchenfeld, the wedding taking place in St. Jakobs church in Bamberg. The von Lerchenfeld family belonged to the old Bavarian aristocracy; Claus's father-in-law had been a consul-general and had served in Shanghai, Warsaw, and Kovno.[9]

In 1933 Stauffenberg returned to the cavalry school in Hannover for the advanced equitation course. He had to ride four horses each day, two from the school and two of his own chargers. In addition to practical and theoretical riding instruction, the course included training in general military subjects.

In equitation Stauffenberg's particular bent was dressage, and this formed a great link between him and his father-in-law, Baron von Lerchenfeld. In 1930 they went shares in buying the horse Jagd. Stauffenberg chose him from a stud farm as a foal and trained him so successfully that he reached the highest standards in dressage. In 1935 Stauffenberg came first in the compulsory military class for his course, in the process beating several members of the team which subsequently won the 1936 Olympic competition.[10]

During this second stay in Hannover Stauffenberg took the military district and English interpretership examinations. The military district examination was compulsory for all officers of about ten years' service; those who got the best overall marks were later accepted for the Staff College, which any officer who wished to become a member of the General Staff had to attend. Competition was at the time extraordinarily severe; only some 15 per cent of officers who took the military district examination reached the Staff College, and of these only approximately one third ultimately qualified for the General Staff.[11]

Stauffenberg took the English interpretership examination, since this qualification was at the time considered of particular value, and he was as a result exempted from taking a foreign language paper in the military district examination. He could therefore concentrate on other subjects. He was determined to pass the examination with the best possible marks, for it was his declared intention to become a General Staff officer.[12]

Stauffenberg's predilection for amassing the fullest possible information on any subject he took up, together with the fact that he had numerous and diverse nonmilitary interests, meant that in his early years he was in danger of dissipating his energies. In addition to attending to his normal military duties, he worked hard to broaden his education. He studied military history, general history, politics, philosophy, literature, art, foreign languages; he played the cello; he went to lectures and concerts and kept up with a wide circle of acquaintances and friends. As time went on he forced himself increasingly to concentrate upon his profession, but there was nevertheless hardly a single field in education or general knowledge of which he did not have some experience and on which he could not express a well-informed opinion.[13]

Stauffenberg was well aware of the fact that he was intellectually superior to many of those around him. Although he did not parade his intelligence, in his early years he undoubtedly had a certain tendency to show off. One report says:

> I have often heard Stauffenberg putting forward his views in the officers' mess, generally to the more junior officers. In most cases he would take the floor at once and lay down the law. This came easily to him, for he was intellectually clearly far ahead of his listeners. Being supremely self-confident and undoubtedly somewhat inclined to show off, he liked the sound of his own voice. Nevertheless his audience enjoyed listening to him.[14]

Another description of him at about the time of his second period in Hannover emphasizes his enjoyment of a forceful and intelligent argument:

> Summing Stauffenberg up, I would say that he had an extraordinary gift of making others feel naturally and completely at ease. This was all the more remarkable seeing that he was generally recognized as being well above average intellectually. He would raise the level of any conversation in which he took part; he particularly liked a stimulating discussion, and with his lively extrovert temperament, the more heated it became, the better.[15] Everything he took up he studied scientifically. He was not satisfied merely with acquiring information, but would go to the root of the matter. On the equitation course he would astound us with his knowledge of the riding and dressage methods of every conceivable period. What is more, he took pains to apply the knowledge which he gained.[16]

The same report includes a special reference to his friendliness, a side of his character mentioned by many of his fellow officers. Another description of him says, "Stauffenberg had no enemies. Everybody liked him and trusted him."[17]

While still a second lieutenant, he was elected to the Court of Honour of the Bamberg regiment, an eloquent proof of the esteem in which he was held.[18] One of his friends described him as follows:

Stauffenberg's outlook on life was firmly rooted in the basic values, and this was all of a piece with his personality and bearing. There were no "two sides" or "double standards" about him. He was always the same—through and through. Herein lay the secret of his personal magnetism, the explanation of the effect he had upon others. He stood by every word he spoke, every opinion he expressed, every decision he took, and every step he made, firm, unshakeable and—in all important matters—uncompromising. It was for this reason that he could always rely upon others paying attention to him and obeying him unhesitatingly when he had to give an order.

Elsewhere in the same account:

Though outwardly invariably genial, his attitude to others was in fact governed entirely by his estimate of their inherent qualities, not by their external circumstances. He was for instance on terms of confidence and friendship with many NCO's and men, whereas he would keep his distance from certain "personalities," a distance which they found it impossible to bridge in spite of obvious efforts to do so. Stauffenberg was indulgent towards other people's weaknesses, but towards underhand behaviour, even in small matters, he was uncompromising to the point of harshness. If the will was there, he was prepared to overlook others' omissions, provided no actual damage resulted. He was an expert at settling differences, acting as a go-between, and smoothing out quarrels; he looked for and found the good side to everybody and had an extraordinary knack of making the best of everything. He was a warm, open-hearted creature, and the best proof of that was his genuinely uninhibited and infectious laugh. Many situations were saved by that laugh.[19]

These various accounts and descriptions by fellow officers and superiors are well summarized in the official confidential report made on Stauffenberg by his squadron leader, Hans Walzer, in October 1933; Walzer still has the draft, which reads as follows:

A reliable independent character, capable of making up his own mind and taking his own decisions. Highly intelligent and of above average ability, both tactically and technically.

Exemplary in his handling of NCO's and men and absorbed in training and raising the standard of his mortar platoon.

Unexceptional in his relationships with others. Shows great interest in social, historical, and religious matters.

A very good, sympathetic rider who loves and understands a horse.

As against these outstanding qualities, mention should be made of certain minor deficiencies and weaknesses. He is well aware of his military ability and intellectual superiority and is therefore apt at times to adopt a somewhat overbearing attitude towards his fellow officers, frequently evidenced by a sarcasm, which, however, never leaves hurt feelings.

He is somewhat sloppy in his dress and bearing, and as a young officer, should take more care of his appearance and give an impression of greater energy. He is rather susceptible to throat infections, which means that his powers of physical resistance are sometimes affected. He fights off illness with energy and determination.

If he goes on as he is, there is every prospect that he will do very well.

[Signed] Walzer

The accounts of Stauffenberg's early years in the army give few concrete details about his political views. It has been said that he tended towards conservatism, but this must be accepted with reserve. He was certainly not a man to get caught up with revolutionary ideas, but in his eyes the existing order of things had no intrinsic value simply because it was old: if he spotted something new which he considered to be good, he would come out in passionate support of it.[20]

Although unconnected with politics, a certain incident shows that Stauffenberg's attitude to tradition was a matter-of-fact one. In 1935 there was an argument over the location of the cavalry school. Owing to the construction of an airfield near Hannover, the school had lost its training areas and the students had to go a long way to reach suitable country. The proposal was therefore made—and later carried out—to move the cavalry school from Hannover to Krampnitz, near Berlin. This roused violent opposition on the grounds that it would adversely affect the world-wide reputation of the Hannover school. Stauffenberg, however, adopted the attitude that preservation of the old must not be allowed to weigh against the practicalities and came out in favour of the move of the school.[21]

There is no record of any remarks by Stauffenberg giving any indication that he belonged to a political party. It was not in his nature to accept or conform to a ready-made line of thought. One account says, "He built his own party."[22]

On the subject of politics the Reichswehr rules for officers ran counter to Stauffenberg's ideas. There was a categorical instruction that a soldier should avoid adopting any definite attitude to current political events, and for a member of the forces, membership of any political party was out of the question; in fact, under the Weimar constitution, soldiers had no vote.[23]

Though Stauffenberg no doubt accepted this rule, he did not take it to indicate that he must concentrate solely upon the problems of his profession. In his view the Reichswehr was not merely a military instrument, but an essential ingredient to the construction of the new state. In Stauffenberg's eyes the armed forces were one of the essential pillars of the nation, called upon to guarantee both its security and reputation.[24] As a result, all questions bearing upon the well-being of the state as a whole interested him immensely. Heinz Greiner says, "His talk was principally of political problems, with a pronounced social tinge."[25]

This does not imply that he gave unconditional allegiance to the Weimar Republic, which in the hurly-burly of political events of this period presented a murky and distorted picture. Stauffenberg felt himself under an obligation to serve the community, the *res publica*; he did not therefore feel that he could stand aside from all politics and treat the subject simply with irony and skepticism. Many of the older officers were still living in the imperial past; democracy was to them something unknown and incomprehensible, which they therefore rejected; they still hankered after a past which could never be resurrected; their obsession with loyalty was expressed in addresses of devotion dispatched to Doorn, to the Kaiser who had abdicated. Stauffenberg was certainly not one of them.

When visiting his relatives in Franconia he would ostentatiously wear his uniform, knowing that people there thought it outrageous that anyone of their circle should join the Reichswehr. Much of the Bavarian nobility still clung to the fiction that the King of Bavaria had not abdicated voluntarily and that the republican leaders were therefore mere usurpers. Stauffenberg remained uninfluenced by such flights of fancy; he may have been a conservative, but he remained a realist.

Stauffenberg was no lover of the Weimar Republic; on the other hand, he did not approve the attitude of some of his fellow officers who, though servants of the state, despised it. In his view it was better to place oneself at the service of the state, even if that state seemed inadequate, rather than stand aside in ineffective arrogance. He would have nothing to do with those who ridiculed or insulted the Republic. He was never one of those who either among friends or in the mess made fun of the republican black, red, and gold flag, calling it "black-red-mustard." He felt that it was after all the flag of the state to which he had sworn his oath.[26]

IV

Hitler's Seizure of Power

On 30 January 1933 Adolf Hitler, the man destined to bring tragedy both to the German people in general and Stauffenberg in particular, became chancellor of Germany. What was Stauffenberg's view of him in the early years of his regime?

Everything so far written about Stauffenberg includes the story that on 30 January, dressed in uniform, he placed himself at the head of a crowd demonstrating in favour of the Nazi seizure of power and marched with it through Bamberg. Critical historical research, however, does not substantiate the tale.

In his book *Schuld und Verhangnis* Hermann Foertsch states that on the day of the so-called seizure of power an enthusiastic crowd collected in Bamberg to celebrate the National Socialist victory, and that Stauffenberg, in the uniform of a second lieutenant, placed himself at the head of the procession. When criticized by his fellow officers and superiors he is supposed to have said that the great military leaders of the wars of liberation had shown even greater sympathy for such popular movements.[1]

Foertsch's account is based upon information from Peter Sauerbruch, Prof. Sauerbruch's son, given while in a prisoner of war camp. Foertsch's version of the story gives the impression of an eye-witness account, whereas Sauerbruch was merely repeating what he remembered of a conversation in the mess.[2]

Sauerbruch was at the time only a nineteen-year-old cadet and was not an officer in the strict sense of the word; he does not even claim to have full knowledge of the matter. All he says is that on a certain day

on or shortly after 30 January 1933, some incident concerning Stauffenberg was discussed in the mess. The story apparently was that Stauffenberg, "who happened to be in uniform, came upon an enthusiastic
crowd and marched along with it, considering that the citizens of
Bamberg would have found it entirely incomprehensible if an officer
had simply stood aside. The problem was whether, faced with such a
situation, an officer ought to have disappeared quickly or taken part
in the demonstration."[3]

The only demonstration, however, which took place in Bamberg
on 30 January 1933, was a National Socialist party procession, reported
as follows in the *Bamberger Tageblatt*:[4]

> The nomination of Hitler as chancellor of the Reich was cele-
> brated in Bamberg by a National Socialist torchlight procession
> or propaganda march through the town. The procession moved
> through the outskirts to the Maxplatz, passing over Chain Bridge,
> from beneath which could be heard whistles and catcalls from the
> Nazis' opponents. In the Maxplatz a speech was made by
> Zahneisen, a member of the Landtag and town council, extolling
> the party's thirteen-year struggle for power; he stated that Adolf
> Hitler would never have become chancellor of the Reich "if his
> opponents had had anything to do with it." The party would now
> continue its ruthless struggle for power and defend the positions
> it had gained; Adolf Hitler would remain chancellor of the Reich
> as long as he wished. The demonstration, which in general was
> completely without incident, closed with a threefold *Heil* and the
> singing of the national anthem.

This was not therefore a spontaneous demonstration by a crowd, as
Foertsch's version of the story would indicate, but an organized party
occasion. Since officers were forbidden to take part in political demon-
strations, the newspaper would hardly have omitted to mention the
fact had there been an officer marching at the head of the procession.
In addition, the incident could hardly have remained unnoticed in
Bamberg. The following, however, have testified that at the time,
they heard no whisper of anything of the sort: Nina Gräfin von
Stauffenberg, then Stauffenberg's fiancée; Lieutenant General (retd.)
Gustav Freiherr von Perfall, then commanding officer of the Seven-

teenth Cavalry Regiment; Lieutenant Colonel (retd.) Hans Walzer, then squadron leader of the First Squadron, Seventeenth Cavalry Regiment; General (retd.) Hasso von Manteuffel, then squadron leader of the Fifth Squadron, Seventeenth Cavalry Regiment; Lieutenant General (retd.) Heinz Greiner, than a captain in the headquarters of the Seventeenth Cavalry Regiment; Colonel (retd.) Bernd von Pezold, a brother officer of Stauffenberg's in the regiment; Dr. Kunkel, an optician in Bamberg.[5]

In addition, there is a statement by a C.I.D. inspector of the Bamberg municipal police who, in connection with enquiries into other matters, had to interrogate a number of members of the former National Socialist organizations and of the SA in Bamberg, some of whom had themselves marched in the 1933 demonstration. He asked whether they could remember Stauffenberg taking part, and his report says, "None of the persons interrogated, members of the former National Socialist organization in Bamberg, had any knowledge either personally or by hearsay of any such incident."[6]

Furthermore, no disciplinary action was taken against Stauffenberg for any affair of this nature. Freiherr von Perfall, his regimental commander at the time, writes:

> I took over command of the Seventeenth Cavalry Regiment on 1 October 1932, and was therefore the responsible commander on 30 January 1933. I hereby state that neither on that day nor at any other time did a member of my regiment take part in a demonstration in favour of the Hitler regime. The story that Stauffenberg took it upon himself to do so as an individual and had to answer to me for his action, is a pure figment of the imagination.[7]

Captain Hans Walzer, Stauffenberg's squadron leader, states:

> He was a straightforward, upright character with a sense of discipline and tradition. This is enough to guarantee that he would never even have dreamed of making so unsoldierly an exhibition of himself as is imputed to him today.[8]

Confusion concerning the seizure of power demonstration in Bamberg may have arisen from an incident connected with the name of Captain (as he then was), later General, Hasso von Manteuffel.

On 31 January[9] the Fifth Squadron, returning from an exercise, rode through the town on its way back to barracks. Its route led through the town hall square, where on this particular day a crowd was assembled waiting for the hoisting of the "new" flag, the swastika. The squadron leader, Captain von Manteuffel, was told that this flag had just been raised to the status of the national emblem. He therefore ordered his squadron to ride to attention as they passed it.[10]

When the regimental commander heard of this incident, he called a meeting of officers and gave Manteuffel, in Manteuffel's own words, "a severe downright reprimand." Perfall in fact said, "This is after all a revolution, and we can have nothing to do with it."[11]

According to Manteuffel, he had had no intention of demonstrating in favour of National Socialism; he had simply omitted to check the truth of the information given him—in fact the swastika was not given the status of the national flag until 15 September 1935, in the first of the "Nuremberg Laws."[12]

This affair, and possibly also the Nazi demonstration march, seems to have been the subject of a conversation in the officers' mess, and it was probably this conversation Sauerbruch overheard. The question was probably raised how an officer should behave should he be involved in a demonstration not organized by any definite party but a spontaneous expression of popular feeling. It is quite conceivable that in this connection Stauffenberg voiced the opinion that in such a situation an officer could hardly stand aloof; when someone took the opposite view, he may well have referred to the great military leaders of the wars of liberation.

A man of Stauffenberg's character and upbringing could never be an enthusiastic member of Hitler's party. There were aspects of National Socialism which he inevitably found repugnant—the crude, ill-bred manners of the National Socialist leaders, for instance, their orgies of invective, and their guttersnipe jargon. An incident which took place in 1934 shows that Stauffenberg was quite prepared to give open and ostentatious expression to his disgust at vulgar demagogic methods. He and one of his friends were detailed to represent the regiment at a Nazi demonstration in Bamberg organized as part of a Party Day. The first speaker was the Reichsleiter, Schemm; he was followed by the Nuremberg Gauleiter, Julius Streicher. The latter launched out into wild invective against the Jews, in such disgustingly pornographic terms —and that in the presence of several hundred B.D.M. girls[13]—that Stauffenberg and his brother officer got up and left the hall down the center gangway.[14]

Although he always found fanaticism and intolerance repellent, Stauffenberg initially saw certain advantages in National Socialism. One account says that he was fired by National Socialism because "the German people were rebelling against the fetters of the Treaty of Versailles and because the movement was endeavouring to do away with the misery of unemployment by creating work and was instituting other social services for the man in the street." The account ends with the sentence: "His attitude to social problems was quite clearly based upon his religious [Catholic] convictions—this is my personal opinion."[15]

The best summary of the attitude of Stauffenberg and the officer corps in general to National Socialism comes from Hans Walzer, his squadron leader at the time: "We were all surprised by the nomination of Hitler as Reich chancellor, and there was no question of anyone being enthusiastic about it. We hoped, however, that it would mean the end of party political wrangling and that instead there would now be a firm, straightforward policy under the direction of our revered Field Marshal, the Reich President [Hindenburg]."[16]

Stauffenberg regarded Hitler's rise to power from an entirely realistic standpoint. "Claus von Stauffenberg was insistent upon judging Hitlerism realistically; any purely derogatory remark about Hitler, therefore, he would regard with caution and skepticism. [He recognized that] despicable though his character might be in many respects . . . Hitler was capable of putting into words certain basic and genuine ideas which could lead to a spiritual revival and that as a result both the idealists and the high-minded might indirectly be attracted to him."[17]

In Stauffenberg's view Hitler's success was the result of three factors:

1. The entire machinery of the state and of German party politics was powerless in the face of Hitler's tactics of destroying democracy by democratic methods.

2. Germany's former enemies must carry some of the responsibility for the emergence of Hitler, since they had thought that they

could build peace on the basis of the Treaty of Versailles. As a result they presented Hitler with his strongest arguments and enabled him to appear as the champion of legitimate popular desires.

3. Hitler's remarkable influence sprang primarily from his social measures. He was thereby enabled to build up an effective counterweight to communism within Germany.[18]

With all his realism, however, Stauffenberg did not feel that he could simply be an observer on the sidelines. He realized that "popular guidance . . . was an inescapable and important part of politics and was something which could not be left to any Tom, Dick, or Harry without disastrous consequences."[19] This being his point of view, he was quite prepared, as were other officers of his regiment, on occasions to direct SA night exercises.[20] This did not mean that he was in favour of the basic objectives of this organization; its pseudo-martial behaviour was, after all, the antithesis of true soldiering. Stauffenberg and his fellow officers hoped that by these exercises they might prevent the SA expending all its energy on beating people up and attending senseless hurrah sessions and instead give it some definite military objectives. Here he was in line with Reichswehr policy, which was striving to bring this private army under control.

Like many others, Stauffenberg did not foresee the ghastly course upon which National Socialism was set. For instance, his reaction to 30 June 1934, the so-called Röhm Affair, was similar to that of the German people as a whole and the vast majority of the officer corps: he regarded it as the lancing of a boil, as a result of which there would at last be some clarity in the direction of affairs.[21]

Tension between the Reichswehr and the SA had been rising ever since the inception of the Hitler regime. The SA considered itself the Praetorian Guard of the new state and was demanding to take over the Reichswehr. The crisis of the conflict came in 1934, each side considering a revolt by the other to be imminent. The SA attempted to supplement its equipment by raiding Reichswehr depots. At the time, the army had secret depots concealed from the Allied control authorities, since they were in excess of the permitted level under the Versailles Treaty; weapons had been cached on estates all over the country. When the SA discovered some of these depots a race between the SA and the Reichswehr began, one trying to lay hands on the weapons, the other to safeguard them. There were incidents of this nature in the neighbourhood of Bamberg, and Stauffenberg himself was responsible for making lorries available to move weapons from one of the secret depots.[22]

The Reichswehr became increasingly insistent on the disarmament of the SA, and Hitler began to doubt the loyalty of Röhm, the SA chief of staff. So on 30 June 1934 he put an end to the dispute by having the leaders of the SA, including Röhm, shot—all within a few hours. The Reichswehr considered that it had won the day, and when, shortly afterwards, von Hindenburg, the old Reich president, died, the army was deluded into swearing a new oath of allegiance, pledging obedience not to the state but to Hitler personally.

Though temporarily relieved, Stauffenberg seems to have been fully aware that the events of 30 June 1934 foreshadowed disastrous developments. The SA had indeed been eliminated as a power factor in Germany, but there could be no glossing over the fact that, without turning a hair and without any pretense of legality, Hitler had had his old comrades shot once they had become tiresome to him. The Reichswehr was subsequently given to understand that "these measures must be considered as having been taken in emergency defense of the state,"[23] but this could not conceal the fact that the government of Germany was now in the hands of men who had no intention of abiding by the normal rules of justice. Even as early as this, Stauffenberg began to play with the idea that it might one day be necessary to use force to get rid of a government such as this. Shortly after 30 June 1934 he had a private talk with his squadron leader, and Walzer states: "We discussed the possibility of getting rid of the National Socialist system by force and the attitude which the churches would adopt to such an eventuality. In particular, we spoke of the influence the Catholic church might have. We agreed that the removal of the regime by force could only take place from above, since a revolution from below, in other words starting from the people, was inconveivable in view of the power and influence of the party."[24]

It would not be right, however, to try to establish any direct connection between this conversation in 1934 and the events of July 1944.

Even at the end of 1936 a fellow officer in the Staff College stated that Stauffenberg had been "impressed" by a speech by the Reichsleiter, Buch, and was "not opposed to the new ideology."[25] Stauffenberg undoubtedly tried for a time to differentiate between the ideals and the reality of National Socialism; many other worthy people in Germany were trying to do likewise and excusing the political amorality of the National Socialists as a temporary inconvenience which must be borne in order to achieve stabilization.

Stauffenberg looked upon Hitler as "the typical modern demagogue, with an astounding capacity for tub thumping, a man who frequently merely took the ideas that came to him and twisted them to his own ends, but who was nevertheless capable of simplifying them and making them politically feasible; he was therefore capable of inspiring the mass of the people to devotion and self-sacrifice, even though to their own disadvantage."[26]

Stauffenberg naturally found the barbaric habits of the National Socialist leaders and their exaggerated insistence on their lack of education repellent; nevertheless, because of his background and his profession, his philosophy had a strong nationalist tinge, and so he was in many respects sympathetic to the National Movement as proclaimed by the National Socialists. In this respect his reaction was similar to that of many of his fellow officers; he differed from them not in their initial misjudgment of National Socialism but in the fact that he did not exclude the possibility of having second thoughts. As soon as he realized that the so-called National Movement was nothing less than a soulless machine, he was ready to do all in his power to set the country on a new course.

V

The Staff College

In September 1936, shortly before starting his Staff College course, Stauffenberg paid a fortnight's visit to England. He had done so well in the English interpretership examination that he was given a grant out of which he could pay for the journey. Writing in English to Prof. Pfau, his English tutor in Hannover, he said (in one of the few of his letters still in existence), that he had first spent a few days in London and had then visited the Royal Military College, Sandhurst, where he had been able to have a discussion with the cadets studying German.[1]

Graf Stauffenberg was among the one hundred officers who entered the Staff College in Berlin-Moabit for General Staff training on 1 October 1936. On 1 January 1937 he was promoted to captain.

The Staff College course was divided into two parts: the junior part dealt with problems of command up to regimental level; the senior, with divisions and higher formations. In each part were five study halls, with some twenty officers in each.

There were twenty-two officers in Stauffenberg's study hall, and from this small circle came three of the most influential leaders of the 20 July coup: Stauffenberg, Mertz von Quirnheim, and Eberhard Finckh. "These three and a few others, though in no sense a clique, were the leading spirits of the study hall; they made a major contribution to the mutual education of the students, stimulated discussion on technical subjects, and set a good general tone."[2]

Stauffenberg was, as always, insistent upon thorough scientific study of any military problem, and while at the Staff College he completed two main theses. The first was the fruit of heated discussion in the

study hall; he submitted it as a competition essay. Unexpectedly it won
first prize and even during the war was still looked upon as a basic
document.[3] Its title was "Thoughts on Home Defense against Enemy
Parachute Troops."

Stauffenberg gave a lecture on the subject to the Lilienthal Society in
Berlin, reproduced in the monthly periodical *Wissen und Wehr*,
published by the Deutsche Gesellschaft für Wehrpolitik und Wehrwissenschaften.[4] Colonel General Student, commander of the German
parachute troops from 1938 onwards, commented, "In view of the
period at which it was written, when this new epoch-making arm of
the service was still shrouded in mystery, Graf Stauffenberg's study
contains remarkably astute, orderly, far-sighted, and progressive thinking; it is noteworthy that he uses the expression 'parachute combat
troops.' "[5]

His second study, on the use of cavalry, was not a success, although
he spent much time and labour in preparing it. Only one copy of it
still exists.[6]

It was criticized at the Staff College as an attempt to perpetuate a
role and an importance for the cavalry which it no longer possessed.
This criticism, however, was based upon a misunderstanding, as the
following extracts from the concluding section of the essay show:

> The question so often asked today, Should we have cavalry or
> tanks? is a bad question. The requirement is for cavalry *and*
> tanks . . . a tactical or strategic break-through is now hardly
> conceivable without the use of tanks in mass. But this does not
> affect the strategic role of cavalry. . . . Looking at the problem
> quite dispassionately, the extent to which either the horse or the
> mechanical vehicle is capable of giving us cavalry-type mobility
> depends upon factors which have only been touched on here;
> among the most important are conditions on and beyond our
> frontiers and the fuel supply problem.[7]

One section of the essay is headed "The Cavalry Commander." The
rest consists primarily of tactical arguments and examples from military
history, but in this particular section Stauffenberg launched out into
ideas which were not of a strictly technical nature.

More than any other arm of the service, he said, cavalry was dependent on the quality of its leaders. "Without great generals, without real
cavalry leaders, cavalry is no more than an expensive impediment. . . .
The qualities of a cavalry leader are inborn and are vouchsafed only
to a fortunate few."

The style of this section differs noticeably from that of the rest of
the essay; turns of phrase appear reminiscent of Stefan George: "Even
these fortunate few only rise to full stature in conjunction with their
arm of the service; only through their arm are they ultimately inspired
to act in the true cavalry spirit—it almost seems as if only a genius in
the art of war is capable of recognizing the cavalry as the arm designed
for major strategic tasks." Qualities of leadership, he went on, were
inborn and could not be acquired merely by technical training and
knowledge. But they were nevertheless "the fruit of long training,
which could not be begun early enough."

The German pre-war Staff College course has frequently been
criticized.[8] It would seem to be generally established that it concentrated overmuch on tactics and that inadequate time was spent on
questions of war economy and on technical problems. The proof of this
was seen during the war in the attitude of the General Staff, which was
frequently reproached for failure to grasp the problems of the overall
direction of the war.

Stauffenberg did his best to close this gap in his education by his own
efforts. He had busied himself with questions of geopolitics while still
at the cavalry school in Hannover.[9] Wedemeyer, later an American
four-star general, was an exchange officer at the Berlin Staff College
on the same course as Stauffenberg; he can still remember discussing
economic questions with Stauffenberg, who seemed to be fully au fait
with, for instance, Keynes's economic theory. In Stauffenberg's view
the catastrophic twentieth-century developments in Europe, including
the First World War, could basically be traced back to economic
causes: during the pre-war period Europe's industrial center of gravity
had moved from Great Britain to Germany, and the British market,
even in distant areas, was being affected by Germany's economic
expansion. "It was Claus's viewpoint that this was the deep-rooted
cause of World War I."[10]

Stauffenberg also discussed with Wedemeyer United States steel production, even then many times larger than that of Germany; he made no secret of his admiration for Roosevelt and the drastic methods he had used to revive the American economy after the 1929 depression. Wedemeyer mentions that he was surprised by Stauffenberg's knowledge of British and American history. He says, "These recollections will indicate to you that Claus von Staffenberg unquestionably was seeking information and thinking about world problems."[11]

Stauffenberg did not, however, discuss with Wedemeyer political questions, particularly conditions in Germany at the time. "I should emphasize that at no time did he reveal his thinking with reference to Hitler, who was at the peak of his power. There could be no doubt about his loyalty to his country, but I did sense that he disapproved of the policies of the Nazi government. However, this was not so evident that one could state categorically his opposition."[12]

Stauffenberg would clearly have been somewhat shy of discussing internal political problems with a foreigner; nevertheless Wedemeyer's assessment gives an accurate picture of Stauffenberg's political attitude at the time. He never allowed himself to be carried away by the National Socialist psychosis; in 1937, however, political developments had not yet reached the point at which his loyalty to his country seemed to him incompatible with his loyalty to the state, whose servant he was.

Stauffenberg made it his business to see a good deal of Wedemeyer in order to practice his English, "which incidentally he could speak very well."[13] As time went on, however, they became real friends and would often invite each other to meals or cocktails at home. Stauffenberg's personality made a lasting impression upon Wedemeyer. "He was a very handsome man—a fine military bearing, courteous, considerate, and sensitive."[14] He was very popular with his Staff College term, Wedemeyer says, and highly respected professionally. When defending the minority point of view he was never dogmatic or arrogant but invariably polite, though quite firm. Though always friendly, he was somewhat reticent, a good listener who, in discussion with others, would only put his point of view forward occasionally. This description by Wedemeyer, in contrast to earlier accounts,[15] shows that Stauffenberg had lost his tendency to push himself forward.

From Stauffenberg's point of view an even more important friendship was formed during this Berlin period, one which exerted its

influence right into the planning phase of the resistance. Stauffenberg
was at the time seeing much of Frank Mehnert, the sculptor from the
George circle, who helped him with his work, even including the
drafting of his essays.[16] Through Mehnert, Stauffenberg came to know
the historian Dr. Rudolf Fahrner, who was at the time working on a
biography of Gneisenau.

Stauffenberg's interest was immediately aroused, since Gneisenau
was one of his ancestors. His fascination, however, extended beyond
mere family connections, for here was an officer who had played a
decisive role in matters of state and governmental reform. One sentence in Fahrner's later book on Gneisenau might well have been
written with reference to Stauffenberg: "His was not a spirit which was
prepared to bow to what to others might seem the inevitable; his mind
was busy thinking how, by his own exertions, a man might liberate
Prussia"[17]—for Prussia read Germany.

Though he never admitted it, Stauffenberg secretly modelled himself
on Gneisenau. It is therefore significant that not only did he follow
Fahrner's work closely but even persuaded the author not to present
Gneisenau's actions too simply as revolutionary or their object as a
popular rising. In Stauffenberg's view any revolt against the state and
its leaders was no business of the irresponsible mass of the people and
should not therefore even be discussed in too wide a circle. He considered that if the use of force against one's own state was unavoidable,
action must be confined to men conscious of their responsibilities and,
even more important, capable of meeting them.[18]

Stauffenberg was always a devotee of history and was apt to slip in
an historical allusion in conversation with his fellow officers. One of
the cavalry school exercises, for instance, took place on the Hohentwiel.
While on the mountain he gave his friends a vivid description of the
far-flung Hohenstaufen empire, "in the center of which you are now
standing."[19] The final exercise of his Staff College year took place in
southwest Germany, on the Rhine.[20] Stauffenberg organized a com-
munal visit to the Imperial cathedrals; during the same exercise he gave
a lecture on the significance of the river in the Franco-German context.
He did no more than outline the events of the centuries-old struggle
between the two countries; his main theme was the significance of this
struggle. In his view, whatever its origin, the decisive battle in the

struggle for hegemony in the West would be fought out on the banks of this river of destiny. He voiced his fear that the resulting self-inflicted wounds would leave the peoples of western Europe morally, ethically, and spiritually exhausted. That the western world had not collapsed after World War I was due only to the fact that it had been possible to avoid the final deadly battle on the Rhine. Stauffenberg ended his talk with a question: what would happen if new developments gave the great power in the East an opportunity to take a hand in the struggle?[21]

VI

Initiation to War

On 1 January 1937 Stauffenberg was promoted to captain. On the conclusion of his Staff College course in the summer of 1938 he was posted to the First Light Division, commanded by Lieutenant General Hoepner and stationed at Wuppertal. With this division he took part in the occupation of the Sudetenland, the Polish campaign, and until mid-May 1940, the French campaign.

Such reports of Stauffenberg as there are from this period concern his military duties and his relationships with his fellow officers; they also give an indication of his attitude to the political events of the time.

Stauffenberg was posted to the First Light Division as staff officer (logistics) in spite of a request for him from No. 2 Section (the organization section) of the army general staff. The request was turned down on the astonishing grounds that there were already enough strong characters in the organization section and that Stauffenberg's appointment might disturb the balance between sections.[1]

Stauffenberg's task consisted of the organization of the division's logistics. There had hitherto been no logistics section as such in HQ of the First Light Division; Stauffenberg therefore had to build up his staff from scratch. His office door was always open; no one ever had to ask or wait for an interview. Anyone could come in to get advice, discuss a problem, or obtain a signature. The senior aide to the divisional commander, Werner Reerink, has given this picture: "Even today I often think back with pleasure to the picture of Stauffenberg at work: the office door wide open, puffing happily away at a black cigar, striding up and down the room, he would dictate the most complicated reports straight onto the typewriter. Though he would often be interrupted by visitors coming in for advice or by the telephone, he would continue with his report from the exact point at which he had been interrupted." Reerink describes Stauffenberg's method of work as "elegant and attractive"; Stauffenberg, he says, was never moody or out of temper but invariably the essence of geniality.

A further description of Stauffenberg's methods of work refers to 1940. It will be noted that this differs considerably from that quoted above insofar as his methods of formulating and issuing orders are concerned. The contrast is explained by the differing situations under which he was working. The first report refers to a period when the requirement was to dictate a fully thought-out concept; the second to Stauffenberg's method of turning all the various reports which came to him into an operation instruction.

I first came to know Stauffenberg during the French campaign, when he was SO (logistics) of the Sixth Panzer Division, advancing through the Ardennes. The "Q" conferences which he held were unforgettable. In general they did not take place at any set time; gradually the section heads, the commanders of special detachments, and the liaison officers arrived. Stauffenberg, tall, slim, lively, and a man of extraordinary personal charm, would welcome us all with genuine infectious geniality; he would make sure that everyone had something to drink, a cigar or a pipe. He would give us the latest information, ask questions, and take interest in apparently trivial matters, tell the latest stories covering the whole divisional area from the reconnaissance detachment back to the field bakery, jump from one subject to another, listen to or ask questions of the latest arrivals. This would go on apparently for ages, and none of our questions had been answered, none of our dispositions made for the next day, or even for the next few hours, and no orders issued. Then quite casually and conversationally would come the words, "Well then, I think we'll do it this way." And then in all its detail out would come the "Q" order, Stauffenberg with his left hand in his trouser pocket, a glass in his right hand, wandering thoughtfully about the room, stopping at one moment here, at another moment there, and then going back to the map. He did not issue a formal order as one would have expected from a General Staff officer; he was in no sense hidebound. He did not find it easy to formulate his orders, and what he said was anything but a fluent order ready for typing; but it was the result of hard thinking, and all the necessary dispositions were there; the essentials were all worked out and complete.[2]

Much of Stauffenberg's job as head of the "Q" (logistics) Section was concerned with organization, and for this he showed a special aptitude.

He was capable of seeing several moves ahead in the chess game and taking account of all the various alternatives. He was quick to grasp a situation, to sort out the important from the unimportant, and could spot the decisive factor with unerring intuition. He was capable of logical abstract thought and possessed a lively imagination, which, however, never led him to overstep the bounds of practicability; both in the operational and organizational fields, he had all the qualifications to do excellent work as a staff officer.[3]

At the outset Stauffenberg found himself faced with the problems arising from the expansion of the army. The First Light Division had been formed on 12 October 1937; it was one of those formations which Hitler had created by ruthlessly overstretching the resources of the state. When Hitler took over power in 1933 the Wehrmacht consisted of seven infantry and three cavalry divisions. Four years later there were thirty-nine infantry and five armoured divisions, together with four light divisions and twenty-two machine gun battalions.[4] The "light divisions" were a compromise between Hitler's requirement for a rapid expansion of the armoured forces and the conservative outlook of the Army High Command (OKH). They consisted of two motorized infantry regiments, one reconnaissance regiment, one artillery regiment, and a tank battalion, together with a number of supporting arms. On the outbreak of war this bastard organization was done away with, and Stauffenberg's division was reorganized as the Sixth Panzer Division.[5]

On 4 October 1938 German troops, including the First Light Division, moved into the Sudetenland. As early as September the division had concentrated in the area Greiz-Plauen-Chemnitz—officially "for exercises."

A copy of the division's war diary covering the period 5 September to 19 October still exists.[6] It comprises twenty-six pages, the first nine of which deal with the activity of the operations section and describe the move of the division to the "autumn manoeuvre" area. On 23 September orders for the attack were issued, and on 27 September the division began to move into its assembly area. On 30 September, however, the outcome of the Munich conference became known. The Sudeten area, which was divided into five zones, was occupied by the German Wehrmacht between 1 and 10 October. The war diary says, "The impression in the staff is that the danger of war has now been finally averted. The tension of the last few days is easing."[7] The division crossed the frontier on 4 October, one of its tasks being to prevent the "Sudeten German Corps" from moving into the Sudetenland on its own initiative.[8] Additional areas were occupied on 5 and on 9–10 October. On 9 October the division reached the town of Mies, where, according to the war diary, the population greeted "each individual vehicle with indescribable jubilation and a shower of flowers."[9] There was a different reception in Nurschan, just short of Pilsen, where the population was Czech; here the Germans were received with obvious hostility. It was not entirely clear whether Nurschan in fact belonged to the area to be ceded to Germany. The British mediation commission, together with a Czech staff officer, appeared at the divisional headquarters and demanded the evacuation of the town.[10] The war diary gives the division's answer; self-confident though it sounds, it does not give evidence of much understanding of the principle of popular self-determination, in the name of which the Sudetenland was being ceded to Germany: "The division replied that any area once occupied by German troops would not be relinquished."[11]

Entries dealing with Stauffenberg's activities—the supply of the troops and the feeding of the population—begin on page 10 of the war diary.

The divisional zone consists almost entirely of a farming area. It is clear that activities have been at a standstill for a considerable period, primarily owing to the Czech mobilization. The standard of living of the population is very simple, due not so much to recent political events as to ignorance of how to live; on the other hand, in the forest and mountain areas there is real poverty. Farming methods are in most cases very primitive. There is a general shortage of horses and vehicles both for the harvest and for ploughing, since everything is requisitioned.[12]

Stauffenberg tackled the problem facing him at once and with energy. With the occupation, all supplies to the Sudetenland from Czechoslovakia ceased abruptly, whereas those from Germany began to come in only gradually:

> The mayor of Haid reports that in Haid and the surrounding area no more yeast is available for bread making. Yeast was therefore bought by the division in Germany and delivered to the population. . . . Labour is not available, particularly on the large estates, to bring in the potato harvest and store the wheat harvest. One supply company platoon was placed at the disposal of the Lowenstein estate manager to help with the harvest. The division managed to obtain two lorries from Germany to assist the local breweries in the occupied area to deliver beer.[13]

Other entries also refer to assistance with the harvest:

> Insofar as manpower can be made available, the troops are helping with the harvest.[14]
>
> The troops were instructed to give any help they could with the harvest in their billeting areas. For any transport vital to the population or the economy, petrol will be furnished at cost price.[15]

Stauffenberg was also responsible for prevention of the spread of animal diseases:

> In the event of any further move, measures must be taken to prevent the spread of foot and mouth disease; all possible precautions must be taken to stop further infection. "Q" branch made contact with the district authorities of Plan and Tachau.[16]
>
> In collaboration with the district officer, the division installed a temporary veterinary officer in the Mies district.[17]

In Hermannshutte, because brown coal supplies were running out, the glass factory was threatened with an enforced stoppage of work.

If the melting ovens have to be let out, three to four hundred men will be thrown out of work; it takes three to four weeks to get the ovens going again. The manager of the glass factory was at once dispatched to Army Group headquarters in Karlsbad to press for an immediate supply of brown coal. In addition, the division itself moved a quantity of brown coal.[18]

On 10 October Stauffenberg called a meeting in Mies town hall.

At the meeting in the town hall under the chairmanship of the SO (logistics) there were present: the divisional medical officer, the divisional supply officer, a representative of the town major, a representative of the district authorities (Karlsbad District Council), the mayor of Mies, a representative of the NSV (National Socialist Welfare Organization) and the SDP (Sudeten German party). The most urgent requirements are:

1. Horses and vehicles for harvesting and ploughing, both of which are well behind schedule.
2. Brown coal, primarily for the bakeries.
3. Petrol, in order that the few available vehicles may be used to keep the population supplied.[19]

Further consequences of the closing of the frontier were that butter and milk intended for Pilsen were threatening to go bad, and hundreds of workers could no longer get to their previous jobs in Pilsen. The "Q" section of divisional headquarters under Stauffenberg was charged with the distribution of passes for work people, and the frontier was opened for supplies to Pilsen.[20]

On instructions from the SO (logistics) the divisional supply officer discussed with the local mayors where supplies were most needed: "The necessary additional supplies will be distributed to the units concerned in accordance with requirements."[21]

The division moved back into Germany on 16 October. On leaving the Sudetenland the divisional commander issued a special appreciation of the work of Stauffenberg's supply units: "In recognition of the work of the rearward services during these exercises, the divisional commander issued an order of the day to the rear services."[22]

After the occupation of the Sudetenland a "Q" exercise without troops took place, attended by Stauffenberg. It is of interest in that at the end of the exercise, Stauffenberg, with two of his friends, produced a military comic turn. Without looking to left or right, an armoured force drove straight through to the Urals. As logistics officer, Stauffenberg improvised the most improbable expedients in order to keep supply going and ended with a *reductio ad absurdum* strategy, recommending that the force should drag itself out of the mess by its bootstraps. When the armoured force ran out of fuel in the Ukraine, his solution was the rapid capture of Baku, whence a land pipeline was laid and petrol pumped through to the force. The motto of the entire show was a favourite phrase of one of the directing staff: "The eye of their master makes the cows fat."[23]

The first serious test of Stauffenberg's organizing ability came during the Polish campaign. Freiherr von Loeper had taken over command of the division from General Hoepner at the end of 1938, and he remembers that Stauffenberg had to deploy all his energy to keep the division supplied, since, owing to the inadequate preparation of the campaign, the supply situation was very bad. "He was outstandingly successful," von Loeper has said. "The division never went short."[24]

The head of the operations section expressed a similar opinion: "Owing to his organizing ability, general level of education, and far-sightedness, Stauffenberg was a very good SO (logistics). He dealt extremely well with the various problems which came upon him suddenly and unexpectedly, such as the feeding of an unexpectedly large number of prisoners of war and assistance with the supply of the civil population."[25]

In addition to dealing with unexpected difficulties and improvising rapid solutions, Stauffenberg attempted to discover the reasons for any hitches which had occurred. The divisional ordance officer reports:

> The Polish campaign of September 1939 was our first experience of the use of motorized formations. This naturally brought out certain shortcomings which we had never suspected during paper exercises, exercises with troops, or manoeuvres. In order to get a grip on these and, even more important, increase the fighting power of the troops, Stauffenberg issued a big questionnaire after the Polish campaign; it was put to everybody from the divisional

commander down to the most junior private soldier in the division. The questions dealt, among other things, with improvements in weapons and equipment, vehicles, tanks, supplies, and treatment of the wounded, etc. The questionnaire was then thoroughly studied by Stauffenberg and worked up into a comprehensive report.[26]

In February 1940 the post of operations officer to the division fell vacant. Everyone expected that Stauffenberg would be appointed, and there was considerable indignation when this did not occur.[27] The new operations officer, Captain Helmut Staedke, therefore found himself faced with a certain ill-will. It was to a large extent due to Stauffenberg himself that Staedke managed to overcome this. He says:

> My first days were not easy, since, owing to his remarkable personality, Stauffenberg was naturally held in such high regard by all officers and other ranks at the headquarters that there was general annoyance that he had not been appointed operations officer. Initially Stauffenberg himself may have been somewhat disappointed, but he was sufficiently broad-minded and selfless to rise above this situation, and from the very first moment, entirely unselfishly, did everything he could to smooth my way into my new surroundings.

General von Loeper still expatiates today on Stauffenberg's extraordinary capacity for hard work. As soon as he had done his own normal jobs, he would offer himself to the divisional commander for other work. "He never seemed to be able to do enough work." As a result, Stauffenberg gained the General's ear to such an extent that anyone who wanted to be sure that his business was dealt with by the divisional commander came to Stauffenberg. The comments on Stauffenberg at this period bear out much which has already been said about him; the mere fact, however, that people who now met him for the first time make a special point of his charm and geniality confirms the earlier reports.

One Christmas he declined to go on leave himself in order to allow a fellow officer to visit his family; he spent many evenings helping a young attached officer prepare for the military district examination.[28] One further description is typical; it is from the wife of the then divisional personnel officer, Captain von Blomberg, who was a particular friend of Stauffenberg's; she describes him as a man "with a deep sense of responsibility, always ready to help, a charming companion, completely selfless and—something which in my view was his finest quality, since it so seldom goes with above-average intelligence —real and patent modesty."[29]

There were strict limits to Stauffenberg's geniality, however, when others failed to maintain a reasonable standard of decency and honesty. After the move into the Sudetenland, both officers and men seized the opportunity to buy things cheaply. They had plenty of money, and the Sudeten Germans badly wanted marks; in addition, many commodities were available which were already in short supply in Germany; Sudeten Germans were accordingly more or less compelled to sell their goods dirt cheap. Stauffenberg protested against this shameless exploitation and plundering of the Sudeten Germans; he got an order issued forbidding large-scale purchases by the men, and if anybody broke this rule, no matter whether he were an officer or other rank, he compelled him to return the goods.[30]

Another instance shows that Stauffenberg could be quite ruthless when anyone broke the laws of humanity which are necessary even in war. This occurred during the Polish campaign, on 4 September 1939, in Wielun. A sergeant major reported to his officer that he had arrested two women who had been signalling with pocket torches from the ground floor of a house and directing the enemy artillery on to Wielun. The sergeant major asked what he should do with the women. The officer without thinking replied, "Oh, get rid of them." This the sergeant major took as an order to shoot them, and he had both women executed. A little later, however, it emerged that the two women, mother and daughter, were well known in the place as being somewhat simple; frightened of the German soldiers, they had hidden themselves away on the ground floor of their house and crept about there with pocket torches. There was no question of signalling. Had there been any form of proper enquiry, this fact would have emerged at once. When Stauffenberg heard of the execution, he made it his business to ensure that the officer was court martialled, regardless of the fact that he happened to be a very old friend. The court martial sentenced him to a reduction in rank.[31]

During the Polish campaign, Stauffenberg's division formed part of Colonel General von Rundstedt's Army Group South, which attacked from Silesia. Geography was in Germany's favour, and the campaign was planned as a large-scale pincer movement. Army Group South was one arm of the pincer, the other being Colonel General von Bock's Army Group North, moving down on either side of the Polish Corridor.

The Sixth Panzer Division first captured Wielun and then, after crossing the Warthe and Vidanka, raced eastwards, south of the retreating Poles, until it reached the Vistula. It then turned north, on the inner flank of the Sixteenth Panzer Corps. Seven Polish divisions were surrounded just short of Radom. Though they put up an heroic resistance, the Poles had not the slightest chance in the face of German numerical superiority.[32]

The divisional headquarters received the news of the British and French declarations of war at a crossroads near Wielun in Poland. The morale of the troops fell to zero, and Stauffenberg made a remark showing how accurately he foresaw the course of the war, its length, and the strategy of attrition it would involve: "My friends, if we are to win the war, it will depend on our capacity to hold out; for a certainty this war will see out ten years."[33]

VII

Stirrings of the Spirit of Resistance

Stauffenberg was with the First Light Division (or the Sixth Panzer Division) for a bare two years—from 1938 to 1940. During this period political developments in Europe revolved primarily around the brutal assault of National Socialist Germany upon the existing system; the result was to drive the nations of Europe into a confrontation calculated to destroy the historic political entities. Eventually this situation exploded into a nationalist conflict, but at the same time, it raised questions as to whether the traditional notions of loyalty to country, nation, and state were still valid unless subordinated to the pursuit of some higher ideal.

Today these developments are clear to us. They were not so clear at the time. Such information as there is concerning Stauffenberg's attitude to the political events of this period gives no definite picture, and the mere fact that the various accounts are divergent is significant. Stauffenberg had not yet realized that the time might come when his duty towards the nation and his loyalty towards the state would become incompatible. Although aware of a rising tension, he did not yet feel himself faced with a crisis of conscience.

In his peacetime station at Wuppertal, Stauffenberg had gathered around him a circle of junior officers whom he frequently invited to his house. The object of these meetings was not simply the enjoyment of good food and wine; Stauffenberg's purpose was to increase the general knowledge and widen the intellectual horizons of his fellow officers by lectures and addresses. During the winter 1938-9, for instance, he invited his friend Rudolf Fahrner to give a talk on

Gneisenau. When it was over, to underline the point that Gneisenau was a pattern for an officer, Stauffenberg said, "There, you see; now we have learned how *he* did things."[1]

The social life of Wuppertal brought Stauffenberg into contact with civilians in the town. He was a member of a businessman's club named Concordia. At a club evening on 20 November 1938 he gave a talk on "The Move of German Troops into the Sudetenland as Seen from the Viewpoint of a 'Q' Staff Officer."[2] There are of course still people alive who heard this talk, but no one can remember any details. The general impression, however, was that Stauffenberg "said nothing critical of the Third Reich."[3]

It could hardly be expected that in 1938, and on a semipublic occasion, Stauffenberg would criticize either the National Socialist party or the government. It seems, moreover, that, like many others both inside and outside Germany, Stauffenberg found his faith in Hitler's diplomatic ability considerably strengthened by the solution of the Sudeten problem. Talking to a friend after the move of German troops into Austria in mid-1938, he voiced the opinion that Hitler would never do anything which might risk starting a war. His friend, who worked in the national defense section of the General Staff and therefore had more insight into the plans and preparations in progress, disagreed. But Stauffenberg stuck to his point of view, saying that Hitler had so far brought off everything without a war; a man who was always emphasizing that as a corporal in the First World War he knew only too well the horrors of war, could not, with his eyes open, head for a war which would in all probability have to be waged against the entire world.

The fact that in spite of a threatening level of tension, the Sudeten crisis was solved without bloodshed no doubt increased Stauffenberg's confidence that Hitler would not embark upon anything which might really lead to the outbreak of war. During this period Stauffenberg put his thoughts on paper in diary form, but unfortunately the papers were destroyed after 20 July. Gräfin von Stauffenberg thinks she can remember that they dealt mainly with the deepening crisis. Stauffenberg was prepared to concede Hitler his success, but expressed a fear that it might have gone to his head.[4]

Stauffenberg was not to know that in Berlin the first steps had been taken to prepare a concrete plan for a coup d'état. The chief of staff of the army, Colonel General Ludwig Beck, had resigned in mid-1938, when it became obvious to him that Hitler was proposing to use force to solve the Sudeten problem. His successor was Colonel General Franz Halder, also an opponent of Hitler; in order to prevent the outbreak of the war which seemed to be threatening, he was prepared to carry out a coup d'état and arrest Hitler. General Hoepner and the First Light Division had a special part to play in the plan. As already mentioned, the division was among the forces which invaded Czechoslovakia and for this purpose had been moved to the area Greiz-Plauen-Chemnitz. If the coup d'état had taken place in Berlin, the First Light Division was to bar the way to the "Leibstandarte Adolf Hitler,"[5] which was in southern Germany at the time. The coup d'état never came because the Munich conference enabled Hitler to solve the Sudeten problem by peaceful means.

It has frequently been assumed that Stauffenberg must have known of his divisional commander's intentions at the time. This is, however, highly improbable. Hoepner seems to have informed no one in his division of what he proposed to do. Neither Major Schöne, his operations officer, nor Freiherr von Loeper, one of his regimental commanders, knew anything about it. To carry out his plan, however, Hoepner would have had in the first instance to tell both these two something, and that before there was any need for him to inform his "Q" officer, Stauffenberg.

During the lunch break there were frequent political discussions in the mess. Officers who worked daily with Stauffenberg have stated that although he was a lively participant in these discussions, he never emerged as a decisive opponent of Hitler.

"During these discussions many things concerning the Nazi party were frequently severely criticized; I cannot, however, say that in this connection there was any indication of Stauffenberg coming out as an opponent of Hitler and the NSDAP. For Stauffenberg, as for the rest of us, Hitler was our country's chancellor, to whom we had had to swear our oath of allegiance."[6]

In this connection a remark by Rudolf Fahrner is of interest; he said that Stauffenberg must not be judged by any oversimplified "for or against" standards. Any attempt to do so overlooked "the independence of his political views; he watched events as they developed with a matter-of-fact, realistic eye and considered the existing situation as something with which one had to live. I never knew him to deviate from his realistic but watchful attitude towards Hitler and National Socialism; he was entirely uninfluenced by emotionalism; however, his rejection of anything mean or underhand was invariably equally unequivocal."[7]

It is therefore no surprise to find a report that early in 1940 Stauffenberg was particularly incensed over one of Goebbels' utterances. Goebbels had said, "The courage with which the German crusaders fought in Palestine has been rightly extolled. How much more bravely, however, will the German soldier fight in this war, which is being fought not for some imaginary virtue but for the daily bread and Lebensraum of the German people." Stauffenberg found the comparison vulgar and intolerable.[8]

The burning of the synagogues on *Kristallnacht* (9 November 1938) seems to have made an especially deep impression upon Stauffenberg, to have marked in fact a decisive turning point in his attitude towards the regime. The change was noticeable even to his fellow officers: "The events of *Kristallnacht* in November 1938 drew from Stauffenberg, always particularly insistent upon justice, decency, and morality, a savage condemnation of what had happened; he emphasized the damage done to Germany in the eyes of the whole world. In the period after November 1938 Stauffenberg criticized more fiercely than before those personalities in the Nationalist Socialist party whose character and behaviour were distasteful to him."[9]

Loeper, also, recalls that it was primarily the persecution of the Jews and action against the churches which gave rise to Stauffenberg's opposition to National Socialism.[10]

In the spring of 1939, when he met his friend Fahrner once more, he told him of an armoured exercise during which he had ridden in a scout car in order to discover for himself what was demanded of soldiers in the armoured corps. In this connection he let fall a remark which showed how far he had already moved from his political optimism of the previous year: "The fool is bent on war." A year earlier he had been insistent that Hitler would avoid anything which might lead to the outbreak of a war. But by the beginning of 1939 things had moved so far that he himself was prophesying war. The thought which weighed with him was the threat hanging over a nation which was prepared to squander the flower of its manhood twice in the same generation.[11]

Stauffenberg was first brought face to face with the idea of an insurrection after his return from the Polish campaign; the occasion was a visit by his uncle Graf Nikolaus von Üxküll, accompanied by the deputy president of Upper and Lower Silesia, Graf Fritz von der Schulenburg. The two men gave him a picture of developments in Germany and told him that it was his duty to act or at least to try to reach a position from which action might become possible.[12] Stauffenberg did not follow up this proposal, considering it unrealistic. With the best will in the world, as "Q" staff officer of a division, he could not initiate anything, nor was there the remotest likelihood that he would be offered a post giving him sufficiently high rank to offer any prospect of action.

Stauffenberg was, however, so shaken by this talk with Üxküll and Schulenburg that those around him noticed a change. Perhaps it was a sense of impotence, perhaps also vexation at the thought that this apparently mighty and victorious army was incapable of ensuring that the state maintained reasonable standards of decency. In another conversation with Fahrner early in 1939 he expressed great pessimism concerning the willingness of the general run of senior officers to resist; it could not be expected, he said, that people who had already broken their teeth once or twice would be prepared to make a stand in the event of some fresh initiative.[13] During this conversation, however, which took place on a walk in the winter woods, he indicated the man around whom German resistance was eventually to crystallize— Colonel General Beck; Beck, he said, was the key figure of the opposition to Hitler from within the Wehrmacht.

VIII

The General Staff

During the French campaign the Sixth Panzer Division was among the forces attacking through the Ardennes. The German High Command had originally intended the western offensive to follow the general lines of the plan for an attack on France worked out by Schlieffen, chief of staff of the army before World War I. Under this plan the main weight of the offensive was to be in the north, and the decisive break-through to take place through southern Holland and Belgium; the bulk of the German forces were therefore to be concentrated in the northern half of the front. General von Manstein, however, succeeded in winning Hitler over to the idea of an armoured break-through in the Ardennes. The French intelligence (Deuxieme Bureau) had in fact realized that the main weight of the German concentration and practically all the German armoured formations were concentrated north of the Moselle. However, Gamelin, the French chief of staff, considered that an armoured break-through in the Ardennes and across the Meuse was impossible.[1]

The offensive opened on 10 May. By 13 May the fortifications in southern Belgium had been pierced and on 13–14 May a crossing of the Meuse was forced at Monthermé. West of the Meuse there was no serious obstacle facing the German armour. A bold armoured operation, later known as "The Sweep of the Scythe," carried it to the mouth of the Somme, at Abbeville.

In the midst of the advance Stauffenberg received his posting to the organization section of the General Staff, the section which had asked for him in vain in 1938. Stauffenberg initially regarded the section head,

Colonel Buhle, with some misgivings, but soon established a good working relationship and the two came to be on terms of confidence.[2]

There had been considerable developments in the General Staff since 1918.[3] The Prussian and southern German staffs had previously been separate entities, and in the days of the kings of Prussia Schlieffen had trained his staff on authoritarian Prussian lines. But the Reichswehr had been formed from the Imperial Army as a whole and the Prussian and German staffs had consequently been merged. Southern German thinking, more liberal and less inclined to narrow dogmatism, dominated the Reichswehr. Proof of the preponderance of south German influence was the fact that when an independent General Staff was resurrected in 1935, the first chief of staff was Ludwig Beck, a Hessian, and the second Franz Halder, a Bavarian. Even the training and education of the younger generation was primarily in the hands of senior General Staff officers originating from the south. Outwardly the General Staff still appeared to be a stiff, strictly hierarchical organization, but in fact the tone was set by the south Germans with their more liberal and uninhibited attitude, particularly to officialdom. Beck and Halder purposely encouraged this tendency, and the change was noticeable in the improved relationships between junior officers and their superiors.

In a letter to me of January 1962 Colonel General Halder says of this relationship:

> Throughout my long service I have never known a staff in which opinions could be so freely and openly exchanged as in the General Staff of this period; although naturally the proprieties were always observed, there were frequently heated arguments without regard for rank or age. The result was that between the senior staff officers and their junior staff there was no parade-ground attitude; all that counted were intellectual and personal qualities. The relationship between the junior officers and their superiors was far closer and more personal than that to which I had been brought up according to the well-known tradition of the General Staff of the kings of Prussia.

Up to the end of 1942—in other words, as long as Halder was chief of staff—this atmosphere of mutual confidence persisted. Even officers opposed to National Socialism felt free to express professional and political opinions without running a risk of denunciation.[4]

There still exists a most informative letter from Stauffenberg to his wife, written about the time of his assumption of duty in the organization section and describing his work and responsibilities; even as early as this he mentions the difficulties with which the General Staff was already wrestling and which were to grow ever more serious as the war went on:

17 June 1940

Yesterday evening (!!) I got my first letter from you via the good Berndt. The army post is apparently in a complete muddle. Probably a lot has gone astray.

You ask about my work. I have the "peacetime army" desk. This may seem a very odd job to take over in the midst of a war characterized by the most mobile and decisive operations imaginable. But this can, of course, become a most interesting job, since after every war, one starts again more or less from scratch. The entire existing organization, build-up, structure, and order of battle, etc., has to be reviewed, and everything must be thought out afresh. So my job will shortly be of the very greatest importance. It is certainly not plain sailing. In so large and high-level an organization a number of parallel authorities are involved in all major questions, even the most important, and then we are dependent upon a dictator who has absolute authority and very definite ideas of his own. Differences of opinion, therefore, even on concrete questions, are unusually wide, and in addition there are invariably the most diverse political, manpower, and tactical considerations to be taken into account. One has to get used to the fact that on major questions all one's work and effort may be rendered useless by some unforeseen decision by the Führer and that in many other cases a compromise, frequently a meaningless one, emerges.

My experience of the operations and logistics of a modern armoured division is of great value to me and is no doubt the main reason why I am occupying this chair. I shall clearly be able to put through many things for which I have fought long and fruitlessly while with troops.

In addition to the basic question of peacetime organization, there
is naturally always a great deal of current business to do in the
organization field, and in general this takes up the greater part of
my time.

My section head is Colonel Buhle, a Swabian, energetic but not
altogether a gentleman. His deputy is Helmut Reinhardt, posted
here at the same time as I was. The wartime army is being dealt
with by Captain Schmidt, an infantryman and also a Swabian, so
the whole office is pure bred.[5]

As the letter shows, work connected with the conduct of the war
took precedence and soon pushed into the background the official
duties of the "peacetime army" section.

Stauffenberg's subjects as head of Group II in the organization section
included higher organization for war and the organization of the rearward services. It was his responsibility to work out and put forward
the organization and responsibilities of the senior command authorities
of the field army, the replacement army, and occupied territories—a
most important task in view of the diffusion of authority in the higher
levels at the time. In addition, he had to deal with all organization
questions concerning the replacement army and the volunteer formations forming part of the army, also with all military formations not
included in the field army, such as police and frontier guard units, and
with the para-military formations such as the SS and SA.

Many of these organizations—for instance, the Oberkommando der
Wehrmacht (OKW), SS headquarters, and the Ministry of the
Interior—had their own responsible authorities independent of army
headquarters (OKH). In these cases, Stauffenberg had to represent the
requirements of the army on the subjects with which he was concerned.[6]

Stauffenberg was at first horrified by the hard-headed skepticism
and the forebodings current in the General Staff. Coming direct from
the front, he felt that victory was round the corner, as indeed did most
people in Germany at the time, even including those opposed to Hitler
and his regime. Stauffenberg believed that the 1918 slate had been
wiped clean and that Germany now held all the cards in her hand to
impose a new order in Europe. His conception of the "New European

Order," however, was something very different from that which the Nazis were planning. In his view the war should not lead to a sort of colonization of Europe but to the final elimination of centuries-old tensions. Stauffenberg later singled out as one of the main causes of the German defeat the fact that Hitler had not been capable of normalizing relations between France and Germany.[7]

In mid-1940 Stauffenberg still thought that all the possibilities for a favourable political outcome were open. When he joined the organization section, however, he found, as he later had to admit, an atmosphere almost of defeatism; people were worrying about steel production and manpower resources, while at the front the army was winning victory after victory. Differences of opinion regarding the overall situation were so sharp that they even threatened to affect the long-standing friendship between Stauffenberg and his predecessor, Major von Pezold. The latter made the desk over to Stauffenberg after only three days, although a fortnight's hand-over had been allowed.[8]

Stauffenberg remained with the organization section until early 1943. He went through all the moves of the headquarters—Godesberg, Chimay in Belgium, Fontainebleau, Zossen, Mauerwald in East Prussia, Vinnitsa in the Ukraine, and then back to Mauerwald.[9] He was there throughout the decisive years of the war and from the headquarters saw the Balkan campaigns, the African campaign, and the German advance into Russia. But he was also there in 1942, when from the German point of view, the war took a catastrophic turn.

In the course of his work Stauffenberg had to travel on duty very frequently, both to the front and to the rear areas. Of all the organization section officers, he is the one most frequently mentioned in the 1942 war diary (which still exists): as examples of Stauffenberg's duties, he had to check unit battle-worthiness, to discuss the question of NCO's battle schools with C-in-C Home Army, to deal with training questions right back to the medical convalescent camps; in addition, he had to handle fundamental questions such as the build-up of the officer corps and to negotiate with police headquarters the regulations for the use of police personnel of Baltic origin.[10]

His polish in negotiation and his charm of manner were a great help to him in these discussions. Müller-Hillebrand, Stauffenberg's immediate superior from April to October 1942, says:

His judgment was sound; he appeared sure of himself, and he had a capacity for carrying on sensible negotiations with all sorts of differing authorities. As a result he became far more widely known than would be expected for one of his age, rank, and position. From the first day to the last, Stauffenberg put into his job all his accustomed concentration and energy. Even when the realization began to grow that the war was threatening to end in immeasurable catastrophe for Germany, he continued to work at the same intensity.

A graphic description of Stauffenberg at work is given by Major Freiherr von Thüngen, a reserve officer posted to the General Staff in 1942 and a personal friend:

What was he like? I had some inkling from the reputation which preceded him: "One of our very best, far above average, his character is his strong point." This was amply confirmed if one had an opportunity of seeing him at work. I never opened Claus's door without finding him on the telephone, mountains of paper in front of him, the receiver in his left hand, turning over the files with his right, a pencil between his fingers. He always looked happy; depending upon who he was talking to, he would be laughing (that invariably came somewhere in the conversation) or cursing (that generally happened too), or giving an order, or laying down the law; but at the same time, he would be writing, either his great sprawling signature or short remarkably detailed notes on the files. His clerk was usually with him, and whenever there was a pause would take down, post haste, notes for the file, letters, or circulars, Claus never forgetting to dictate with almost pedantic accuracy such tiresome accessories to General Staff work as letter heading, reference number, and subject. Claus was one of those men who could do several things at once, all with the same concentration. He had an astounding capacity for working through files, in other words, reading them and sifting the important from the unimportant at a glance—an enormous advantage in his type of work. Equally astounding and equally striking were his capacity to concentrate, his clarity of expression, and his sudden asides, which invariably hit the nail on the head and frequently took his listeners aback. When I used to visit him he was generally at the end of a twelve-, fourteen-, or even sixteen-hour day filled with telephoning, conferences, visits, dictation, working on files, notes for conferences, etc. He worked at an incredible pace, with unyielding concentration, and yet he appeared just as fresh late at night as he did in the morning. I envied him both his strong nerves and his health, neither of which he spared.

Stauffenberg expected his staff to show a similar unsparing devotion to duty. "They often looked overdone and tired to the point of exhaustion; the pace in their offices was killing; their master was ruthlessly demanding. Nevertheless, every little incident and sidelight which gave any indication of the relationship between them showed that the staff regarded their chief both with affection and respect and would therefore work themselves to the bone for him. They were carried along by his energy, efficiency and devotion to duty."[11]

Young though he was, Stauffenberg soon came to be trusted by everybody. Anyone who got to know him, went to him whenever he wanted to pour his heart out, and this applied not merely to men of his own age and rank; even generals visiting headquarters from the front or from the replacement army would often seize the opportunity of having a talk with him. Whenever Stauffenberg was late for lunch, the word went round: "He's got some general weeping tears in his office again." Matters came piling in on him which were really not his responsibility. The fact that he was thereby contravening an order from Hitler did not bother him in the least.[12] He busied himself with anything that interested him, even if outside his official competence.

What attracted his visitors so much was his capacity for clear un-hurried decision, his courage in speaking his mind, and his ability to find time for every visitor and listen calmly to his troubles.[13]

In many people's eyes, therefore, he was "the ideal of a young General Staff officer, a go-getter whose natural impulsiveness was tempered by common sense and strict General Staff training, so that with him one could get business done quickly."[14]

Primarily, however, he was attractive because of his immense charm and his infectious, appealing sense of humour. This enabled him to say things to his superiors which they would never have accepted from anyone else. He never failed to give his opinion, even though to do so might require considerable courage. He was capable of expressing a flatly opposing point of view in such a way that the impression given was neither offensive nor presumptuous.[15]

Opinions expressed concerning his work in the General Staff bear out previous descriptions. In his 1933 confidential report Walzer referred to professional competence and integrity of character; similar comments are to be found in accounts of Stauffenberg's tour of duty with the First Light Division, and they appear again in the statements by his fellow officers and superiors in the General Staff. Colonel General Zeitzler, Halder's successor as chief of staff, considered Stauffenberg "even then a good future corps and army commander."[16] Major General Kleikamp, colonel in charge of the General Staff personnel branch (Generalstabs-Zentralabteilung) from 1942, recalls that all reports on Stauffenberg were very good. "Graf Stauffenberg had both the character and ability to rise to the very top one day. He was undoubtedly the best stamp of young officer, the type we required for the highest command positions."[17]

Stauffenberg worked in this headquarters for more than two and a half years; all that time he was in the immediate vicinity of the Führer's headquarters, in constant touch with the senior officers of the army, and continuously wrestling with the manifold military and political problems of the war. His entry into the camp of Hitler's active opponents undoubtedly stemmed from his experiences of these two and a half years.

He was particularly influenced by the fact that ever since 1940 he had been on terms of friendship and confidence with Colonel General Halder.

There was nothing unusual about the chief of staff dealing direct with junior officers; nevertheless, Stauffenberg's personal relationship with Halder was considered as something exceptional by his fellow officers. Major (as he then was) de Maizière, for instance, says, "Although two or three rungs down the ladder, Stauffenberg was the only one of the organization section apart from the section head who from time to time did business direct with Halder and with whom Halder would discuss things personally."

The invitation to Stauffenberg to discuss matters outside the realm of strict military business came from Halder himself.

> My private talks with junior staff officers invariably grew out of discussion of some strictly military problem. Officers would never have broached world or political questions had I not given them the opening during some private interview. I knew Stauffenberg's attitude to Hitler and by making some comment or asking some question, would lead him on to speak his mind. But as soon as it was clear that we were on the same side and Stauffenberg had realized that my attitude was even more extreme, though perhaps more considered, than his own, there was no further need for me to give him a lead. Once he had dealt with his military business, he would speak his mind openly and even ask whether he might tell me what he was thinking.[18]

As a character, Halder found Stauffenberg "magnetically attractive"; he said, "I recognized in Claus von Stauffenberg a born leader, one whose whole outlook on life was rooted in his sense of responsibility towards God, who was not prepared to be satisfied with theoretical explanations and discussions, but who was burning to act."[19]

Halder explains that the words "born leader" should be understood "in the sense given them by the previous generation, to which Stauffenberg in spirit belonged." The words carried no hint of the class-war "master and servant" idea. "My concept of a born leader is a man who, unlike most people, does not allow his thoughts and actions to be dictated by external influences; by 'born leader' I mean a man who has both the courage and the will power to deal with the problems of life on his own responsibility. There is no incompatibility between 'leadership' and 'service' when a natural leader of his own free will decides to serve, for instance, his country or an ideal."[20]

Next to Beck, chief of staff of the army until August 1938, the name most intimately connected with the first concrete plans for a coup d'état against Hitler was that of Halder. When the Sudeten crisis reached its height in September 1938 and it was obvious that Hitler was determined, in his own words, "not to shrink from a world war in order to bring the Sudeten Germans back home," it was Colonel General Halder, together with General von Witzleben, Colonel Oster,

and Admiral Canaris, who were determined to put an end to the
adventure. As already mentioned,[21] the plan was to arrest Hitler and
arraign him before the Reich high court, but it was not put into effect
because, at the last minute, Hitler agreed to Mussolini's proposal for
the conference which led to the Munich agreement of 29 September
1938. This deprived the opposition of the argument that Hitler was
heading irresponsibly towards a new world war,[22] and they were afraid
that under these circumstances there would be no popular support for
a coup d'état. As a result of the collapse of this plan and of the fascination which Hitler's successful brinkmanship exerted even over his
opponents, when war did in fact break out in 1939 there was no
section of opinion to refuse to follow Hitler's lead.

Plans for Hitler's arrest came to the fore once more between the
Polish and French campaigns. Early in November 1939 Halder instructed Colonel Oster to check the 1938 preparations and bring them
up to date. On 5 November, however, while this check was still under
way, came a violent disagreement between Hitler and von Brauchitsch,
the commander-in-chief of the army. Hitler complained bitterly about
the attitude of the generals as a whole and threatened to "exterminate
the spirit of Zossen." Zossen being the location of the army general
staff, Halder became apprehensive lest Hitler should have learned of
the plans and ordered Oster to destroy all material concerning the
projected coup d'état. It later emerged that Hitler's threat was not based
upon any definite suspicion but was merely an expression of his general
dislike of the "prophets of gloom," as he used to call the General Staff;
by then, however, it was too late to reconstruct the plans. Another
factor contributing to Halder's hasty decision to cancel his plans for a
putsch may have been the fact that his soundings of commanders in
the field had shown that the number of those prepared to play an active
part was so small as to make the plan barely viable.[23]

Halder was also involved in a third attempt to bring about a change
of regime. Early in 1940 a lawyer, Dr. Joseph Müller, on instructions
from Beck, entered into negotiations with the British chargé d'affaires
in Rome, the object being to discover what the attitude of the Western
Powers would be in the event of a change of regime in Germany.
Contact was established through the Vatican, Pope Pius XII taking a
personal hand as intermediary. The Western Powers showed them-

selves ready to make considerable concessions in the hope that the change of a regime might come before the opening of hostilities in the west. Halder was given the report on these negotiations, which he laid before his commander-in-chief. Brauchitsch, however, could not be persuaded to take any further action. So this golden opportunity for Germany to reach an agreement vanished. On 10 May 1940 the offensive opened in the west.[24]

When Stauffenberg was posted to the army general staff, he found all those who were not obsessed by blind faith in the Führer's genius, and who were therefore still capable of independent thought on the military and political situation, asking the same question, "What next?" Stauffenberg's view was that victory in France was meaningless unless its outcome was to bring Germany and France closer together; some new order must eventually emerge to replace the old emnity between the two nations.[25] But although Hitler was now at the peak of his success, in Halder's view he failed at the very moment when he might have shown real stature as a statesman. He had loosed war upon the world without having first thought out what the possible results of his decision to make war might be. There was no political concept for the treatment of defeated France. While the war continued, the outward trappings of military occupation were no doubt justified, particularly since England was still fighting, and even Hitler agreed that she could not be attacked.[26] With her victories over Poland and France, combined with the occupation of Denmark, Norway, and the Benelux countries, Germany had subjugated all her territorial neighbours, but the question remained how to re-establish real peace.

Quoting from one of Halder's letters:

> In spite of all our victories, we were not victorious—a thoroughly unsatisfactory situation which, to anyone not under the spell of Hitlerism, could only be dealt with by political means, in other words, by forfeiting any further expansion of German power in the west and concluding an early peace based on far-reaching German concessions. This problem gave rise to lively discussions among the younger General Staff officers in army headquarters. On one side were the protagonists of cool reflection and wise moderation; on the other, the fire-eaters defending

Hitler's insatiability. . . . Claus Stauffenberg was, of course, on the side of calm reflection and moderation.[27]

In a letter of 19 June sent from the field headquarters, Stauffenberg made certain comments on the outcome of the French campaign; they sound more like a lament over the collapse of a great nation than some jubilant song of victory. "The French debacle is frightful. They have been totally defeated and their army annihilated, a blow from which this people is unlikely easily to recover."[28]

In another letter, two days later, Stauffenberg reverted to the question of the French collapse, which seems to have affected him deeply. France had been rudely awakened from the security born of her 1918 victory, he said; the same fate might await any nation which felt over-sure of its achievements. It is astounding that a thirty-three-year-old officer could show such clarity of vision; at the moment of greatest military triumph he was still able to see that the true aim of national education must be to make the youth of a nation aware that only a continuous quest for renewal could guarantee national well-being.

> A week from today is the anniversary of the Treaty of Versailles. What a change in so short a time: while rejoicing over our triumph, we should cast our minds back over the three decades through which we have lived and realize how little finality has been reached; abrupt change or indeed a complete reversal of the situation is more probable than even a few years stability. We must teach our children that salvation from collapse and decay lies only in permanent struggle and a permanent quest for re-newal; the greater our past achievements, the more essential renewal becomes. We must teach them, too, that stagnation, immobility, and death are synonymous. Only then shall we have fulfilled the main part of our task of national education.[29]

The central theme of Halder's discussions with his friends who held views similar to his own was invariably the question of preventing Germany from being bewitched by a man who had neither balance nor morality. The circle of those who were unquestionably of the same mind as Halder, "in whom the spirit of resistance to Hitlerism was more or less inborn" (Halder's words), consisted of officers of a certain age whose duties brought them into close contact with the chief of staff—Generals Fellgiebel and Wagner or Admiral Canaris, for instance. Halder was always on the lookout, however, for "promising young General Staff officers." He says, "In spite of the fact that I knew that they could help little towards the solution of these great problems, I felt that they could assist in forming a correct estimate of the popular mood towards the dictator."[30] Both Halder and Stauffenberg reached the conclusion that Hitler must be removed from control of the state. They were, however, opposed to an attempt at assassination:

> For hours at a time we would mull over and over possible methods of removing this monster without in the process seriously damaging the army now in contact with the enemy in fulfillment of its duty to defend the Fatherland, and without destroying the entire structure of the state. Large sections of the German populace had been captivated by Hitler's success in the French campaign. In addition, however, to the prospects of an insurrection and the methods by which it might be launched, a continuous subject of discussion was its timing. Insofar as I remember I discussed all these ideas with Claus Stauffenberg. Later, when Hitler's decision to take the offensive against Russia was becoming ever clearer, and finally in the period when the war was being carried into Russia, our discussions revolved round the question of the way in which military means might be used to remove Hitler from the saddle without turning him into a martyr, and how the party's grip might be broken.[31]

Halder and Stauffenberg did not discuss the question of who should take over the leadership of the state after a coup d'état; it was not for the soldiers to "waste their breath over Steps Nos. 4 and 5 before the possibilities of Step No. 1 had been established." According to Halder, Stauffenberg leaned towards a "strictly controlled democracy" on the British model. Both men nevertheless realized that in the first instance there could be no question of anything other than a military dictatorship, which, however, must give way to civilian leadership at the earliest possible moment. "It was equally clear that this civilian leadership must be organized democratically."[32]

Halder was ultimately to have no part in the events of 20 July. It is certain, however, that conversations with Halder contributed to that clarification of Stauffenberg's political views which, combined with his natural energy, gave him the ability to carry the German resistance along with him in his historic act of courage. It has been said that Stauffenberg's rejection of Hitlerism as a system dated from the period of the Stalingrad catastrophe,[33] but this is contradicted by Halder, who says, "His criticism was based simply and solely upon the revolt of his whole soul against the spirit of Hitlerism."[34]

Criticism alone, however, does not imply active opposition. Stauffenberg was not the only one who had the courage to express strong views. The majority, however, with Halder himself the outstanding example, did not go further. There can be no doubting Halder's deep-rooted antagonism to Hitler, but he felt his hands tied by the responsibilities of his office and eventually, after a stormy scene, was dismissed by Hitler. It is clear from Halder's own statements that he had allowed himself to become entangled in a web of second thoughts—what would be the effect on the army facing the enemy?—how would the wider circles of German public opinion react?—how could the martyrization of Hitler be avoided?—it was a web which prevented him from acting. In this he was typical of many other senior officers of the Wehrmacht. Stauffenberg's conversations with Halder were undoubtedly of great value to him personally, but in the ultimate issue, other influences were decisive in turning him on to the path of definite resistance. These influences stemmed directly from his day-to-day military duties.

IX

1942

The direction of the war on the German side revealed far more than Hitler's dilettantism as a strategist. Under the cloak of military necessity the whole evil of National Socialism was allowed to run riot.

The first instance was the higher organization for war. Stauffenberg found himself wrestling continuously with difficulties stemming from the nonsensical command set-up upon which Hitler insisted, and he had no hesitation in giving vent to pungent criticism in public. In 1941 he gave a lecture to Staff College graduates in Berlin and opened with a sentence which one of the audience remembers ran as follows: "If our most highly qualified General Staff officers had been told to work out the most nonsensical high level organization for war which they could think of, they could not have produced anything more stupid than that which we have at present."[1]

Hitler was not prepared to leave the conduct of the war in the hands of a single responsible headquarters, but insisted upon the constitution of a whole series of competing authorities. Being profoundly mistrustful of army headquarters and the General Staff, he made every effort to restrict their influence. He downgraded the General Staff to the status of a theatre command, limiting its responsibility to the eastern front alone; all other theatres of war were dealt with by the OKW operations staff. As a result the latter was prevented from fulfilling its true role and assuming responsibility for the Wehrmacht as a whole; in the end there was total lack of co-ordination not only between theatres of war but between the three services.[2] The whole set-up was a chaos of competing authorities, each in its own watertight

compartment; there was the army headquarters with its General Staff
and the OKW intelligence directorate under Admiral Canaris; there
was the OKW with its operations staff; there was Göring; there was
the Reich Security Service. As time went on the situation deteriorated
even further, as organizations from individual ministries and the party
made their appearance; the foreign ministry competed with "Ribbentrop's office"; the Ministry for the East, under Rosenberg, with the
party "External Organization," under Gauleiter Bohle. Hitler was
obsessed by a suspicion mania. Instead of a sound, sensible organization
for war, he preferred this total confusion, since it prevented any
potential concentration of power in the hands of any one authority.

For one short moment at the end of 1941 it looked as if the jungle of
command authorities might be cleared up. After the failure of the
German offensive against Moscow there were bitter disagreements
between Hitler and Brauchitsch, the latter considering withdrawal
unavoidable. When Hitler yet again hauled the commander-in-chief of
the army over the coals Brauchitsch handed in his resignation. Hitler
thereupon took over command of the army himself, saying, "Anyone
can do the little job of directing operations in war."[3]

The ultimate consequences of Hitler's decision were disastrous.
Temporarily, however, it did raise the morale both of the army and the
home front. Confidence in Hitler was still unshaken, and Goebbels'
propaganda made much of the Führer's profound sense of responsibility, which had moved him to leap into the breach himself.[4]

Oddly enough, even Stauffenberg allowed himself to be carried
away by this temporary optimism. As seen from his desk there was
now some hope that a more sensible war organization would be
adopted and that the change might work to the army's advantage. As
he told a friend, Brauchitsch had reached the end of his tether, and
when faced with Hitler, no longer had the energy to represent and
insist upon the interests of the army when they conflicted with those
of the other services, and even more important, the party organization.
Now, he went on, there would at last be an opportunity for the chief
of staff of the army to do business direct with Hitler; Hitler would now
have direct contact with "his army" and be far more interested in its
welfare than hitherto. Stauffenberg even expressed confidence that the
situation on the eastern front could be put right.[5]

The Russian campaign had brought the German army to the brink of defeat for the first time in this war. The army general staff had initially planned the main thrust direct on Moscow, but two months after the opening of the offensive Hitler reverted to his original intention and ordered two widely divergent attacks, one in the north on Leningrad and the other in the south towards the Donetz Basin. In his diary Halder recorded the Führer's order as follows: "The most important objective, which must be reached before the onset of winter, is not the capture of Moscow; it is to deprive the enemy of the Crimea, the industrial and coal resources of the Donetz, and to cut off their oil supplies from the Caucasus; in the north the object must be to encircle Leningrad and effect a junction with the Finns."[6]

From the outset the German General Staff had realized that in the Russian army the German Wehrmacht was facing an adversary superior both in manpower and resources, whose strength must inevitably grow in view of its inexhaustible reserves of human material. Towards the end of 1941 General Köstring, who had been military attaché in Moscow for many years and was later commander of the Russian volunteer forces, remarked sarcastically that if the war went on like this, the Russians would have to mobilize.[7]

German inferiority was initially offset by the versatility of the German commanders and the greater war experience of their troops. Even so, however, a campaign against Russia was from the outset so risky an undertaking that Hitler was given urgent warnings against it. When it was clear that he was not to be moved from his purpose, the only possibility of scoring a decisive success seemed to be to direct the main weight of the offensive on Moscow. Hitler refused to adhere to this plan, and the initial successes seemed to prove him right. But in spite of enormous gains of territory and the capture of a vast number of prisoners, it soon became clear that the defeats inflicted on the Russians were tactical only, not strategical.

As a result, Hitler finally made up his mind to launch an attack on the Russian capital. But it was then too late; the attack took place in early October and was soon bogged down in mud, winter having started earlier than anticipated. On 10 October 1941 the *Völkische Beobachter* carried a red banner headline "Campaign in the East Decided." Two months later, however, the "attack on Moscow" petered out in the outskirts of the city, and over the next few months the initiative lay with the enemy. The Germans had passed the peak of their success.[8]

Stauffenberg was not basically opposed to Hitler's strategy of an attack on Moscow. At the end of April 1942 he met von Loeper, his former divisional commander, in Wuppertal. The two went for a walk lasting several hours and discussed affairs at the front. Loeper told Stauffenberg that in December 1941 he had been ordered to advance with his division over a distance of about four hundred miles to Gorki, well east of Moscow, in order to capture the vital rail junctions east of the capital and cut its communications to the rear. In his opinion, Loeper stated, the order was crazy. Stauffenberg, however, did not agree: one must on occasions, he said, stake everything on a single card if one wished to reach a decisive objective, and the capture of the enemy capital was such an objective.[9]

A measure of agreement with Hitler's strategic decisions did not, however, prevent Stauffenberg condemning his internal political measures in no uncertain terms. During this talk with Loeper they had touched on Hitler's speech to the Reichstag on 26 April 1942, in which he had demanded that henceforth he should be the sole and supreme judge, empowered to decide what was necessary for the "good" of the German people, "without being bound by any legal regulations."[10] Stauffenberg and Loeper both agreed that this demand and its fulfillment meant the end of the rule of law.[11] An arbitrary system of justice had now been given legal recognition; this was the natural sequel to the events of 30 June 1934, when Hitler had had the SA leaders liquidated without finding it necessary to have recourse to any court of law. Legislative, executive, and judiciary powers were now in the hands of one man. Anything was right which was good for the German people—in Hitler's opinion. So deliberate a rejection of any standards of legality was bound to have some side effects in the military field. On 6 June 1941 the so-called Commissar Order—that all Soviet commissars captured should forthwith be handed over to the SD for liquidation— had given an indication of the way in which Hitler intended to use his new plenary powers. A year later came other orders, such as that for the shooting of prisoners from the so-called Allied commando units and the "Order for Guerrilla Warfare," laying down that any methods, even including the shooting of women and children, might be used if they produced success.[12]

Stauffenberg's hope that Hitler's assumption of the command of the army would lead to the adoption of a more realistic strategy and a more clear-cut command set-up was soon disappointed. The old rivalries between army, air force, SS, and other organizations broke out afresh. Hitler continued to give preference to the branches of the Wehrmacht which he considered more reliable in the National Socialist sense.

In his 1941 lecture to Staff College graduates, referred to above, Stauffenberg had put the question, "What is the difference between an SS division and an army division?" and had given the sarcastic reply, "Simply that SS divisions have better equipment but no divisional chaplains."[13]

In April 1942 Stauffenberg came across Werner Reerink (the ex-aide of the Sixth Panzer Division) in army headquarters and gave him a vivid picture of the difficulties with which the General Staff had to contend in keeping the army supplied. For instance, he said, if the organization section had ordered a certain number of vehicles required for the formation or reconstitution of certain divisions to be ready for delivery from the factory on a certain date, they would find either that the SS had already laid hands on them or that, via Göring, the Luftwaffe had already "pocketed" the lot and used them as they thought fit. The same applied to ammunition, tanks, and even to recruits. In this atmosphere of barely concealed hostility common sense no longer counted for anything.[14]

The 1942 war diary of the organization section of the army general staff gives chapter and verse to prove Stauffenberg's point. Volunteers, for instance, were much sought after, since from the military point of view they were likely to give better service than conscripts; the war diary, however, shows that the army allocation was only 45 per cent in spite of the fact that the army had by far the largest number of fighting troops and was suffering the severest losses. But Hitler thought it more important to allocate the volunteers to the National Socialist formations, and in spite of a personal protest by the chief of staff refused to make any change in the quota.[15] SS units invariably had their full complement of equipment, even if this meant keeping the army short.

Between 1 July and 30 September 1942 SS formations laid hands on twice their allocation of personnel- and load-carrying vehicles, receiving nearly half as many as the army. From the Opel works they could even count upon a quota of their own, produced by their own labour.[16]

The Luftwaffe was also allotted a disproportionate share of available volunteers, and it was allowed to make the wildest demands for personnel and equipment. At one time it was proposed to make good the army's manpower shortage by the use of women, but the entire program was nullified by the exorbitant demands of the Luftwaffe; at a conference in OKW on 23 October 1942 the following figures were given for requirements in women: army, 31,000; navy, 33,000; Luftwaffe, 136,000.[17] In mid-September 1942 OKW issued an order for the formation of ten to twelve Luftwaffe brigades, the personnel to come from the Luftwaffe, but equipment to be provided by the army. In theory they were to support the army in land operations. A month later the formation of twelve more Luftwaffe divisions was ordered, a program which ran counter to all military common sense. Because the new formations were totally inexperienced in infantry methods, it was obvious they would not be equal to their task, and wastage would therefore be far too high. The sensible course would have been to incorporate the Luftwaffe personnel in experienced army units, possibly as junior NCO's, after the necessary training. The equipment of these Luftwaffe formations obviously made considerable inroads into supplies for the army; the army organization section war diary, for instance, says: "The requirement in load-carrying vehicles for eleven to twelve Luftwaffe divisions is approximately 6,000; the result will be to postpone, yet again, bringing four to five armoured divisions up to establishment."[18]

The head of the organization section, Lieutenant Colonel (as he then was) Müller-Hillebrand went so far as to set down on paper the disadvantages he foresaw in the formation of these Luftwaffe divisions. Göring, however, took care to ensure that the Luftwaffe personnel remained under his command. In spite of the protests of the organization section, the supreme command adhered to the plan of forming Luftwaffe units.[19]

From the winter 1941–2 the available reinforcements were no longer adequate to make good the army's losses. On 20 January the war diary

recorded a shortage of 93,000 men. Losses had been most severe in
Army Group Center, which showed a total of 95,000 killed, wounded,
and missing as against reinforcements of only 10,300.[20]

Forecasts predicted that by 1 June 1942 the overall shortage would
have risen to 340,000 men.[21] The reality turned out to be worse. On
1 June available strength was set against the estimate, and it was found
that losses were 25,000 men greater than anticipated.[22] On 1 November
1942 the army was 800,000 men short, and it was anticipated that by
the spring of 1943 the overall shortage would rise to 1,200,000.[23] Army
losses were particularly severe in August and September 1942, when the
gap between losses and reinforcements was no less than 270,000 men.[24]

Stauffenberg and his staff in the organization section found themselves engaged in a desperate search for any method of arresting this
development, but were blocked at every turn. Their request for an
additional call-up of men in reserved occupations was refused, owing
to the requirements of industry.[25] A proposal to disband weak and
disorganized formations and use the personnel thus made available to
form new full-strength units was "categorically" turned down by
Hitler "on political and propaganda grounds."[26] On this subject the
war diary says: "The manpower shortage affects some 110 infantry
formations on the eastern front. In the case of these divisions shortages
are so great and fighting power therefore so low that there is little point
in maintaining the divisional organization. The best solution would be
to disband a sufficient number of infantry divisions to ensure that in the
remaining formations fighting efficiency bears some acceptable and
reasonable relationship to organization."[27]

This solution being barred by Hitler, the organization section took
refuge in the reduction of divisional strength from nine to six battalions
and the organization of differing types of division, "however un-
palatable it may be for commanders to have to deal with formations of
differing fighting capacity and mobility." In addition, in March 1942
a cut in the administrative and headquarters strengths in the west was
ordered.[28] On 8 October an instruction, drafted by Stauffenberg's
section, was issued, the object of which was "to increase fighting
strength." It ordered a 10 per cent personnel cut in headquarters on the
eastern front and in army headquarters. In addition, all formations not
actively engaged were placed "on call," and all officers, NCOs and

men who could be spared were posted temporarily to these divisions, where they were given training in infantry tactics. The intention was that these divisions should either provide temporary reliefs for units at the front, or in the event of particularly severe fighting, be put into the line as reinforcements.

This picture of the situation would seem to be contradicted by the fact that during 1942 the "ration strength" of the field army rose. In June overall strength was 3,954,862 officers, NCOs, and men, and on 1 November 4,207,000.[29] The demands of the fighting, however, rose at a far higher rate than available strength.

In Africa the German offensive had ground to a halt before El Alamein, and the general situation of the German-Italian force was deteriorating.[30] Apprehension increased that the Allies might attempt a landing somewhere along the French or Norwegian coastline. Troops had to be withdrawn from the eastern front to strengthen the coastal defenses, and divisions destined for Russia had to be retained in the west and reinforced.[31] Towards the end of the year developments in Africa necessitated hasty reinforcement of the Italian coastal defenses.[32]

The mid-1942 offensive in southern Russia was, however, the decisive factor in overstraining German potential. The Führer's new "Directive for Army Reorganization and Recuperation in Preparation for Operations in 1942" was issued as early as 21 January.[33] The organization section's comment was that it was no longer possible fully to equip the forces detailed for this operation. They could "only be brought to full strength in time for the operation if, in addition to the personnel reserves initially allocated, further trained personnel could be obtained from Germany" (by releasing men in reserved occupations).[34]

To ensure that Army Group South, which was to carry out the operation, was brought to full strength in personnel, it was necessary in May and June 1942 to reduce training time for recruits destined for Army Groups Center and North from six to two months.[35]

A full scale of equipment could not be made available for the forces destined for the offensive. The organization section's comments include the following: "It is not possible to bring the operational formations or Army troops up to full strength in vehicles. The estimated requirement in vehicles can only be met as to 50 per cent from new deliveries unless an equivalent number of formations and Army troops are to go short."[36]

One month before the opening of the offensive the war diary noted that "unless preliminary operations result in sizeable further losses and delays in re-equipment, the formations of Army Group South can in general be classified as adequately mobile for the opening of the offensive. Equally, adequate reinforcements up to 100 per cent strength must be made available if possible. A decisive factor for the conduct of operations, however, is the fact that the stamina of formations can no longer be brought to the level of summer 1941."[37]

On 28 June 1942, when the offensive opened, the war diary noted that the first-priority mobile formations, in other words the most important spearhead troops, were at only 80 per cent of establishment in tanks.[38]

The army had in fact managed to assemble an offensive force which, though no longer at full fighting effectiveness, could nevertheless be considered as adequately manned and equipped within certain limits. But this had been made possible only by stretching resources to the limit; there were no further reserves of any size available. The German Wehrmacht was playing its last card.

The offensive consisted of two main thrusts, southwards into the Caucasus and eastwards against Stalingrad. Despite certain initial successes, neither of the principal strategic objectives could be reached; strength was dissipated by attacking in two widely divergent directions, each attack aiming at far distant objectives. The end result of this strategy was "Stalingrad," and before the 1942 summer offensive had even begun, this catastrophe had been foreshadowed in the organization section's war diary.

At the end of 1942 the Führer's orders for operations in 1943 arrived in the organization section. Though the collapse of the summer offensive had long since become obvious, Hitler was still apparently unable to take a realistic view of the situation. The organization section laboured dutifully, working out the necessary equipment demand for the planned operations; but, as if they wished to guard against any suspicion that they themselves might have thought up these totally unrealistic figures, they added: "These demands have been worked out on the basis of orders received from the Führer."[39] Shortly thereafter the head of army ordnance stated that "only a fraction of this demand can be met."[40]

X

The Russian Volunteer Formations

Of all the various methods used by the German army to make good its colossal manpower losses in the east, the most important was the incorporation of Soviet prisoners of war in German units.

After the initial great victories of the Russian campaign, it was found that many prisoners of war were quite prepared to work in German formations. At first they were used only as auxiliaries—cooks or drivers, for instance. But as time went on they were employed to carry machine guns and ultimately became an integral part of the fighting troops. In certain divisions no less than 15 per cent of personnel consisted of these volunteers, and in the end approximately a million former Soviet soldiers were serving in the German army.[1] An entry in the war diary of early January 1942 is as follows: "At the request of a number of corps headquarters, caused by the serious shortage of personnel for guard duties, an order was issued to constitute companies composed of released prisoners of war and anti-Bolshevik members of the local population. . . . In addition, consideration was given to the formation of legions of up to regimental strength for employment at the front."[2]

Prisoners of war were initially recruited by individual units according to requirements, without higher headquarters bothering to give authorization. When, however, the supply and equipment of the volunteers became more than individual units could handle themselves, the organization section of army headquarters had to take a hand, and Group II was detailed as executive authority for all questions concerning the Russian volunteers. According to one of the officers involved, it was primarily due to the efforts of Stauffenberg and his staff that the volunteers were made the responsibility of army headquarters and not of the SS.[3]

Prior to all this, in October 1941, two senior Turkish officers had visited the Führer's headquarters. They had suggested that a Turkish-Mohammedan volunteer formation be constituted on the eastern front from Mohammedan prisoners of war organized on the lines of the Mohammedan legion formed in Wunsdorf during World War I.[4] The Ministry for the East took up the proposal and eventually achieved the incorporation of all prisoners of Caucasian or Turkish origin into military formations. Ultimately there were units for Armenians, Azerbaijanis, Georgians, North Caucasians, Turkestanis, and Volga Tartars. Later in fact a Cossack corps under General Helmuth von Pannwitz was formed, Hitler having been assured that the Cossacks were a people of unknown origin and not basically Slav. Pure Russians were at the time not being admitted to the volunteer formations.[5]

Hitler was not, however, enamoured of these volunteers. He was afraid that their use might carry with it certain obligations which would later prevent him from establishing his "New Order" in the east. The war diary says, "The volunteer companies having proved a success, units are asking for the formation of as many as possible. The Führer, however, is insistent on the principle that these units are to be approved only in the most urgent cases. He fears that otherwise there may be political repercussions which might prejudge a later decision on the question of the treatment of the occupied areas in the east."[6]

In addition, Hitler was convinced that the peoples of the east were not natural fighters; this was of course completely contrary to the facts, but it accorded with his preconceived ideas. Hitler was convinced that it was the prerogative of the German soldier to shed his blood in battle; all the Russian was fit to expend was his sweat. Hitler either could not or would not recognize the political possibilities opened up by the fact that hundreds of thousands of Soviet soldiers were prepared to fight on the German side against their own countrymen. Probably he realized instinctively that the volunteers' readiness to change sides carried with it a danger to his own system—the acceptance of Russian volunteers might imply that there were men in the German army ready to liberate their own country from totalitarian tyranny. In addition, use of these volunteers would destroy the convenient theory used by Goebbels' propaganda that the Russians were subhumans and that the people of Russia and the Soviet system were one and the same thing. Hitler's opposition to the volunteer formations was therefore based on ideological grounds; in the case of the majority of German senior commanders, however, the idea of making war with the assistance of foreign volunteers was something for which they were not mentally prepared. It is a striking fact that the men who fought most passionately for humane treatment and a just political settlement for the peoples of the east were to be found primarily among the younger generation of the German officer corps.

Stauffenberg and his staff maintained that in justice to the volunteers they should be organized in their own units, with their own uniform and their own officers—in short, that a "Russian Liberation Army" should be formed. He thought it possible that the war against the Soviet Union might be turned into a Russian civil war. These ideas came to nothing, however, since they did not accord with the views of the National Socialist leaders.[7] Stauffenberg therefore had to content himself with trying to ensure that the Russian volunteers were treated on the same basis as members of the German Wehrmacht. Because they were grouped in units not larger than a battalion, were under German command, and had German cadres, he contended that they should be treated on exactly the same footing as German soldiers.

When Hitler learned that the number of these locally raised battalions was still on the increase, he issued an order, on 10 February 1942, forbidding any further recruitment.[8] Stauffenberg watered it down somewhat at the drafting stage, but as issued to corps HQs it read: "The Führer has decided that the constitution of additional Ukrainian or Baltic formations for guard duties or for use as field units at the front will cease."[9] The order was not strictly observed, and in June Hitler was compelled to intervene once more and issue a categorical instruction that from 1 August no further units of this nature were to be formed.[10]

But this did not mean that the existing locally formed units were to be disbanded. Group II of the organization section therefore continued to work to eliminate the discriminatory treatment which was still the rule. On 25 June 1942[11] a conference dealing with the volunteer battalions took place in the office of General Wagner, the quarter-master general. One of those present was Dr. von Mende, representing the Ministry for the East; his account is as follows:

> General Wagner himself presided at the conference. With him as advisers were Lieutenant Colonel Schmidt von Altenstadt and Graf Stauffenberg, representing the organization section of army headquarters. The political side—in practice the Reich Ministry for Occupied Territories in the East—was represented by myself together with the director of the political division of the ministry and OKH liaison officer, Dr. Otto Bräutigam. . . .[12] Prior to this official conference I had held a series of internal discussions, either in Berlin or Rastenburg, with Schmidt von Altenstadt and Graf Stauffenberg on the question of the Russian volunteers and policy in the east. The conference had therefore been well prepared beforehand. After a short introduction by General Wagner, Dr. Bräutigam dealt with the political aspects of granting the volunteers a status equivalent to that of German soldiers; I then followed up with a reference to their organization into national units. The next to speak was Graf Stauffenberg, who, in accordance with our preliminary discussions, took up the political point and gave a masterly exposé, ending with an extempore draft of an instruction laying down equality of treatment for the volunteers. He insisted most adroitly that those present should either voice any misgivings they might have during the conference or, if they had none, give their agreement to his proposals. His object here of course was to prevent the volunteer question being discussed in wider circles and by a variety of authorities, and so being un-necessarily delayed. He gained his point without difficulty.[13]

Dr. Bräutigam adds: "In all these questions it was a pleasure to work with Graf Stauffenberg; he showed himself fully aware of the political problems involved in the formation of these units."

Initially there were differences, basically discriminatory in nature, between the treatment of the volunteers and that of German soldiers in almost everything—general conditions, provision of canteen goods, pay, family allowances, badges of rank, and decorations. Hitler wished to give the volunteers a uniform similar to the German, but of another

colour. Stauffenberg opposed this plan with his usual energy; he
equally scotched another idea—that prisoners of war should be
recognizable by a tattoo mark on the right buttock (he told a General
friend that if this rule was introduced, whenever he met anyone in
Unter den Linden in future he would first have to ask him to take
down his trousers to prove that he was not a Russian POW[14]). In
addition, he succeeded in obtaining agreement that members of the
locally raised units should be entitled not only to their special "bravery
decoration for personnel of Eastern origin" but to the Iron Cross also.[15]

In August an "Instruction regarding locally raised Auxillary Forces
in the East" appeared, followed by a separate order concerning
"Turkish Units in Rear Areas."[16] Both originated from Stauffenberg's
section.[17] The instruction contained everything concerning the
formation, employment, status and conditions of locally raised forces;
they were divided into four groups:

> 1. Turkish and Cossack units whose use in battle was permitted.
> 2. Locally raised guard units for use in rear areas and against
> guerrillas.
> 3. Locally raised police forces for use as the executive arm of
> the local German authorities.
> 4. Auxiliary volunteers—a new term introduced into the
> military vocabulary by this order. They consisted of local in-
> habitants and released prisoners of war employed as volunteers
> for technical assistance.[18]

Insofar as the scope of his office allowed, Stauffenberg did everything possible to improve conditions for the volunteer units. On 5
November he held a conference with representatives of the administrative section, supply section, and medical section at which the main
lines of further measures concerning supplies and amenities for these
units were agreed on.[19] In one instance he had to intervene to prevent
Turkish battalions from being sent into action without adequate winter
clothing.[20]

Of all the occupied areas of the Soviet Union, the most leniently
treated was the North Caucasus. The population was not of Slav origin,
and there were no German plans for colonizing this area. In addition, it
seemed advisable to guard against any reaction from Turkey. Stauffen-

berg therefore began looking for a suitable person to undertake the functions of special military representative in the Caucasus, an authority to be recognized both by the Germans and the volunteers. One of his staff, Hans von Herwarth, suggested to him the former German military attaché in Moscow, General Köstring, to whom reference has already been made. He had been born in Russia of German parents and had incurred Hitler's displeasure for having given emphatic warnings against an attack on the Soviet Union.[21]

Herwarth knew Köstring from the time when they had worked together in the embassy in Moscow, and he arranged a meeting between Stauffenberg and the general. "It was obviously going to be difficult to persuade this man to accept the post of organizer of the volunteers, since he wished to have no part nor lot in an undertaking he regarded as a crime." His meeting with Stauffenberg, however, convinced him of the necessity of accepting. Each felt himself drawn to the other by some indefinable influence. When General Köstring left the room Stauffenberg exclaimed, "What a wonderful personality!" Köstring, too, recognized the ability of the young General Staff officer. This meeting—an historic moment for humanity—was the genesis of the idea of a real war of liberation for the peoples of the Soviet Union, in alliance with a different type of Germany.

Stauffenberg had hoped to entrust Köstring with the whole organization of the volunteers *ab initio*, but the idea was scotched by resistance from Hitler's entourage. All Stauffenberg could achieve was to get Köstring nominated as "General Officer attached to Army Group A for Caucasian Questions." As such, however, he was able to work closely with his old friend Field Marshal von Kleist, and instructions were issued to the German troops to behave towards the population of the Caucasus exactly as they would behave if they were on manoeuvres at home. The collective farms were broken up, and the population given a wide measure of self-government. "The success of these measures was soon to be seen. There was no guerrilla warfare in the Caucasus, and the North Caucasian people were soon fighting enthusiastically on the German side."[22]

An entry in the war diary, most probably drafted by Stauffenberg, describes the nomination of General Köstring as follows: "With the backing of General Köstring's authority it is far easier to get various offices such as armaments, reinforcements, propaganda, quartermaster, etc., to take proper interest and give help in practical ways. The organization section suggested that General Köstring be nominated OKH representative in Army Group A area, with the idea that he might later be employed as military commander in the Caucasus, or in some similar capacity. After obtaining the approval of the Führer, the chief of OKW agreed to Köstring's appointment as Special OKH Representative."[23]

Under pressure from General Wagner, Hitler issued a directive on 8 September 1942 that local puppet governments might be set up in the Caucasus. A few days later, on 13 September, Stauffenberg, Altenstadt, and Bräutigam met and drew up a detailed program laying down that the guiding principles in the Caucasus area were to be "freedom, independence, and collaboration."[24]

Stauffenberg stated quite openly that the war in Russia could only be won, if at all, by renouncing the National Socialist concept that the populations in the east were creatures of a lower order.[25] He criticized German policy severely, not merely among his friends but in a memorandum sent to OKW in which he stated that the existing treatment of east European workers constituted "an irresponsible challenge to the east."[26]

In October 1942 Stauffenberg attended a conference at Vinnitsa with Schmidt von Altenstadt in the chair and some forty staff officers present. According to Otto Schiller, who was there, Stauffenberg got up and made a half-hour extempore speech amounting to a passionate condemnation of German policy in the east. Germany was in the process, he said, of sowing such hatred in the east that "our children will reap the reward of it one day." The war could be won only if it was possible to win over the eastern peoples to Germany's side. At present Germany's eastern policy was calculated to turn this mass of humanity into enemies. It was a scandal that, at a time when millions of German soldiers were risking their lives daily, no one was to be found among the senior commanders with the courage to put on his steel helmet and go and tell the Führer quite openly about these things, even at the risk of losing his life as a result.[27]

At the end of 1942 Stauffenberg scored an important success. On 15 December he was given authority to set up a special headquarters for the locally raised units known as "General, Eastern Forces". This was of course primarily an administrative measure, but it nevertheless "legitimized" these forces as part of the German Wehrmacht.[28]

Thanks to Stauffenberg, a propaganda school was formed and maintained in Dabendorf. Here Russian officers and soldiers were given a short course and then dispatched to the prisoner of war camps and volunteer units. Thanks to them, and with the help of the Wehrmacht propaganda section (OKW/Wpr IV), the more flagrant abuses in the prisoner of war camps were brought to an end, and some improvements were made in the Russian workers' camps.[29]

On 18 December 1942 a meeting took place in the conference room for the Ministry of the East in Berlin to discuss abuses in the treatment of the civilian population in the east. A large number of officers and officials were present, the former, one of whom was Stauffenberg, representing the various General Staff sections and also Communications Zone Headquarters.[30] According to the minutes a lively discussion took place on maltreatment of civilians by German officials, forced labour, food shortages, and the general disillusionment of the population. It was agreed that the army was in no sense responsible for this state of affairs in the operational area and that the political authorities must answer for it. There could be only one conclusion: the present abysmal situation regarding treatment of civilians was no longer tolerable; in view of the seriousness of the situation and the necessity to reinforce the fighting troops, active collaboration by the population in the east was essential.[31]

Alfred Rosenberg, the Minister for the East, himself tended to favour more humane treatment of the population. Spurred on by the support of the officers, he sent a personal memorandum to Hitler, outlining the main points emerging from the conference. However, although he was the minister responsible for policy in the east, Hitler questioned his competence in such matters, saying that he "had no business to meddle in military affairs." At the same time, Hitler gave the Wehrmacht representatives to understand that they were not to concern themselves with political questions without the agreement of OKW.[32]

Rosenberg took his rebuff lying down, but the officers took up the question once more. General Reinhard Gehlen, head of the Intelligence Section, Foreign Armies East, had already prepared a memorandum

on the subject; now Colonel Schmidt von Altenstadt and Colonel
Hans-Henning von Tresckow, head of the operations section of Army
Group Center, each prepared a memorandum,[33] the salient points of
which were reproduced in the "Pamphlet on Relationships with
Auxiliary Volunteers" issued by the organization section in January
1943.[34]

According to Hans von Herwarth, the collective farm issue provided
the best illustration of Stauffenberg's attitude to the treatment of the
Russian population. In Stauffenberg's view it had been an error to
retain the hated *kolkhoz* system after the German conquest; it would
have been better, as in the Caucasus, to break up the collective farms
and so prove to the people of the Soviet Union that the Germans'
object was to liberate them and that they were not being asked merely
to exchange one form of slavery for another.[35]

XI

The Path of Decision

Hitler's hatred of the Slav race was such that he was incapable of treating the Russian volunteers justly or, from the political point of view, wisely; he was equally incapable of appraising the military situation realistically. The more menacing the military situation became, the more frequently he interfered in the conduct of operations and the more obvious became his dilettantism based on pure wishful thinking. The further divorced he became from the views of his military advisers, the more obdurate and obstinate were his reactions to any sober proposals. Goebbels wrote in his diary for 9 March 1943, "The Führer thinks nothing of the generals. They throw dust in his eyes whenever they can. Besides, they are ignoramuses and do not even understand their own job of making war."[1]

The staff had all it could do to translate Hitler's sudden ideas or his "orders" into terms which preserved some semblance of military logic; they could not, however, eliminate his party jargon—"political guidance" to the fighting troops, intended to fill them with "fanatical determination" or "righteous wrath." In contrast to this propagandist verbiage was the calm, matter-of-fact attitude of the General Staff, which was unanimously of the opinion that: "Whatever comes from Hitler is nonsense."[2]

Stauffenberg became increasingly convinced that in some shape or form active resistance must be offered to these misconceived orders and above all to the crimes ordered from on high and perpetrated in the occupied areas. In his talks with Halder or discussions with other officers, however, he was not at this stage envisaging some funda-

mental sweeping change brought about by the removal or murder of
Hitler; his thoughts were turned more towards improving the general
atmosphere by putting right certain individual abuses and effecting a
general amelioration of Hitler's misguided policies by directing
attention to certain definite points. This idea was based primarily upon
the belief that Hitler was under the influence of a misguided and
depraved camarilla from whose grip he must be freed.[3] When, however, in spite of all efforts, no change was apparent, discussion turned
towards the necessity of removing Hitler from supreme command of
the Wehrmacht.[4] But even this line of thought meant that the attempt
to solve the problem was being made from far too narrow a standpoint.
Hitler, after all, could hardly have maintained his political authority if
he had allowed himself to be forced to renounce the combination in his
own hands of political and military leadership which he had imposed
on 4 February 1938. That would have been tantamount to an admission
that he was not the "greatest warlord of all time." There was in fact
no feasible method of curtailing Hitler's power by legal means.

During the second half of 1942 Stauffenberg was forced to the conclusion that Germany's political and military situation could only be
bettered by ruthless action against Hitler himself. It was Hitler after all
who against all sound advice had ordered the disastrous dual offensive
against Stalingrad and the Caucasus in the summer of 1942; the orders
legalizing crimes under the cloak of military necessity could be traced
back to Hitler himself.

Gradually it was becoming questionable whether a favourable ending
to the war was possible at all—a brilliant German victory was now
more or less unthinkable. This question was the main subject of a conversation between Stauffenberg and his section head, Müller-Hillebrand,
during a morning ride in the Ukraine countryside around Vinnitsa in
August 1942. Discussing an incident when Hitler had broken out in
wild invective against the generals, Stauffenberg exploded "in words
totally uncharacteristic of him, 'Is there no officer over there in the
Führer's headquarters capable of taking his revolver to the brute?' "[5]

A similar comment of Stauffenberg's in the autumn of 1942 shows
how he was reacting to the current but totally useless idea that the
Führer must eventually be told the truth: "The point is not to tell him
the truth but to put an end to him, and I am prepared to do that."[6]

Although as early as the winter of 1941-2, when asked what the solution was, Stauffenberg was heard to reply, "Kill him", his fellow officers, looking back to that time, do not believe that he was then already toying with the idea of a coup d'état and an attempt at assassination.[7]

It was hardly likely that a major on the staff, who hardly had an opportunity of entering the presence of the Supreme Commander, would discuss concrete plans for an assassination and coup d'état with other equally junior officers. A number of his remarks, however, passed on by other people, show that Stauffenberg was already expressing himself with unwonted determination and vehemence.

Moreover, he actually did something. During the second half of 1942 he began to look round to see whether there were not some influential personalities prepared to come out into the open against Hitler. Stauffenberg was of course thinking primarily of the generals. On certain of his trips to the eastern front he made efforts to discover whether the senior commanders, in particular the field marshals, could not be persuaded to unite in common action against Hitler. But, as he later told his divisional commander in Africa, he invariably came back disappointed. "They all told him that they entirely agreed that things could not go on as they were and that something must happen. But no one showed himself ready to act or to take the lead."[8]

Stauffenberg's reaction to this attitude was one of unconcealed contempt. Shortly after the dismissal of Halder a number of the more junior officers were discussing matters among themselves, and several of them said that they were sick of General Staff work and wanted to get away to the front, primarily to escape from what went on in headquarters. Stauffenberg came out in passionate opposition:

What is this sham heroism, going and getting yourselves shot like hundreds of thousands of others "in faithful performance of duty." This is nothing but cowardly evasion, no better than the field marshals who make the excuse of their duty to obey and their "purely military outlook." We have to have something quite different. When, by reason of his office or his upbringing, a man reaches high rank, a moment arrives when the man and the job are identical and no second thoughts can weigh with him; it is his duty to represent the general concensus of opinion. How few there are now who behave that way or even feel that they should do so. We have now got butchers and bakers and candlestick makers dressed up as generals. They draw their pay, do their "duty," put their trust in the Führer, and look forward to their next leave. What a way to run a country![9]

In mid-June 1942, shortly before the opening of the disastrous offensive in the south, Stauffenberg wrote a letter to General Paulus in which he lamented that it was difficult "to keep up one's enthusiasm" when one saw the troops "staking their all . . . while the commanders, who should set an example, squabble about prestige and are unable to pluck up the courage to put forward their views or indeed their convictions even though thousands of lives may depend on them."[10]

It has sometimes been stated that Stauffenberg discussed the possibility of action by the opposition with the majority of senior commanders on the eastern front, but there is no definite evidence to support this. Of the three field marshals still alive today, Georg von Küchler, Wilhelm List, and Erich von Manstein, the first two never even knew him.[11] He did, however, have a conversation with Field Marshal von Manstein which the latter has described as follows:

> I only spoke to Stauffenberg once, when he came to Army Group South on behalf of the organization section of army headquarters to discuss the question of reinforcements. He then asked me for a personal interview, during which he spoke his mind about the errors being made by the Supreme Command—in other words, by Hitler. I could not but agree with him. I told him that I too was only too well aware of Hitler's military shortcomings (the political system was not referred to) and that I considered a change in the Supreme Command to be urgently necessary. My idea was that a responsible chief of staff of the Wehrmacht should be appointed and that he should undertake the real military direction of the war, alternatively that at least an overall commander-in-chief should be appointed for the eastern front. I told him that I would try—as indeed I did—to get Hitler to agree to a change on these lines. There was nothing in what Stauffenberg said to indicate that he was thinking of a concerted move against Hitler

by the commanders-in-chief—in other words, of a coup d'état. My impression rather was that he was in despair over what he saw going on in OKH, and so I advised him to get himself posted to some staff job at the front in order to get away from the unhappy atmosphere of the Führer's headquarters. . . . If I had thought that in view of the situation on the eastern front, a coup d'état against Hitler was either possible or inevitable, then I would . . . have acted myself. I was and still am of the opinion that any such action must have led to the collapse of the eastern front, and until the very day of my dismissal that was what I was hoping to avoid.[12]

Stauffenberg was most disappointed by his conversation with Field Marshal von Manstein. "That is not the answer I would have expected from a Field Marshal," he observed.[13]

Stauffenberg's object in this conversation was far more than mere criticism of the conduct of the war. Why did he ask Manstein for a personal interview after he had done his official business? There would have been no need for that if all he wished to do was to express views current in practically every staff at the time—Army Group South headquarters was criticizing the Supreme Command like everybody else. Moreover, in a conversation with Colonel Busse, chief-of-staff of Army Group South, immediately before his interview with Manstein, Stauffenberg had made his views quite clear. Busse says, "We touched on the overall war situation, on which Stauffenberg's view was very pessimistic. He was troubled by the same problems that had been worrying us in the Army Group for a long time. In the inner circle in Army Group headquarters extremely sharp criticisms of Hitler were frequently being voiced at this period. So with us Stauffenberg must have found an atmosphere which almost invited him to speak his mind."

The fact that Stauffenberg nevertheless asked Manstein for a personal interview can only mean that he intended to go further than the usual criticism. Although Manstein says that Stauffenberg never referred to anything in the nature of a coup d'état, this was almost certainly his original intention. On hearing Manstein's ideas concerning a change in the military command, Stauffenberg probably abandoned his real subject for discussion of Manstein's—that Hitler should be forced to give up military command. Manstein's aim was simply to put some sense into the direction of military operations. Busse says, "The Field Marshal and I were continually cudgelling our brains at this period as to how Hitler might be forced to give up supreme military command." But this was an idea Stauffenberg had already considered and found inadequate.

In the light of the situation Manstein's primary purpose was to obtain freedom of action in the direction of the war. As he himself says, his guiding principle was: "We must hold the eastern front." Why a collapse of the eastern front should necessarily have followed if the senior commanders had told Hitler that they no longer proposed to follow his instructions Manstein does not say. In any case, anyone who knew Hitler's mentality must have realized that he would never willingly give up military command. In order, therefore, to achieve even the more restricted objective, to "put sense into the direction of operations," there was no alternative but to take the bull by the horns. Manstein was fully aware that a military catastrophe was threatening and according to his lights did what he could to prevent it, but Stauffenberg quickly sized Manstein up: no decisive action—in Stauffenberg's sense of the word—was to be expected from him. Everything that Manstein had in mind was to be done by legal means.

When Manstein finally advised Stauffenberg to get a posting to the front in order "to get a breath of fresh air,"[14] the thoughts running through the latter's mind were no doubt similar to those to which he had given vent earlier (see pp. 107–8).

By the end of 1942 Stauffenberg was finally convinced that only the fall of Hitler could save the situation.[15] All of Halder's objections to the use of force, all arguments that the time must be ripe for Hitler's removal, now seemed invalid to Stauffenberg, who felt that they had been overtaken by events. The development of the Stalingrad catastrophe and the realization that Hitler was the cause of it finally confirmed him in his determination that the opposition must take action.

On 24 September 1942 Halder was dismissed as chief of the General Staff after bitter disagreement between him and Hitler over the conduct of the war around Stalingrad. When Halder pointed out that the Russians at Stalingrad had fresh formations totalling one and a half million men and that they had raised their tank production to 1200 a month, Hitler shut him up, calling it "idiotic twaddle"; the task now facing the army, he went on, could not be fulfilled by professional ability but only through the "ardour of belief in National Socialism."[16]

The change at the top had its effect upon the position of the General Staff. Hitler became increasingly impervious even to the factual arguments of the new chief of staff, Colonel General Zeitzler, and the influence of those prepared to tell him what he wished to hear increased.[17] Stauffenberg was most depressed by this change in the influence of the General Staff. He visited Halder one evening in his Berlin villa a few weeks after the latter's dismissal. Halder, who was under Gestapo supervision, was worried that he should have come, but Stauffenberg told him that he was determined to bring about some change and had come to Berlin to discuss the matter with his brother Berthold. The atmosphere in OKH was no longer to be borne, he said; with Halder's departure all resistance to Hitler had vanished; it was now hardly possible even to exchange ideas, and one was expected to head for catastrophe with one's eyes open and without lifting a finger.[18]

On 14 January 1943 Stauffenberg met Werner Reerink once more. They talked about the Stalingrad army, the capitulation of which was imminent. Stauffenberg told Reerink of the decision made on 23–24 November, which sealed the fate of that army and finally proved that Hitler was now no longer open to any argument which did not accord with his own wishful thinking.[19] In more detail, Reerink says:

> In the evening Stauffenberg took me for a walk through the Mauerwald, since, as he said, one could talk more freely in the open than in the office huts. He told me the detailed story of the vain efforts by OKH to persuade Hitler to order the break-out from Stalingrad and so save the lives of 300,000 men. OKH had been supported by Goebbels, who had shown himself most sensible—he had been the only party man to take the attitude that the German people must be told the truth about Stalingrad and about the general situation. With Goebbels' help they had almost got Hitler to issue the order for the break-out while there was still time. At the decisive briefing conference, however, Göring had taken the floor with the words: "My Führer, I guarantee that my Luftwaffe will keep the Stalingrad army supplied." Hitler had

thereupon decided: "Sixth Army will remain in Stalingrad."
Stauffenberg was totally and obviously shattered by such irresponsible and treacherous behaviour. He told me this in so many
words.

Stauffenberg described Göring's attitude as sheer betrayal.[20] After
Stalingrad Stauffenberg was clear that the war could no longer be won
by military means and could only be brought to an end by diplomatic
methods.[21]

At this point it is worth looking back over the changes in Stauffenberg's attitude. He had throughout been watching developments in
Germany with a keen and critical eye, but had not jumped to the
conclusion that the regime must be brought down by force. The
thought had passed through his mind from time to time, but had not
yet become a conviction. He went through a number of phases during
which he hoped that affairs might still take a turn for the better; for
instance, in 1938 he refused to believe that Hitler was deliberately
heading for war; in 1940 the thought uppermost in his mind was pride
at the German victory over France; early in 1942, when Hitler assumed
command of the army, he was optimistic. During that year, however,
the military catastrophe for which Hitler personally was responsible
and his method of conducting the war, which revealed his complete
disregard of human life, forced Stauffenberg to take a more radical
view of the military and political situation.

Freiherr von Thüngen says, "He was deeply depressed and completely convinced that there was now no way of avoiding catastrophe.
His feeling that 'he' must be got rid of was more definite than ever
before."

XII

Africa

On 1 January 1943 Stauffenberg was promoted to lieutenant colonel. Shortly thereafter, without having asked for a move, he was posted to Africa. The posting in fact took place on instructions from Colonel General Kurt Zeitzler, the chief of staff of the army, who said, "I wished to give him experience as a staff officer with troops and in command, in order to prepare him for later command of a corps and an army." The move suited Stauffenberg very well.[1] Owing to casualties in Africa, he had to take up his new appointment so quickly that the three weeks' leave to which he was entitled was cut to eight days.

An incident which occurred during this short leave illustrates his state of disillusionment. During a short stay in Berlin he met Colonel Bürker, one of his predecessors in his future post in Africa. They had a talk at Kempinski's, one of those present being Frau Beate Bremme, whom Stauffenberg had known from the Wuppertal days. Her account is as follows:

> On 2 or 3 February 1943 . . . I happened to meet Gräfin Stauffenberg in Berlin; she took me to lunch at Kempinski's. At lunch were the Stauffenbergs and Colonel Bürker and his wife. Bürker, who was Blomberg's son-in-law, had been summoned back from Africa on Hitler's orders because both his Blomberg brothers-in-law had been killed. Bürker's successor, Bürklin, had been wounded, and so Stauffenberg was to take over the job previously held by them both. Accordingly, during lunch there was a kind of hand-over between Bürker and Stauffenberg. Stalingrad had just happened, so the two naturally discussed the

war situation. They talked loudly and very critically, Stauffenberg more than Bürker. During lunch the army communiqué was broadcast. The waiter came along and insisted that they talk more softly, but they took not the smallest notice and in fact talked even louder.

Stauffenberg's new post was Senior Staff Officer (Operations) of the Tenth Panzer Division. Before taking over he visited his predecessor, Colonel Wilhelm Bürklin, in Tunis to be put in the picture regarding the division. Bürklin had been severely wounded by a mine, and the divisional commander was also a casualty. Bürklin says, "I was at the time in a very bad way and could not carry on a long conversation. I still remember, however, that, seeing he had no experience of war in the very open African country, I warned him particularly against low flying enemy aircraft. Shortly afterwards he was severely wounded by low flying aircraft."[2]

The new divisional commander, Major General Freiherr von Broich, took over at the same time as Stauffenberg, and the two soon established a very good working relationship. Colonel Reimann, commanding one of the armoured regiments in the division, says, "The harmonious teamwork of these two produced most happy results from the point of view of the division, particularly seeing that heavy fighting was in prospect." And the divisional commander himself says, "After a short while we became real friends. . . . Whatever the situation, he was calm, balanced, and personally courageous. The armoured division's tasks changed almost daily. For instance Stauffenberg once said to me, 'Here in the African theatre we practice a different phase of operations almost every day; today it is attack, tomorrow defense, then withdrawal, then attack again, then delaying action, etc. In a fortnight one will have put into practice everything one learned at the Staff College.' As SO (operations), he was equal to any situation."[3] Colonel Heinz Schmid, commander of the divisional artillery regiment, was particularly struck by Stauffenberg's capacity "to grasp a tactical situation rapidly and formulate orders in excellent style, at the same time giving a vivid picture. The drafting of his orders was never stereotyped, but highly personalized."[4]

In the spring of 1943 the Tenth Panzer was continuously in action.

It was involved in the heavy fighting on 14 February around the Faid and Kasserine Passes and on 6 March in the major Afrika Korps attack from the Mareth line in southern Tunisia against the advancing British Eighth Army.[5]

In spite of the severity of the fighting, "divisional orders always arrived in time and crystal clear. The troops felt they were being well led. Even when disengaging there was no confusion; the divisional commander and his staff officer dealt with all difficulties with cool self possession; their calm solidity had its effect upon the troops."[6]

Colonel Schmid gives the following account of the Mareth battle:

When the British Eighth Army, which was in strength, had been brought to a halt before the Mareth position in southern Tunisia, an attack was to be carried out from the western sector of this position and from the mountainous country southwest thereof. In that area, the *djebel*, One Hundred Thirty-fourth Infantry Division was strung out over a wide sector. The Fifteenth, Twenty-first, and Tenth Panzer Divisions had in all more than a hundred and fifty battle-worthy tanks. The Tenth Panzer proposed that all three divisions should be placed under single command and attack from the *djebel* against the left flank and rear of the British Eighth Army, but unfortunately the proposal was turned down. According to several experienced regimental commanders this plan had excellent prospects of success. I do not, of course, know to what extent Stauffenberg was responsible for the idea, but the proposal was definitely made from his divisional headquarters, which up to the time of the unhappy Medenine battle had given striking proof of efficiency. In fact, instead of striking at the enemy's flank and rear with a superior force of armour, we launched three separate armoured attacks against his front and defensive areas, which were prepared for just such an operation. We split into penny packets instead of concentrating. While a prisoner of war I learned from a senior officer, who was actually on the spot, what the situation was in rear of the British left flank during the Medenine battle, and so could see how apt the Tenth Panzer's proposal had been. Stauffenberg certainly had some hand in it.

All who knew Stauffenberg during his tour of duty with the Tenth Panzer Division stressed his excellent relationship with the troops. "He soon became very popular in the division and was very highly thought of for his efficiency, reliability, and energy, still more for his frank, cheerful manner and helpfulness."[7]

Stauffenberg was an attractive and very gifted officer whom commanding officers in the division soon learned to appreciate. A few days after his arrival I asked him how he was settling down with the Tenth Panzer. His reply was that he had been most impressed by its excellent spirit of co-operation, its astonishingly rapid and invariably accurate reporting, and the healthy self-confidence of the troops. He had never imagined that life could be so good from a soldiering point of view. This was said without any intention of buttering me up; it was quite clear that he was saying exactly what he thought.[8]

In spite of all his office work, the Staff Officer (Operations) invariably found time to keep in touch with the troops. He would frequently visit regiments and battalions to discuss personal or official problems with commanding officers. By informal discussion on the spot, he would deal with a whole mass of business which would otherwise have had to be cleared up through official channels. His conversation was not, however, limited solely to official matters; he would range over history, geography, literature, and of course, politics. Though he was clearly opposed to the existing system, he never tried to persuade or influence anybody. He did not seem to me to be in any sense fanatical, impetuous, or a go-getter trying to change everything all at once. Whenever opportunity offered he would talk to men of all ranks; he was often to be seen conversing with drivers, NCOs and private soldiers, and they would not just stand and say "Sir," but would ask him definite questions, which he would answer with equal clarity. He had the natural charm of the Swabian, which everybody found irresistible.[9]

A good illustration is the following report from a young officer due to take over command of a company and who therefore had to report

to Stauffenberg—which he did on 6 April, the day before the latter
was so severely wounded:

The divisional command post was in an olive grove west of
Sidi Mansour. As I arrived there, I ran into the converging British-
American attack of 6 April. . . . When I got to the command post
I found that it was under artillery fire. I waited for the attack to
cease and then went in to report to the Senior Staff Officer. As I
entered the command caravan, I found myself facing a tall, slim,
young-looking officer occupied in wiping mud and splinters of
glass from the maps. He was wearing American trousers and the
Afrika Korps shirt with lieutenant colonel's badges. This was
Graf Stauffenberg. As soon as I had reported, he took me to a
window, and pointing to two foxholes, said, "If that starts again,
you take the right one, and I'll take the left one." I was in the
caravan for about forty to forty-five minutes. There was no
question of having a quiet undisturbed talk—quite the contrary.
He talked to me during pauses in other, more urgent business.
The American attack was in full swing and the noise of battle very
loud; infantry fire could be heard. An uninterrupted stream of
messages came in, not only from the division's own sector, but
also dealing with the situation in the south. Commanders were
sending in desperate requests for reinforcements or permission to
withdraw, all of which Operations had to refuse. There were no
reserves available, and the positions had to be held until the
evening if the Italians fighting in the south were not to be taken
in the rear. This was quite clear to me from a glance at the map
and what I had seen on my journey. Commanders at the front,
however, knew nothing of it all. Speaking politely but quite
firmly, in a friendly conversational tone, Stauffenberg assured and
reassured them, from time to time slipping in a crack that he had
been lying on his face in the mud too. From the way in which he
carried on these conversations, I had the impression that the man
at the other end of the line must have felt comforted in spite of
having got "no" for an answer. Although I was only a twenty-
two-year-old subaltern, Stauffenberg's manner to me was just as
frank and friendly. Although there were many interruptions, he

asked about my personal affairs, every now and again slipping in
an explanatory word about the situation in the divisional sector
and in Tunisia in general; he asked about my experiences as a
railway transport officer. Then, more or less out of the blue, but
in a lower tone of voice, which demanded a frank answer, he said,
"What do you think; what is the point of your coming to Tunis,
just now?"

I replied, "I suppose to get taken prisoner."

Laughingly he replied, "That's it; we shall be in luck; that will
be the end of the war for us." Then he sent me on my way.

I was extraordinarily impressed by Stauffenberg's personality.
He seemed to me the ideal of an officer. His manner was so frank
and friendly that one did not get the impression of being a
subordinate. His thoughtfulness inspired one with confidence.
On the other hand, the incision with which he spoke drew respect;
he was a man possessed of natural authority. It was typical of
Stauffenberg's way of going about things that he was determined
to get to know personally all officers in the division, down to
company commander, as soon as he could—which was why I was
ordered to report to him. This was not normal procedure. He was
determined that there should be close contact between the staff and
the troops.[10]

The good relationship between the divisional commander and his
staff officer was not limited to official matters; they were soon on
terms of personal friendship and so, when talking together, would
discuss wide-ranging political problems in addition to the general war
situation. After the day's orders had been issued, they would often sit
together in the command caravan "until midnight, discussing politics,
philosophy, and literature. . . . Even at that time, Stauffenberg was
playing with the idea of using force to bring about a change of those
in power."[11]

Stauffenberg told General von Broich of his fruitless attempts to get
the senior army commanders to take action against Hitler. "His view
even then was that no change was possible without the assistance and
leadership of the military and that the change must involve the use of
force, since from his personal knowledge of the headquarters, he

believed, indeed was convinced, that Hitler and his criminal regime would never willingly give up their power. But if they did not lose their power soon, he said, Germany was lost. The decision to use force he found particularly difficult and serious, being a confirmed Christian and Catholic."[12]

Stauffenberg's Christian convictions were in fact the basis of his opposition to Hitler. "Not only did his opposition spring from knowledge of the hopelessness of the military situation (into which he had had only too good an insight as head of the organization section, responsible for the supply position), but as a believing Catholic he was opposed to National Socialism on principle."[13]

When, early in April, the end of the Tunisian campaign was obviously in sight, Broich agreed with Stauffenberg that he should be flown back to Italy; his commander thought he would be more valuable to Germany at home than in Africa.[14] Back he did indeed go, but not in the way intended; he was in one of the last hospital ships to leave Africa.

The Allies had gained complete air mastery in Africa. They could therefore afford to use whole squadrons of fighters to attack individual German vehicles. Stauffenberg was one of their victims. Freiherr von Broich writes:

> I can see him now as he took leave of me out here in the country. We were once more "practising" "withdrawal and delaying action." Because of the air threat, the rule was that the divisional commander and his staff officer were not to travel in the same vehicle. So he took leave of me to go to the new command post, farther back. I said to him once again, "Look out for aircraft. I will follow in about an hour, when the last battalion is through here." When I drove back myself, accompanied only by a wireless truck and two dispatch riders, as we crossed a completely open plain we were at once attacked by about twenty fighters. However, we managed to scramble out of our vehicles and disperse, and it so happened that the machine gun bursts missed us. Driving on, we came shortly afterwards to Stauffenberg's vehicle, full of bullet holes. We knew what must have happened and feared the worst. This time he was severely wounded but had escaped with his life—fate had preserved him for a later occasion.[15]

XIII

Commitment

Stauffenberg was taken to a Carthage hospital. He had lost his right hand, the third and fourth fingers of his left hand, and his left eye, and for some days there was no certainty that he would retain the sight of the remaining eye. Although hardly fit to travel, he was moved to a hospital in Munich. He ran a high temperature for weeks; the doctors were by no means certain that they would succeed in saving his life. Even after the immediate crisis was passed, recovery was slow and difficult, with continuous complications. Stauffenberg was hospitalized for a full three months.

In June, using the three fingers of his left hand, he attempted a letter to his friend Wilhelm Bürklin, telling him that he was to be operated upon for an infection of the middle ear and had had to have an operation on his knee. The letter was interrupted by a fresh attack of fever, and when Stauffenberg continued, he wrote laconically, "In my state one must always reckon with complications and setbacks."[1]

With his usual determination, however, Stauffenberg overcame all the results of his wounds. He refused all pain-killing and sleeping drugs.[2] An officer who visited him reported: "It was heart-rending to see him so badly shot up. His mother was taking care of him. In spite of his pain and mutilation, Stauffenberg's spirit was unbroken."[3]

Although his movements were naturally very restricted, he later contrived to do a very great deal without help. On one occasion a fellow officer, who happened to be travelling with him in a sleeping car, offered to help him undress, but he refused "with a chuckle, and in a flash had undressed himself, using his three fingers and his teeth."[4]

Wilhelm Bürklin later asked him why he did not spare the time to have an artificial hand and eye fitted; he replied laughingly that he was quite all right as he was and now really hardly knew what he had done with all ten fingers when he had them.[5]

The general regard in which Stauffenberg was held was proved by the intense interest taken by everyone in his progress while in the hospital. He was visited by Colonel General Zeitzler, the Chief of Staff, who handed him the Golden Badge for War Wounded, together with a personal present.[6] Other senior officers looked up Stauffenberg, often in order to get him on their own staff. He never gave a firm answer to such offers, saying that it was for his superiors to scratch their heads about his future employment.[7]

Meanwhile, the personnel department was proposing to appoint him Chief of Staff to the head of the General Army Office (Allgemeine Heeresamt—AHA).[8] Early in May he dictated to his wife his first letter to his new chief, General Olbricht, in which he said that he hoped to be "available" in three months' time.[9]

While in the hospital he was also visited by his uncle Graf von Üxküll, who once more besought him to take part in active opposition to the regime. According to Graf von Üxküll's daughter, who gave the story to Wilhelm Bürklin, Stauffenberg asked for time to think the matter over. When his uncle visited him a second time, Stauffenberg said, "Since the generals have so far done nothing, the colonels must now go into action."[10]

It is more than likely that Stauffenberg learned through Graf von Üxküll that his new master, General Olbricht, was one of the confirmed opponents of the regime.

At this point there are certain contradictions, difficult to disentangle, between the various accounts. Colonel General Zeitzler, for instance, recalls that Stauffenberg reported to him almost before he was fully recovered and asked for a fresh posting to the front.[11] But Zeitzler "wished first to give him further opportunity of rising to the very top and offered him to C-in-C, Replacement Army, as a staff officer."[12]

This request to return to the front hardly makes it look as if Stauffenberg had any precise knowledge of what awaited him in Berlin. One can only suppose that he had not yet fully realized that the post proposed for him by Zeitzler would place him at the focal point of anti-Hitler action.

Early in August he was to have an artificial hand fixed. The operation was, however, postponed for a month because a bone splinter suddenly began to grow out.[13]

Stauffenberg then went to Berlin, probably on a summons from Olbricht and on the assumption that the head of the army office wished to talk to him about his future work. It seems reasonably certain, however, that the conversation took a very different turn and that Olbricht faced him with making the decision about whether he was willing to take part in the plans, then already in train, for a coup d'état against Hitler. Stauffenberg pledged himself to do so. He was then examined by Prof. Sauerbruch, the surgeon. When told that he would have to have two more operations, followed by a long period of convalescence, Stauffenberg refused, saying that he had urgent work to do.[14]

Though perhaps unexpected, Olbricht's question had not caught Stauffenberg unprepared. A profound psychological change had taken place in him as a result of his wounds. He was convinced that only by some disposition of Providence had he survived such serious wounds; the conviction began to grow that he had been preserved in order to fulfill some nobler task.[15] Many who met him at this period were struck by the fact that his whole outlook on life seemed more concentrated, more sharply focussed, and more purposeful than before. "As General Staff officers we must all carry a share of the responsibility," he said to his wife while still in the hospital. And then, in that half humourous, half serious tone which concealed a genuine impulse behind a façade of overstatement, he said, "You know, I have a feeling that I shall now have to do something to save the Reich."[16]

A little later he told a friend, "I could never look the wives and children of the fallen in the eye if I did not do something to stop this senseless slaughter."[17]

After a full discussion with Olbricht, Stauffenberg went to Lautlingen. Here he met his brother Berthold, with whom he discussed the repercussions of his decision. The question principally taxing them was the system which should replace National Socialism.

In late August they were visited by Rudolf Fahrner, who joined in their discussion. He has recorded its general lines in note form as follows:

Men not guaranteed a civilized existence by a state without religious background. No one for whom this background is still provided by the Christian churches should be disadvantaged or prejudiced thereby.

Planning based upon material advantage no substitute for advanced conditions and manner of life, since certain things must be allowed to develop gradually.

Necessity to eliminate from among the men of a nation inhibitions stemming from differences in position, wealth, and standing which will inevitably persist.

Extent to which international understanding is a natural desire of all peoples—perhaps now nearer than ever before, provided that those who happen to be in power do not stand in its way but insist that differences between the European peoples, for instance, are similar in nature to the ancient tribal differences and can be made similarly fruitful.

Methods of drawing into government circles the right influences from all classes; possibility and methods of establishing a form of popular representation in Germany based perhaps upon an entirely different system from that of political parties, possibly something founded upon the political realities—communities, professional groupings, and common interests; such organizations would openly represent their own interests in parliament and would not pursue their aims by tortuous methods, by manipulating political parties, or by party negotiations.

The relationship between employer and employee to be based upon the concept that they are engaged in a common task, are together responsible to the community, and are obliged to ensure decent standards of treatment of human beings.

Relationship of technology, industry, and commerce to the state—important as they are, their role is to serve the community rather than deliberately and systematically to create requirements and so rule the lives of men.

The strength given by voluntary self-denial; freely accepted division of the great estates undertaken by the landed proprietors themselves (of which they are already indications) would set a positive and promising example and might lead to new forms of socio-economic activity; both for planning and execution, leaders require the help and advice of non-official independent thinkers similar to those whom intelligent rulers formerly gathered around them by various means.

Necessity to guard against fixations and dogmatism, the important point in any given set of circumstances and with any given set of human beings, invariably being to create and hold open possibilities of development potentialities.[18]

This list of thoughts, though expressed in Fahrner's language, is an indicative document insofar as Stauffenberg's political concepts are concerned. Though it clearly does not justify any conclusion that politically he was a definite adherent of one side or the other, it does show certain definite tendencies which coloured his political thinking.

The consequences of the unhappy experiences of the Weimar period stand out clearly; the most obvious example is the question whether, in setting up the future system of popular representation, political parties should be done away with. These ideas had clearly not been fully thought out, for the question might well be asked, how would the "political realities" (*e.g.*, local communities) emerge and on what principles would the professional and interest groupings be constituted? Moreover, would not conditions in a parliament so constituted be chaotic?

But on all these subjects set out by Fahrner the Stauffenberg brothers were only posing the problem. Many of the questions about which we still argue today were raised by them at this time, and although no definite answers to them were given, it is noteworthy that the Stauffenberg brothers already had a correct instinct for the problems of the day.

They were in no doubt that after the war it was essential that there be some permanent settlement between the European peoples, and it is significant of the lines upon which their thinking ran that they did not produce some formal plan for the creation of European institutions but were looking for some starting point from which to turn the experiences of history to good account. In their search for a new political path the brothers were always conscious of the legacy of history. They were not striving for any unprecedented innovations. They did not

wish to exacerbate existing differences but to find the happy mean
between them; they had no intention of trying to start with a clean
slate but were looking for some common basis behind the existing
antagonisms. This is clear from the statements that "inhibitions" stemming from the continuing differences in status must be "eliminated"
and that employer-employee relationships must be founded upon
common "responsibility to the community."

The final paragraph is especially indicative of Stauffenberg's political
attitude. The two brothers were no day-to-day rough-and-tumble
politicians; they made no attempt to work out demagogic formulas.
One must guard, they said, against fixations and dogmatism; it is easy
to guess what they meant. The two brothers foresaw the dangers
inherent in class warfare, nationalist or utopian clichés. For them
politics was the art of dealing with circumstances as they arose; any
other method carried with it the danger that facts might bear no
relation to preconceived theory, and reality might have to be forced
to accord with dogma.

On his return from Lautlingen Claus von Stauffenberg spent a few
days with his family in Bamberg. His wife found him noticeably
changed and said to him that he gave the impression of being involved
in a conspiracy. He made no attempt to evade the issue and replied that
he was. Olbricht had put the question to him, and he had given his
word.[19]

From Bamberg Stauffenberg drove straight to Berlin. Henning von
Tresckow was due to spend a few weeks in Berlin, and so Stauffenberg
called off the fitting of his artificial hand due to take place early in
September and took up residence with his brother. Officially he spent
the few remaining weeks before taking up his appointment on a further
period of sick leave; in practice he devoted this period to intensive work
on plans for the coup d'état.

XIV

The Men of the Resistance

Once having committed himself to collaborate, Stauffenberg rapidly gained contact with the various personalities in Berlin opposition circles. In August Tresckow introduced him to Dr. Goerdeler, who thereupon informed the lawyer Joseph Wirmer that a particularly highly qualified staff officer had been found who, together with General Olbricht, would make all the military preparations. Goerdeler and Stauffenberg discussed the various civil and military measures involved in a proclamation of a state of emergency, the arrest of ministers and other political leaders, and the occupation of ministries, railway and communication installations, and important through roads.[1]

Stauffenberg was put in touch with other personalities, such as Fritz-Dietlof Graf von der Schulenburg, a well-known expert on rationalization and co-ordination and a member of the special staff under General von Unruh charged with combing through Wehrmacht and civilian offices to ensure that all men fit for service had been drafted into the forces.[2] In this position Schulenburg naturally came into contact with many personalities well suited to occupy important posts after a change of regime.

One of Stauffenberg's most valuable contacts was Dr. Julius Leber; the introduction to Leber was arranged for him by Schulenburg. Leber had been a Reichstag Social Democrat deputy and therefore an opponent of National Socialism. Immediately after Hitler's seizure of power he had been arrested and was only released from a concentration camp years later, when it was assumed that he would have lost his taste for political activity. Leber, however, immediately regained contact with his political friends and brought them together again.[3]

Stauffenberg and Leber soon became firm friends. Both had the capacity of devoting themselves selflessly and whole-heartedly to any cause they were convinced was right. In Leber Stauffenberg found a friend who was not prepared to be satisfied merely with the re-establishment of the old state of affairs in politics. He was particularly impressed by Leber's concept of a socialist state—a subject in which Stauffenberg had always taken particular interest. From this experienced politician Stauffenberg learned much concerning the structure of a state and the alliances and antagonisms between the various groups and organizations upon which a state is built. He held long discussions with Leber far into the night and emerged from them convinced that it was not enough simply to plan the military organization of a coup d'état, and that anyone preparing a stroke of this nature must carry responsi-bility for the political consequences of his action—a thought, be it noted, foremost in the minds of the Stauffenberg brothers during their Lautlingen discussions in August 1943.[4] As a result, from this time onwards Claus von Stauffenberg played an increasing part in the political planning, a fact which was to lead to disagreement between him and Goerdeler.[5]

Fritz Graf von der Schulenburg had known Stauffenberg of old, although up to this time he had never been in any very close personal contact with him. Working together on plans for the coup, however, they soon became close friends, as did Stauffenberg and his cousin Graf Yorck von Wartenburg.[6] Of these two a mutual friend said, "Stauffenberg had the greatest respect for Yorck and his political views. Had these two not been so close, Stauffenberg would never have come to the vital decision to make the assassination attempt himself."[7]

In Yorck's house Stauffenberg also made the acquaintance of Graf Schwerin von Schwanenfeld, who had been actively engaged in plan-ning a change of regime ever since 1938.[8] To avoid the frequency of their meetings exciting suspicion, they immediately used the familiar *du* and let it be known that they were old friends.[9] This circle of young counts soon came to be known as the "count gang."

In November 1943 Lieutenant Werner von Haeften joined the group, having been posted to Olbricht's office and allotted to Stauffen-berg as ADC. His brother Bernd von Haeften, who was a counsellor in the foreign ministry, introduced Stauffenberg to another counsellor, Adam von Trott zu Solz, who became a special friend.[10]

Nevertheless, the man with whom Claus von Stauffenberg was in the most intimate and closest touch was his brother Berthold. Claus did not lift a finger without his brother's knowledge and approval. The latter was, as someone remarked at the time, "his brother Claus's conscience incarnate."[11]

The two brothers lived together in the Tristanstrasse in Berlin-Wannsee. During the autumn and winter 1943–4, their uncle Graf Üxküll was with them, and he became especially close to Claus von Stauffenberg, for both were similar characters. Graf Üxküll's daughter, Olga von Saucken, says that both were "gay, optimistic characters, full of enthusiasm." Her account, although it deals with much which will be mentioned later in other connections, is given now, since if quoted piecemeal, much of its vividness would be lost.

> I must try to give you the essence of what my father said to me in October 1943 when he told me of the conspiracy for the first time. He said, "I have been trying for years to convince the younger generation"—in which he included also my other cousins Hofacker, Yorck, and his young friend Schulenburg—"that some move against this regime must be made in Germany by Germans. At last I have got somewhere. Unfortunately I must admit to you that I think it is now too late, and the moment is past; naturally, however, although I think this, I am still heart and soul behind this business, for, even though I believe that it has in fact no chance of success, it at least has the advantage that we shall have shown the world that some attempt has been made by Germans to rid themselves of these criminals.
>
> "Any small chance of success which this conspiracy may still have is due to the adherence of Claus. He is now the driving force, the force which has brought some actuality to all our efforts over the years. His is now the finger on the trigger. I am an old man now, and at the moment I regard my primary task as looking after Claus, for he is now the heart and the brains of the entire affair. He is so handicapped. And I think I am still doing something useful in caring for his physical needs. I help him in the bath

and I help him to dress, for instance. It is incredible how that man stands up to this colossal exertion. Both his regular job and this secret business require a fit man. But he has the most incredible capacity to relax. He comes home and after a minute or two's sleep is bright as a button once more and ready to carry on discussions requiring the utmost concentration. Although most of the time we are in fact living in a state of considerable nervous tension, good old Claus's infectious laugh frequently comes booming through it all."[12]

Claus and his uncle often worked together on drafts of documents; when Graf Üxküll met his daughter for the last time, on 20 July, he told her that amendments in his handwriting were to be found on most of Stauffenberg's papers.

Graf Yorck von Wartenburg was the contact man between the soldiers, primarily Stauffenberg, and the Kreisau Circle, which used to meet in the evenings in Yorck's house. For security reasons Stauffenberg was only present on rare occasions, but he was invariably kept informed of the discussions.[13] Although not a member of the Kreisau Circle in the literal sense of the word, he was with them in spirit. The Kreisau Circle was so named after Helmuth Graf von Moltke's estate in Silesia, where a group of men met in 1942 and 1943 to try to work out how Germany might be reconstructed after the anticipated collapse of National Socialism. Their object was to elaborate the principles upon which their country, now being rotted spiritually and destroyed materially, might be brought back to health. The guiding spirits of the circle were the two friends Graf Yorck von Wartenburg and Graf von Moltke, but around them were gathered men of the most diverse views and backgrounds. "There were east Germans, west Germans and south Germans all with their differing views, priests, schoolmasters, farmers, civil servants, socialists of every shade of colour."[14]

The fundamental basis upon which, in the view of these men, the future German state must be founded was set out in an "Initial Directive to State Administrators" dated 9 September 1943. It ran: "The liberal minded German working class together with the Christian churches will lead and represent those popular forces upon which reconstruction may be based."[15]

The second draft—"Principles of Reorganization"—predicated consciousness of his responsibility on the part of every citizen and stressed
the importance of the concept of nationhood, perverted though this
had become at the time: "The personal political responsibility of each
individual necessitates his active participation in small controllable
communities, through which the practice of self-government will be
resurrected. The special responsibility and loyalty which every
individual owes to his national origin, his native language, and the
spiritual and historical heritage of his people must be respected and
preserved. These sentiments must not, however, be perverted nor lead
to overconcentration of political power or to degradation, persecution,
or oppression of foreign peoples."[16]

In November Stauffenberg was invited for the first time to the house
of the lawyer, Prof. Jessen, who was in contact with Beck via an
academic club.[17] Here he was introduced to the former German
ambassador in Italy, Ulrich von Hassell, together with the Prussian
finance minister in office at the time, Johannes Popitz.[18] During the
next few months Stauffenberg met these two several times, as Hassell's
diary shows. The entry in this diary for 7 February 1944 describes one
of these meetings and at the same time throws some light upon the
differences of opinion within the opposition:

> In this connection it is thought that Geissler [Popitz] is in some
> danger. Sophie's nephew [Schwerin] confirms this and also
> Zollerndorff [Stauffenberg], to whom I was introduced in
> November at the Nordmann's [Jessen's] and of whom I got an
> excellent impression. He considers that we must be quite extra-
> ordinarily careful both in what we say and in whom we see; the
> latter applies particularly to Geissler, who is under close observa-
> tion. Zollerndorff does not think that anything special is being
> planned against me at the moment. Our conversation was inter-
> rupted by an air raid warning which drove us down to the cellar.
> Contrary to our previous agreement, Nordmann had asked
> Geissler to be present (I wanted to be alone with Zollerndorff),
> but he left after the air raid warning. Geissler is understandably
> bitter against Pfaff [Goerdeler], who has treated him incredibly
> badly; he is consequently nervous and irritable. He takes things

far too personally, which hurts no one but himself. His objections
to Pfaff's methods are in fact justified. During the discussion
Zollerndorff was extremely adroit but could not overcome all
Geissler's factual objections, with which to a certain extent he
himself agreed. The nub of the problem is the fact that Geibel
[Beck] is a complete political simpleton and is entirely under
Pfaff's thumb."[19]

Details of other meetings between Stauffenberg and opposition personalities are known only through the Gestapo reports. For instance,
he had several conversations with Hermann Maass, director of the
German Youth Movement prior to 1933. They were introduced by
Dr. Brücklmeier, a counsellor in the foreign service, who presented
Stauffenberg as a senior officer interested in socio-political questions.
The talks between Maass and Stauffenberg, in which Graf Schwerin
later also took part, dealt primarily with the question of the new social
order in Germany. Maass was in favour of a pronounced socialistic and
trade-unionist trend. Stauffenberg was in agreement with this idea; he
also thought a new social order necessary. He stressed, however, that "the
inherited virtues should not simply be thrown overboard" and that
"account should be taken of the past achievements of the aristocracy."[20]

Stauffenberg thought these questions so important that he drafted
an outline of his views on socio-political problems and submitted it to
Maass at one of their later meetings.[21]

Through Graf Bismarck, local government representative in Potsdam, Stauffenberg was introduced to the Berlin chief of police, Graf
Helldorf, who was of course a man of extraordinary importance for
the coup d'état. Stauffenberg invited him home and there introduced
him to Goerdeler. In Helldorf Stauffenberg found that he was dealing
with a man of very different views on social and political problems.
Helldorf stated flatly that it was a mistake to give the working class too
extensive rights and to make too many concessions to them; in his
view the right course was "to keep the working class within bounds
by strong-arm methods."[22] Remarks such as this were no doubt one of
the reasons why Stauffenberg and his friends looked upon their
relationship with Helldorf merely as a short-term marriage of
convenience.[23]

XV

The "Valkyrie" Plan

During the weeks preceding Stauffenberg's arrival, the leading personalities in the circle of conspirators had been holding intensive talks.[1]
Tresckow was pressing for a renewal of activity, since he feared that
sooner or later the eastern front would collapse. Early in September
Beck summoned Generals Fellgiebel and Stieff; it was agreed that
preparations must be made for early action. Beck put Olbricht and
Stauffenberg, whom he had recently met in the house of the surgeon
Prof. Sauerbruch, in charge of the military planning.[2] Dr. Goerdeler,
the Reich Chancellor-designate, however, proposed that before action
was undertaken the army leaders should present themselves to Hitler
and issue him an ultimatum. All the generals present, knowing the
attitude of the commanders-in-chief, rejected this proposal and decided
that Hitler must first be eliminated and that action should then be set
in train, starting from the home army.[3]

In September 1943 the first important army commander declared
himself ready to work with Beck and Goerdeler—Field Marshal von
Kluge, whom Goerdeler had visited on the eastern front as early as
1942 to persuade him to join the conspiracy. Now, a year later, Kluge
arrived in Berlin "most anxious over the future course of the war from
the military point of view"[4] and met both Beck and Goerdeler in
Olbricht's house. Goerdeler explained his political ideas on both internal
and external policy but, as in previous conversations, raised objections
against the use of "extreme force." Kluge's view was, however, that
assassination was the only way. Goerdeler thereupon said, "The
military leaders who have allowed things to come to such a pass

through being afraid to tell Hitler the truth must now find the right way to produce a satisfactory peace instead of a lost war."[5]

Contact had therefore been established with one of the most senior generals. But by a stroke of ill-fortune this was broken shortly afterwards; a few days later Kluge had so serious a motor car accident that he was in the hospital for months and so could not be counted upon for the coup d'état, which Berlin was hoping could take place at the end of the year.[6]

The idea of attempting to assassinate Hitler during the daily briefing conference originated with Tresckow.[7] This seemed to be the only method of guaranteeing success, since the Führer was not in the habit of keeping any fixed hours and continually altered arrangements for any journey. In one of his talks Hitler had said, "I understand very well why ninety per cent of the assassination attempts throughout history have been successful. The only effective precaution is to lead an irregular life—to take a walk or a drive at a different time each day and always travel unexpectedly. Whenever I go anywhere by road, I do so as far as possible unexpectedly, and without warning the police."[8]

The conspirators were therefore faced with two problems:

1. To find an officer who had the opportunity of attending the briefing conferences and who was at the same time sufficiently determined to make the assassination attempt.

2. To work out a plan to mobilize the necessary troops for the security measures which would become necessary.

The origins of the military resistance have already been mentioned. The central figure, in addition to Colonel General Beck, was Dr. Carl Goerdeler, former mayor of Leipzig and now the Reich government Prices Commissioner. Ever since the outbreak of war these two had been trying to find senior officers prepared to undertake a coup d'état against Hitler. Generals Oster and Olbricht were only too ready to act, but they had no troops under their command. There was another group, mostly composed of junior officers, whose guiding spirit was Major General Hans-Henning von Tresckow, Chief of Staff, Army Group Center. Early in 1943 agreement was reached between Beck and Field Marshal von Witzleben;[9] he also had no troops under his command, Hitler having placed him on "Supreme Command Reserve," but his was a name to conjure with, and it was thought that if he took over command of the Wehrmacht after a coup d'état, all military units would follow him.

On 13 March 1943 the first assassination attempt was made by the conspirators in Army Group Center. A bomb was smuggled into Hitler's aircraft, but it did not go off. A few days later a second attempt, made in the Berlin Arsenal, also failed.

But Tresckow was not discouraged. He set to work to eliminate the causes of failure and perfect his plans. In doing so, he reached the conclusion that an attempt at assassination was only likely to succeed if it could be made during the briefing conference in the Führer's headquarters.

Meanwhile, in April 1943, the Gestapo had arrested certain of the conspirators from General Oster's office (OKW Intelligence) for having illegal connections with foreign countries. The Gestapo knew nothing of the real intentions of those they had arrested, but Oster was dismissed from his office, and so the military resistance lost the man who had hitherto worked out all the plans for the coup d'état. In discussing who should replace Oster on the General Staff side of planning and bring the plans up to date, Olbricht proposed Stauffenberg, who was due to become his chief of staff on 1 October. Tresckow immediately agreed.[10]

Stauffenberg was able to base his planning upon the "Valkyrie" plan, which had been worked out in 1942 with Hitler's full agreement. Olbricht had told the dictator that there was a danger of internal disturbances from the large numbers of foreign workers in Germany or as a result of enemy commando raids. Plans must be prepared for such eventualities, Olbricht said, providing for the mobilization of the replacement army even should communications between him, Hitler, and the home army be cut. In such circumstances the commander-in-chief of the replacement army should be authorized to set "Valkyrie" in motion on his own initiative. Hitler accepted the proposal and authorized the plan to be worked out. The resulting orders for "Valkyrie" were issued to military district (Wehrkreis) headquarters in sealed envelopes, to be opened only on receipt of the message "Internal disturbances."

This was the official plan, but Oster and Olbricht now worked out secret supplementary orders designed to set the "Valkyrie" plan in motion should an assassination attempt against Hitler succeed. Thus, apparently perfectly legal action would be used for the purposes of the coup d'état.[11]

In mid-1943 General Olbricht, probably with the assistance of Tresckow, checked the "Valkyrie" plan once more and reissued it on 31 July.[12]

Early in September 1943 Tresckow was able once again to spend a few weeks in Berlin; he and Stauffenberg, assisted from time to time by Major von Oertzen, whom Tresckow had brought with him from Army Group Center, checked the existing plans and drafted the secret supplementary orders.[13] There is no evidence that Stauffenberg and Tresckow formed any closer personal friendship as a result of their work together. It would be surprising, however, if two men of their type, working together in such a highly dangerous situation, did not find bonds forming between them closer than generally implied even by the word friendship. We only know of one comment by Stauffenberg concerning Tresckow, namely that "Stauffenberg would occasionally refer to Tresckow as his instructor."[14]

Frau von Tresckow and Fräulein von Oven acted as clerks for the preparation of the supplementary "Valkyrie" orders concerned with the conspiracy. Fräulein von Oven, now Gräfin von Hardenberg, has given a vivid picture of the conditions under which these discussions were held: "The work covered the period from the middle to the end of September 1943. Various places in the Grünewald were used as meeting points, since discussions in a house were thought to be too dangerous. The arrangement of meetings was a matter of considerable difficulty, since, for security reasons, neither the telephone nor the post could be used and, in addition, laboriously arranged rendezvous could often not be kept, owing to air raids and the resulting disorganization of public transport."[15]

Stauffenberg and Tresckow would bring sheets of notes or sometimes even drafts, and during their discussions these would be worked up into formal military orders, which were then dictated to Fräulein von Oven for her to type. This she did, following Tresckow's instructions to wear gloves, to ensure that the paper carried no fingerprints. In addition, her typewriter was kept concealed at all times so that, should any papers be discovered, the machine could not be used as a means of identification.

Gräfin Hardenberg recalls an incident illustrating the nervous tension under which this work was carried on: after one of these discussions she was walking down the Trabener Strasse near the Grünewald with Stauffenberg and Tresckow. All the details of the conspiracy were under her arm. Suddenly an official SS car came towards them and braked immediately beside them. As the SS men jumped out, she, Stauffenberg, and Tresckow all thought that the conspiracy had been discovered and that they would be arrested at any moment. But the SS men took no notice of them and disappeared into a house. "Even those two war-hardened officers were white as sheets."

In the September–October 1943 period the supplementary orders had not yet reached their final form—they had to be continuously revised to keep pace with changes caused by the war situation; in the essentials, however, plans for the coup remained unchanged right up to 20 July 1944.[16]

Fritz Graf von der Schulenburg described Stauffenberg's style and method in dealing with the overall planning as nothing short of "classic"; he said to his wife one day, "We should have got further if Stauffenberg had made up his mind earlier."[17]

The post-20-July Gestapo reports give the following summary of the dispositions of the "Valkyrie" plan:

> The orders provided for the formation of effective combat groups, which were to be alerted in two stages by a given code word. Field army units in course of formation, recuperation, or reorganization and located in the home forces area were to be included in the framework of the "Valkyrie" order. It was laid down that as far as possible they were to be used as fighting troops, that in any case they were to be kept as separate units and were not to be combined with other "Valkyrie" formations from the military district in which they happened to be. Armoured and armoured infantry units, including schools with courses in progress or demonstration troops available, were to be formed into special combat groups to be used alongside the infantry formations. The order was worked out in great detail and laid down that military

district headquarters were to undertake the protection of vulner-able points and the guarding of important buildings "in the event of emergency." . . . No further indications were given as to the object of the "Valkyrie" plan. There were, however, very strict instructions regarding secrecy; it was laid down that "the number of those involved in the preparatory work was to be kept as small as possible" and that in no case were headquarters or individuals outside the Wehrmacht to have knowledge of the intentions or preparations. In addition, in the executive instructions it was laid down that "prior to the issue of the code word no discussions were to take place with authorities outside the Wehrmacht"—e.g., offices of the Reich food ministry—"regarding preparations for requisitioning" of horses.[18]

The Gestapo later gave grudging recognition to the method of camouflaging the plans for a coup d'état under a mobilization plan approved by Hitler himself: "In general it is clear that the method adopted by Stauffenberg and his clique of conspirators to camouflage their true intentions in the "Valkyrie" plan was highly sophisticated."[19]

As regards the method of setting the plan in motion, on Hitler's death the only man authorized to put the order in force was the commander-in-chief of the replacement army, Colonel General Fromm. Should he, however, realize that he was being used by a revolutionary movement and therefore refuse to issue the code word, General Olbricht was prepared to sign the order. It was not, of course, within his competence to do so, but the recipients of the code words, the commanders-in-chief of the military districts, would have no means of knowing that the order was being issued illegally, since Olbricht proposed to make use of Fromm's name. All offices in the army headquarters in the Bendlerstrasse, Berlin, used the same signal center. Once the order had gone out over the teleprinter there would be no method by which units could establish whether or not it had been issued from the authorized headquarters; the only man who might spot this and check back was the officer in charge of the signal center. This was the system eventually adopted on 20 July.

The object of the supplementary orders was to turn the "Valkyrie" plan into a plan for a coup d'état. "Measures for the protection of vulnerable points," the official phrase for the posting of guards on ministries, radio stations, and headquarters, would serve to secure the conspirators' position from the military point of view. In addition, the SS, the "Imperial Guard" of the National Socialist system, had to be brought under control of the Wehrmacht as soon as possible. It was realized that there would be a crisis lasting some twenty-four hours, since initially the SS forces within Berlin would be considerably stronger than those of the army. It was hoped, however, that after the first day, so many Wehrmacht soldiers would have been moved into the city that superiority would have swung over to the army. It was the intention of those drafting the supplementary orders that they should be not only orders for action but at the same time a demonstration that a new respect for legality was the rule; for instance, the orders contained statements such as that in the concluding paragraph of Supplementary Order No. 2: "Though extreme force may be used, no arbitrary methods or acts of revenge will be tolerated. It must be brought home to the population that the arbitrary methods of their previous rulers have been abandoned."[20]

In addition, proclamations were drafted, to be broadcast forthwith over all radio networks. In October Stauffenberg called his friend Rudolf Fahrner to Berlin by telegram to help him in the drafting of these proclamations.

> Since I had to work out the proclamations, I was first told of the plan to occupy all radio stations immediately on Hitler's death and give out the various declarations. Members of government and all party leaders down to Kreisleiter were to be arrested, all SS barracks surrounded and SS officers and men forced to surrender. These tasks were to be undertaken by the forces of the home army in each military district. There was general certainty that they would co-operate once Hitler was dead. The orders were worked out in great detail and, in addition to the necessary instructions, in some cases included a short legal justification and and explanation of their purpose. I remember working out with Berthold Stauffenberg a whole series of such orders, in particular those for dealing with the SS and police; I also remember discussing measures for the maintenance in force or alteration of

existing regulations on the most diverse subjects. The principles we worked on were that, although ruthless action must be taken against criminals and their accomplices, no lawlessness was to be tolerated and that sensible and proven arrangements should not be upset by any temptation to condemn the existing system lock, stock, and barrel. The concentration camps and other places of internment were to be occupied and a legal procedure instituted to examine each case of arrest and establish the status in law of those under detention.[21]

The conspirators realized from the outset the importance of the most rapid possible announcement over the radio. They were therefore fortunate in having among their number men like Major General Fellgiebel, the Wehrmacht chief signal officer, and Lieutenant General Thiele, chief of staff in the signal corps inspectorate. Moreover, early in October Stauffenberg came across a friend whom he had known from his Seventeenth Cavalry Regiment days and who was a member of the propaganda service. Talking to each other, they found that they were completely at one in their estimate of the situation. When his friend remarked that Hitler must be arrested, since he would never give up, Stauffenberg replied that in his view that would be no solution; it would only lead to civil war, since the youth of the country was to a large extent still infected by Hitlerism; the Hitler Youth, the SS, and a considerable part of the SA still believed in their Führer's mission. Hitler must be killed, he said. Men such as Thiele, Stieff, Olbricht, and Mertz von Quirnheim thought so and were busy with plans for Hitler's downfall, as he (Stauffenberg) was also. His friend thereupon assured him that he, too, was ready to play his part.[22]

Stauffenberg charged him with the collection of a group of trained speakers from the Wehrmacht propaganda office; they were to be divided into two sections, each with a group of radio operators selected by Lieutenant General Thiele, and as soon as Hitler had been assassinated were to occupy the Deutschland and Nauen radio stations. The officer in charge was to be given a sealed envelope which he was to open on arrival and the contents of which were to be broadcast both on the home and overseas service.[23]

Although their intention was to bring the war to an end as quickly as possible, the members of the military resistance envisaged a complete revision of the higher organization for war. This they were determined to achieve for two reasons; in the first place, criticism of the existing organization had been one of the main subjects of discussion among the officer corps for years; secondly, the existing arrangement, with its jungle of overlapping authorities and intentional perpetuation of rivalries, was so typical of Hitler that a reorganization would constitute a political gesture in addition to being a military necessity.[24]

On these questions there was clearly no more expert officer than Stauffenberg in military resistance circles; he had, after all, wrestled with just these problems for years while in the organization section. It may therefore be assumed with some certainty that the reorganization proposals, a draft of which is still in existence, were primarily his work.[25]

Their principal points were as follows: the existing parallel staffs—the OKW operations staff, the general staff of the army, the general staff of the Luftwaffe—to be combined into a "Great General Staff"; the Waffen-SS to cease to be an independent force; the base and supply organizations of the army, Waffen-SS, labour service, and Todt organization to be amalgamated.[26] In addition, it was proposed to re-establish a Reich war ministry, incorporating the staff of home forces and all offices dealing with armaments and war production; the independent "Reich ministry for armaments and munitions" was to be disbanded. An independent air ministry was also to be abolished. Apart from the general staff of the Luftwaffe, the staff of the ministry was to be placed under a permanent secretary for air; the army and Luftwaffe personnel offices were to be amalgamated into a single "officers' office." A "Commander-in-Chief East" was to be nominated to take charge of the Army Groups on the eastern front. Although the navy was to remain organizationally independent, the general staff of the Wehrmacht was to be empowered to issue directives to it.

In addition to all this organization planning, Stauffenberg and his friends had to ensure that there were a sufficient number of officers determined to carry out the orders for the coup during the decisive phase. Of the greatest importance were commanders who knew their units intimately and were sure of their loyalty. But even though such-and-such an officer might pledge himself to act, this might well mean

nothing when the decisive moment came, since the personnel department was continuously transferring and reposting officers. Under these
circumstances it was hardly possible to find commanders who could
rely upon their troops to carry out any orders, even those for a coup
d'état. For this reason it was arranged that in each military district
(Wehrkreis) there should be at least one officer to act as liaison officer
in a state of emergency, to ensure that orders were carried out and
keep headquarters informed of what was going on. Stauffenberg began
selecting these officers in the autumn of 1943 and eventually had found
thirteen reliable officers for the seventeen military districts.[27]

On the civilian side, political representatives were nominated to give
political direction in the various military districts and take over the
civil administration. The choice of these people—they were not all let
into the secret, since it was assumed that they would come forward
voluntarily—was primarily the business of Dr. Carl Goerdeler, who
discussed the appointments with Beck and Stauffenberg.[28]

In the summer of 1943 the Berlin plotters established close contact
with General von Stülpnagel, the military commander-in-chief in
France, the contact man being Lieutenant Colonel Cäsar von Hofacker,
a cousin of Stauffenberg's.[29] The conspirators did not, unfortunately,
manage to establish similarly close relationships with commanders in
other theatres, and this was one of the reasons for their failure on
20 July.

XVI

Assassination Plans

In parallel with planning for the future, the military conspirators had to look for a possibility of carrying out the attack on Hitler. Opinions were divided regarding the advisability of assassination; Goerdeler was continually raising the question of whether there was not some other method of "sparking things off"; Moltke and Yorck also, and with them many of the Kreisau Circle, considered that the military situation should be allowed to develop and that the groundwork should be prepared for a new state structure to be set up after the collapse. Stauffenberg and Tresckow opposed this point of view, saying that force must be used, since simply to await the catastrophe would be irresponsible. As soldiers they could see only too clearly the chaos into which Germany would be plunged in the event of total military defeat. In the face of Stauffenberg's arguments many members of the Kreisau Circle, notably Graf Yorck von Wartenburg, accepted the necessity for assassination.[1]

Moreover, the officers knew that a coup d'état against Hitler had little chance of success while he was still alive; in the eyes of many, indeed the majority of soldiers, their oath of allegiance bound them irrevocably to Hitler. This question of the oath may not seem a very convincing argument today, but at the time the majority of soldiers felt that, although they had been more or less compelled to swear it, it did constitute a vow made "before God," pledging them to "unconditional obedience." Although Stauffenberg and his friends had already brushed the question of the oath aside insofar as they were concerned, they knew the views of their fellow officers. In this connection a conversation between Dr. Bräutigam and Stauffenberg's friend Colonel Schmidt von Altenstadt is a good illustration. Bräutigam put forward the view that it would be better to attack the Führer's headquarters, take Hitler prisoner alive, and arraign him before a court. Altenstadt's objections were:

1. A regiment could not detrain in Rastenburg without Hitler's knowledge.
2. One could not be sure of the attitude of the junior regimental officers; they had risen from the Hitler Youth and were not fully informed regarding the seriousness of the situation.
3. For soldiers the oath of allegiance was something so sacred that both officers and men would feel themselves released from it only when the Führer was no longer alive.

Bräutigam added: "In view of the close relationship between the two men, I am convinced that Altenstadt's views were considerably influenced by Graf Stauffenberg."

The man who seemed most suitably placed to carry out the assassination attempt was Major General Helmuth Stieff, head of the organization section of the army general staff. He was the only one of the conspirators who had regular access to the briefing conferences. In October Tresckow handed to Stauffenberg some British explosive which he had obtained, and the latter passed it on to Stieff at the end of the month.[2] But no action resulted; Stieff maintained that he could find no possibility of getting the explosive into the conference room unnoticed.[3]

In November 1943 a second plan for the assassination failed, owing to Hitler's continuous alteration of his plans. As a result of conditions on the eastern front, some alterations to the German uniform were thought to be necessary. The new patterns had to be presented to Hitler and approved by him. It was planned that the assassination attempt should be made on this occasion, provided someone could be found who fulfilled the following three conditions: he must be an officer involved in the presentation of the new uniforms; he must be convinced of the necessity to eliminate Hitler; and finally, he must be prepared to sacrifice his own life in the process. The plan was that he should have a bomb sewn into his equipment and jump upon Hitler, thereby setting off the detonator.

Schulenburg proposed his friend Captain Axel von dem Bussche, and Stauffenberg arranged that Bussche should be given leave from his unit on the eastern front. The two met in the neighbourhood of Berlin. Their conversation must have been a bizarre one, for here was a young officer ready to sacrifice his life to save his country from a terrible fate. The main subject of their discussion was not whether the elimination of Hitler was desirable or expedient—that question had long since been decided. The problem was whether for a Christian the murder of Hitler could be morally justified. Stauffenberg stated that in matters such as this the Catholic tradition was more liberal than the evangelical but that even Luther had considered the use of force permissible if the state was facing a situation endangering its very existence. Bussche declared himself ready to make the attempt, but then the presentation of the new uniforms was postponed several times. When finally, in November, it seemed certain that Hitler would appear, the railway wagon carrying the experimental patterns to east Prussia was destroyed in an air attack. Before new models of the uniforms could be made Bussche had to return to the front.[4]

A third attempt at assassination was made shortly after Christmas 1943. In mid-November Stauffenberg made an excuse to summon Freiherr von Leonrod, one of his brother officers in the Seventeenth Cavalry Regiment, to Berlin; after completing their official business he told Leonrod that he was hoping for his assistance in connection with the coup d'état. Leonrod declared himself ready, and Stauffenberg told him that he might under certain circumstances be wanted even before Christmas.[5]

Goerdeler was informed that he might expect action to take place between 25 and 27 December, and he was asked to alert the political representatives. But nothing happened; whatever the plan was—and we know nothing about it today—it could not be carried out.[6]

When once again no action took place Goerdeler reproached Stauffenberg, primarily because of the danger to the political representatives implicit in passing on the information to them. Stauffenberg assured him that he would not do it again. Goerdeler, who had never been basically in favour of the plan for assassination and had merely turned a blind eye to it, once more questioned whether consideration ought not to be given to finding some method other than assassination of depriving Hitler of his power. But Stauffenberg would have nothing to do with such ideas. He gave Goerdeler his word that the military would definitely take action, saying that he would rather make the assassination attempt himself than have to fall back on some other solution.[7]

XVII

Conspiratorial Ways

As 1943 drew to its close all the conspirators' attempts to initiate the
coup d'état had gone awry. Tresckow had twice tried to get himself
into a position giving him direct access to Hitler, first via Major
General Schmundt, the senior aide, and then via Lieutenant General
Heusinger, head of the army operations section. Both attempts had
failed. Towards the end of 1943 Tresckow had also failed to persuade
Field Marshal von Manstein to act.[1]

But the resisters did not give up. They continued to search, though
with increasing desperation, for some way to put their plans into action.
Moreover, they did not confine themselves merely to the planning of
their coup d'état and the search for an opportunity of assassinating
Hitler. Insofar as they were able, they tried to counteract orders issued
by Hitler which were of a criminal nature or contrary to international
law.

Early in 1944 Hitler learned that the Hungarian government was
proposing to renounce its alliance with Germany and sue for a separate
peace. He thereupon produced a plan to disarm the Hungarian troops
fighting on the German side in Russia, to occupy Hungary and install
a new regime in Budapest. The conspirators, including Stauffenberg
and Olbricht, considered whether the Hungarian government should
be warned. They could not, however, find any suitable opposite
number in Hungary with whom to deal.[2]

This plan is reminiscent of an incident connected with General
Oster, Stauffenberg's predecessor as the coup d'état planner.[3] In 1940,
shortly before the opening of the western offensive, Oster had passed

to Colonel Sas, Netherlands military attaché in Berlin, the date for the attack on the Scandinavian neutrals. In doing so, he was giving warning of an attack which was contrary to international law, but at the same time, he was endangering the lives of German soldiers. A warning to Hungary in 1944 would have been a similar case.

Strictly, that which Oster had done and Stauffenberg planned to do in the case of Hungary was high treason—indisputably a serious crime. At the time, however, there was an even more serious crime of high treason being committed, although it was one that was not strictly judiciable as such—a government recklessly gambling away the life-blood of a nation. What should a man do if he feels it his duty to warn a weaker state against an unexpected act of war when the price may be the lives of soldiers of his own country? A dilemma such as this falls into the category of the great tragic conflicts of conscience with which any right-thinking man was bound to be faced by Hitler; it illustrates the moral turmoil into which any totalitarian system must throw its subjects.

In another case Stauffenberg and his friends were more successful. Hitler had ordered that all Allied airmen who fell into German hands should be shot in reprisal for the bombing of German cities, an order obviously contrary to all the rules of war. The members of the resistance in the OKW intelligence office dealing with international law were worried lest this illegal order be held up against Germany even after she had freed herself from Hitler and attempts to come to some under-standing with the West be hindered thereby.

It was the duty of OKW intelligence to report fulfillment of this order to Hitler; Graf Moltke made use of his position in that office to falsify the reports. The numbers of airmen shot down and captured were correct, but their names were not. Stauffenberg had taken it upon himself to obtain from the prisoner of war camps the names of those who had died in captivity. These names—the "dead souls"—were entered in the lists and reported as "executed," whereas in fact those captured were alive in the prisoner of war camps.[4]

In Stauffenberg's view it was self-evident that policy must be con-ducted on a basis of "morality firmly rooted in religion."[5] He once said, "A people which does not know how to pray is not fit to live."[6] This being his background, it is not surprising that he made frequent use of religious arguments to win his brother officers over to his views. In his vital conversation with Freiherr von Leonrod, for instance, the latter objected that he felt himself bound by his oath of allegiance. Stauffenberg replied, "In a case like this and in an emergency such as this an oath, which intrinsically may be considered sacred, is no longer valid." He went on to describe the political and military situation and then to tell Leonrod that if he was a "believing Catholic," he "owed it to his conscience" to act contrary to the oath.[7]

It is known that Stauffenberg discussed these questions with certain Catholic dignitaries,[8] and from the arguments he used—for instance, in his talk with Axel von dem Bussche—it is clear that he had come to terms with theological dogma. In the spring of 1944 he had had a talk with Conrad Cardinal Graf Preysing, the bishop of Berlin. Although he did not let the Cardinal into the secret of the plans for a coup, the necessity of a change of regime was discussed, in which connection the question of justification of an assassination attempt must at least have been hinted at. After the collapse of the conspiracy, Cardinal Preysing wrote to Stauffenberg's mother that although he had not been able to give Stauffenberg the blessing of the Church, he would not withhold from him his personal blessing as a priest.[9]

The discussions about religion, Christianity, and politics continued right up to 20 July. One of Graf Yorck's favourite subjects was the reform of the liturgy and the union of the Protestant and Catholic churches. In mid-June 1944 Stauffenberg, Yorck, Schwerin, and Schulenburg held an exhaustive discussion on the theme that "Christianity should again become the overriding spiritual force of the future."[10]

All these ideas, however, were no more than castles in the air so long as it proved impossible to initiate the coup d'état by the assassination of Hitler.

In January 1944 a discussion took place between Stauffenberg, Tresckow, Schlabrendorff, Colonel Rudolf-Christof Freiherr von Gersdorff, and Colonel Wessel Freiherr von Freytag-Loringhofen, the head of Security Section II in Admiral Canaris' office. The last named had been security officer in Army Group Center and had been persuaded to join the opposition group by Tresckow. The main subjects of discussion were the lessons to be learned from previous failures and, more important still, the provision of a fresh supply of explosives. Freytag-Loringhofen volunteered to deal with this matter.[11]

Prior to this an attempt had been made to persuade Hitler to pay a further visit to Army Group Center, where a number of officers were ready to make a combined revolver attack upon him. But Hitler could not be moved to pay a further visit.[12]

Early in February 1944 the new uniforms were to be demonstrated once more and Stauffenberg once again succeeded in finding a young officer prepared to sacrifice himself—Ewald von Kleist. Though he talked to him on the same lines as he had a few months earlier to Bussche, explaining the political and military situation, he did not press him or try to persuade him to make the attempt. After thinking the matter over and discussing it with his father, Kleist declared himself ready to do it. The attempt was to be made on 11 February, but once more the demonstration was cancelled.[13]

The conspirators' situation was now desperate, as shown by a plan which another officer, Captain von Breitenbuch, declared himself ready to carry out. As ADC to Field Marshal Busch it was possible for him to accompany his commander to the briefing conferences in the Führer's headquarters, and he was prepared to shoot Hitler down with his revolver at the next conference. As he was about to enter the conference room, however, the SS officer on duty announced Hitler's arrival and held him back, saying that ADC's were not to attend the conference that day.[14]

As time went on, the danger of the conspiracy attracting the attention of the Gestapo and SD increased. Early in 1944 Himmler told Admiral Canaris that he was well aware that certain well-known army circles were planning a coup. Let no one think, he said, that he was not going to intervene in good time; he had only allowed the affair to run on so long in order to see who was really behind it; people like Beck and Goerdeler would be run out of business quick enough. Canaris at once gave this menacing news to Olbricht, who passed it on to Stauffenberg and the other conspirators.[15]

In January 1944 the Gestapo arrested the members of a tea party gathered in the Solf house, and among them was Helmuth Graf von Moltke, the head of the Kreisau Circle. (The police did not, however, succeed in uncovering his conspiratorial connections and shortly

before 20 July were in fact thinking of releasing him.) This blow was
soon followed by another—Himmler succeeded in pushing out his
old rival Canaris and getting the OKW Intelligence Office subordinated
to the Reich Central Security Office.[16]

In March the word went round that Captain Gehre, who was on
Oster's staff in intelligence, was under Gestapo supervision. Stauffenberg had to warn all his friends not to try to telephone to or get in
touch with Gehre.[17]

As time went on, therefore, indications multiplied that danger was
in the offing. In addition Beck fell seriously ill at about this time and
had to be operated upon.[18]

In view of the increasing nervous tension, it is not surprising that
after the failure of the assassination attempt planned for February,
Goerdeler should have complained to Beck about the continual delays.
In all his dealings with army leaders over the years, he had gained the
impression that they were only too ready to talk and make promises
but much less ready to act. Beck attempted to explain to him that they
were still trying to find a suitable moment but could give no set date.
Stauffenberg passed through a message to Goerdeler that, having had
his (Stauffenberg's) word of honour, there was no need for him to go
on agitating all the time.[19] Goerdeler was clearly getting the impression
that Stauffenberg was doing nothing, or at any rate not enough. The
reason no doubt was that Stauffenberg naturally did not publicize all
he was doing and planning; probably Goerdeler never knew of the
efforts he was making to find an officer both able and willing to carry
out the assassination.

Captain (as he then was) Dr. van Husen of the OKW Operations
Staff, Berlin Rear Link Headquarters, tells the story of an attempt by
Stauffenberg to recruit a brother officer for the assassination:

> One day I had to go to Berchtesgaden by overnight train
> together with the head of the OKW Operations Staff, Rear Link
> Headquarters, Colonel Meichssner. Shortly before the train left,
> Stauffenberg appeared . . . and was given the other bunk in my
> compartment. I knew that Stauffenberg had some connections
> with Meichssner and assumed that Meichssner would be one of
> the main participants in a coup d'état. His outlook, his character,

and his energy all combined to make him ideally suited for such action, and in addition, he had a permanent entrée to the Führer's headquarters and to the briefing conferences. Recently, however, Meichssner's nerves had gone to pieces. He had been grossly overworked and was keeping himself going with drink and other stimulants. Meichssner did not at the time know that I was part of the conspiracy. Stauffenberg took two bottles of Burgundy out of his bag and said, "Now we'll have a talk with Meichssner." He invited him into our compartment. He then began a general disquisition on the military and political situation, and although he was playing a cat-and-mouse game and speaking in riddles, the question he was really putting was quite clear, How could one best get rid of Hitler? When the bottles were empty and Meichssner was on his way back to his compartment, Stauffenberg asked him whether he would not next see him *chez* Brücklmeier, to which Meichssner gave an evasive reply. Stauffenberg then said to me laconically, "It is quite clear; he does not want to play any more." If Meichssner had been willing to be responsible for action in Wolfsschanze, so leaving Stauffenberg free to direct matters in Berlin, the whole course of events would probably have been very different.[20]

Another brother officer of Stauffenberg's, when asked whether he would be willing to carry out the assassination, did not give a flat refusal but did not agree either. He rejected on principle the idea of using a bomb, because people other than Hitler would be endangered thereby; he was not confident of being able to shoot straight enough to use a revolver. Moreover he was still beset by doubts which with Stauffenberg were things of the past; he wondered, for instance, whether there was not some solution which would avoid bloodshed and whether the elimination of Hitler would not produce such a shock at the front that it might have a most serious effect on the stability of the eastern front.

Haeften, Stauffenberg's aide, also refused to make the attempt on religious grounds.[21] In spite of all this, there were plenty of younger officers ready to carry out the "dirty work," as the assassination was called in resistance circles;[22] the majority, however, could not even be considered because either they had no entrée to Hitler, or were at the front, or had been wounded.

Consideration was even given to entrusting an officer ready to do the deed with some form of enquiry of importance in Hitler's eyes, on which he would then have to report to the Führer. But to be entrusted with such a task the man concerned had either to be some senior staff officer or some well-known senior commander whom Hitler already knew and trusted and who also was not under suspicion by the SD. Such an officer was not to be found.[23]

It is not possible now to work out exactly which plans were considered, which were rejected, and which failed. Nor is it possible to say exactly who were the officers to whom the question was put, which of them were willing, which refused, and what their motives were, though these motives ranged from abhorrence of assassination on moral grounds to straight lack of courage. One thing is certain: there was no lack of effort to find a suitable man. In spite of the unnerving effect of their failures, the conspirators did not fold their hands, but were continuously revising their plans and making every effort to bring them to fruition.

In March General Olbricht instructed Colonel Hassell, who, as head of Section VII of the Signals Inspectorate, was well placed to make unobtrusive enquiries, to check any changes in the signal system caused by air attacks.[24]

On 1 April Stauffenberg received his long-standing friend Major Roland von Hösslin and gave him a general picture of the situation, emphasizing the catastrophic German manpower losses by quoting the official figures. "Losses are considerably higher than the replacements which can be furnished from home. The strength of the field army is sinking by the equivalent of an army corps a month, and this loss cannot be made good. . . . We are heading for a military collapse. In that case the officer corps must not fail a second time and allow the initiative to be snatched from it as it did in 1918; it has a moral responsibility to act," Stauffenberg said. Passing to the external political situation, he pointed out that in his view there was no possibility of Hitler renouncing his plans for world conquest and being satisfied with a Germany confined to her ethnic boundaries. No other state would or could conclude peace with the National Socialists because the whole spirit of the movement must inevitably be regarded by other peoples as a permanent menace.[25]

As this talk with Hösslin shows, Stauffenberg's method of argument was to use the catastrophic military situation as a starting point but to proceed from there to compel the other partner to the conversation to draw the political consequences. Stauffenberg's general attitude, his remarkable power of expression, and his unswerving conviction combined to cast a spell over anyone to whom he spoke openly.[26] An account of one of these conversations says that if anyone to whom he was talking tried to evade the inexorable conclusion that Hitler must be got rid of, Stauffenberg knew how to disarm any argument: "He would force the man opposite him into a pitiless examination of the factual position. He made no attempt to persuade him, but simply compelled him to think logically. Stauffenberg had already passed through the crisis of conscience inevitably caused by the thought that he and his friends might well go down to history as traitors."[27]

Stauffenberg almost invariably adopted the same technique to win over new adherents. He would summon certain officers to Berlin on some official pretext. They were selected either as being relatives of members of the opposition or as being known opponents of National Socialism or as having swung away from it as time went on. When they appeared in his office he would launch into his subject without beating about the bush; frankly and with crystal clarity he would set out the catastrophic war situation and using the official information at his disposal work back pitilessly to the causes of it. When Lieutenant Colonel Bernardis, for instance, remarked that he could not help thinking that Hitler was surrounded by men who gave him bad military advice, Stauffenberg replied bluntly, "Bernardis, it is not the staff; it is the Führer himself."[28] When asked whether a sufficient number of commanders in the field would support a coup d'état he would reply with every appearance of assurance that the majority of the field marshals would fall into line once action had been launched and would indicate that he had solid grounds for this assumption.[29]

An officer for whom Stauffenberg had arranged a Berlin posting gives the following account of his first conversation with Stauffenberg, who, as soon as they had finished discussing their official business, turned to him and said, "Let us get down to brass tacks; I am carrying on high treason with all the resources at my disposal."

We then discussed the hopeless military situation, the fact that a coup d'état could do nothing to improve it but would at least avoid further bloodshed and the final ghastly chaos. The stigma of the present government must be removed. With particular seriousness he added that it was questionable whether the coup would succeed, but even worse than failure would be the shame of submitting tamely to oppression and allowing oneself to be paralyzed by it. Freedom, both internal and external, could only be won by action.[30]

Stauffenberg could be utterly frank when he had to, but equally, when there was no particular object in frankness, he kept his mouth shut. However convinced he might of the loyalty of the man to whom he was talking, as soon as he realized that any attempt to win him over was useless, he would refuse to give him even an inkling of any of his plans. Dr. Georg Freiherr von Fritsch says:

From time to time we lunched together in the officers' mess near the Bendlerstrasse. As before, we were still entirely agreed in our estimate of the overall situation; yet he never said a word to me of his plans for a coup d'état. This was entirely understandable, since, realizing that the war would be lost and the occupation of all Germany unavoidable, I had at this time reached the conclusion that the German people must bear the uttermost consequences of its behaviour in order from the outset to cut the ground from under the feet of some stab-in-the-back legend. . . . I think I remember expressing this view to Stauffenberg; in any case, I know that something I said obviously hit him hard, and from then on I sensed an attitude of reserve towards me.

Whenever an officer declared himself ready to collaborate Stauffenberg would put him in the picture, but only so far as was necessary for the task he was intended to fulfill. The degree of information imparted was graded on a definite system, described to the Gestapo by Graf von der Schulenburg as follows:

On certain matters—the whereabouts of explosives, for instance —only a very small number of persons were let into the secret.

A somewhat larger circle was informed of the plan for the assassination, but even this circle was very small.

A somewhat wider circle again was told that an action involving the use of force was to be initiated, leaving open the question of whether this would include the elimination of the Führer.

Finally, there was a circle which was told only of the seriousness of the situation, its catastrophic deterioration, and the necessity for the declaration of a state of military emergency. Information was given only to those directly involved in any particular matter, and no more information than was strictly required.[31]

Only in the rarest cases were names given. Stauffenberg adopted this technique even to his closest friends in order to ensure that should anyone fall into the hands of the Gestapo, he would not be able to give information endangering his fellows, however severe his interrogation. On one occasion this secrecy led to a quarrel between Stauffenberg and his cousin Hofacker, with whom the feeling of being no more than an accessory to the conspiracy went against the grain.[32]

Irrespective of the degree of information he was willing to impart to any one of them however, in all that he did, Stauffenberg had the full confidence of his friends. They admitted as much even to the Gestapo. Von Hagen, for instance, said, "I felt confident that Stauffenberg would only resort to such methods [i.e., assassination] if after careful consideration of all the circumstances, he had come to the conclusion that this was the last and only method of bringing the war to a tolerable conclusion." Kranzfelder said that the fact that "the two Stauffenbergs had a hand in the game" was enough to convince him that the undertaking had right on its side. Finckh simply said that he felt himself bound by loyalty to his friend Stauffenberg.[33]

The bonds of personal friendship and the unquestioning solidarity existing between these officers were responsible for the remarkable fact that throughout the entire period of the conspiracy in no single instance did anyone betray the secret. From the point of view of the Gestapo this was a highly displeasing phenomenon, to which they devoted much attention; the Kaltenbrunner report contains the following revealing comment: "They all set less store by their oath to the Führer and their loyalty to the National Socialist Reich than by the bonds, in many cases only loose bonds, of comradeship and friendship uniting them to the officers involved in the conspiracy."[34]

In addition to all this, a special type of link united Stauffenberg and his closest friends. Stauffenberg's thinking was still much influenced by that of his master, Stefan George, and with many of his friends he found a meeting of minds easier to achieve through the medium of a George poem than by discussion of the catastrophic war situation. The poem "Anti-Christ" served almost as a password. In September 1943 the friendship between Tresckow and Stauffenberg was cemented by George's poems.[35] Talking to Lieutenant Colonel Bernardis, Stauffenberg merely quoted "Anti-Christ," made no comment, and simply left the poem hanging in the air like a question mark. Bernardis was hesitant and Stauffenberg relied solely upon the force of the poetry to convince him.[36]

During April 1944 Stauffenberg paid a number of visits to his friends' estates in the neighbourhood of Berlin; he twice visited the Hardenberg estate near Küstrin and spent Easter on the Trebbow estate in Mecklenburg. Schulenburg, whose brother-in-law owned Trebbow, was anxious to give his friend a few days' rest away from the city and away from all politics; his wife says he asked her to "make everything as pleasant and as homely as possible so that Stauffenberg could for once have a real rest. In general there was to be no talk of politics."[37] This was a well-intentioned instruction, which, however, Schulenburg himself did not obey.

XVIII

Stauffenberg and Goerdeler

Whenever occasion offered, the resisters would discuss Schulenburg's particular subject—future state structure. *Mutatis mutandis*, the problems in the civilian field were no different from those in the military. In civil administration the practice of the National Socialist regime consisted on the one hand of the same catastrophic system of a hotch-potch of special plenipotentiaries and special authorities, on the other hand of such a high degree of centralization that even minor administrative matters had to be dealt with by the central Reich authorities. What had once been a logically organized structure designed to meet its responsibilities had in Schulenburg's words become "an amorphous mass of machines large and small labouring without purpose."[1] Since no one knew what his competence or authority was, the result was a widespread lack of sense of responsibility.[2]

Other participants in the administrative planning were Dr. Goerdeler and Graf Yorck. They were agreed that the number of ministries must be reduced, that the responsibilities transferred to special authorities should return to the regular civil administration, and that local government powers should be restored, leaving the Reich administration free to deal with the major problems.[3]

It was of course inevitable that as planning proceeded there should be differences of opinion between those involved. There had long been a certain degree of tension between the members of the Kreisau Circle and Goerdeler. As early as 1942 Father Delp[4] had warned a friend against having too close contact with Goerdeler, saying that on economic matters his leanings were far too conservative.[5] Early in 1943 a talk which took place in Graf Yorck's house between Goerdeler, Beck, and the most important members of the Kreisau Circle ended in total disagreement, neither side being willing to change its views. Moltke, who was convinced that collaboration with both church and trade-union forces was essential, reproached Goerdeler with planning a German Kerensky regime.[6]

The tension grew when Stauffenberg appeared and demanded that he too should take part in the political planning. He staked his claim at one of his very first meetings with Goerdeler, whose reaction was one of astonishment and vexation. Stauffenberg's demand cut across the hitherto accepted principle that the soldiers should be responsible only for the technical side of the coup d'état, leaving the political side solely to the civilians. As a result of intervention by Beck, however, Goerdeler eventually agreed to talk politics with Stauffenberg.

Goerdeler could of course justifiably lay claim to be far more experienced in political matters than a young General Staff officer; he failed, however, to see that the latter had a moral right to air his thoughts on the political background to the coup d'état, which, after all, was entirely dependent upon his plans and his actions. Goerdeler was not apparently prepared to accept the old established truth (propounded in the eighteen-eighties by Field Marshal von Moltke to Kaiser Wilhelm I, and still valid today) that in the ultimate issue—such as the situation in this case undoubtedly was—no hard and fast line can be drawn between the military and the political.

A further factor was that Stauffenberg in general leaned towards the views of the Kreisau Circle. Graf Yorck made no secret of the fact that he did not consider Goerdeler to be the right man to be Reich chancellor. He thought him too old and too conservative. In his view the government required a far broader basis than Goerdeler was either able or willing to give it; it should take in the working class as far left as the Social Democrat left wing.[7] Graf von der Schulenburg held similar views.

Dr. Leber also considered Goerdeler's program insufficiently constructive. In his view an attempt "to return to Weimar" was not good enough; it was, in fact, the conditions of the Weimar period which had given rise to National Socialism. Now some "positive aim" must be put forward to take its place,[8] and that aim must be the product of a

combined effort by all "surviving social and democratic forces possess-
ing adequate vitality." Dictatorship could not be immediately replaced
by democracy; the executive authority set up by the dictator could
only be dismantled gradually. The best solution in his view was to
restrict the system to a two-party one in order to avoid the formation
of the splinter groups characteristic of the first republic; one party
should be based upon the Social Democrats and trade unions, the other
tending more towards conservatism.[9]

It was not in fact Goerdeler's intention simply to revert to an out-of-
date system, although from time to time he would give vent to ideas
which laid him open to the suspicion of being ultra-conservative; for
instance, he was heard to wonder whether it would not be a good idea
to work towards the re-establishment of the monarchy. Beck agreed
with him, but when they tested the opinion of their fellow conspirators
—Goerdeler himself discussed the matter with Stauffenberg—they
found no support for the idea.[10]

Stauffenberg took part in the discussion of Goerdeler's suitability for
the chancellorship, not so much from the point of view of political
concepts as on practical grounds. On one occasion Brücklmeier, a
counsellor in the foreign service, was introducing Stauffenberg to
Wilhelm Leuschner, the former minister of the interior in Hesse and
president of the General German Trade Union Council; he described
Leuschner as a man particularly interested in working-class problems
and opposed to Dr. Goerdeler personally, although generally in agreement with his political ideas. Talking to Leuschner, Stauffenberg said
that it might perhaps be better for a working-class representative to
head the new government.[11] He was clearly apprehensive that
Goerdeler might not have the popular touch or be persuasive enough
to win over the mass of the people to the new regime.

In the view of Stauffenberg, Schulenburg, and others of their circle,
Dr. Julius Leber was the man best suited to be Reich chancellor. They
felt that he had more of the right ideas on building up a state founded
on a new social order and, more important still, that he had the
necessary political appeal to gain popular support for a change of
regime. Even Beck toyed with this idea; he had two conversations with
Leber on the subject, one shortly before the latter's arrest on 5 July
1944. Leber, however, was opposed to the idea; he thought, as did

Leuschner, that it would not be right for social democracy to appear too much in the forefront in the immediate post-Hitler regime; in fact the Social Democrats did not wish their party to have to shoulder once more, as it had done in 1918, responsibility for bringing to an end a war for the outbreak of which they were in no way responsible.[12]

Goerdeler reacted violently against this contact between Stauffenberg and the Social Democrat politicians, and he particularly opposed Stauffenberg's friendship with Leber. In Goerdeler's view political negotiations were his prerogative, not that of the officers.[13] He may well have seen in this contact between the military and the left wing the possibility of a coalition which would not have accorded with his political ideas.

In May and June two meetings took place between Goerdeler and Leber; economic and foreign policy problems were discussed. Both meetings ended in violent disagreement, and Goerdeler suspected that there was some machination of Stauffenberg's behind Leber's criticisms.[14] Goerdeler must have been particularly touchy at this time to be able to convince himself without more ado that there was some connection between his irritation with Stauffenberg over his independent attitude and his vexation with Leber over his criticism. In fact, in foreign policy questions Stauffenberg tended to share Goerdeler's optimism as was shown by the 11-point programme put forward by Stauffenberg in mid-May which had been drafted by a friend of Goerdeler's, Captain Kaiser.[15] Goerdeler was incapable of taking the discussion regarding his own personal position calmly, though that would have been his best course; he clearly found it difficult to accept that, after having worked himself to the bone for years to consolidate the anti-Hitler opposition, he should now have to allow his qualifications to be discussed by young men who had only comparatively recently become active members of the opposition. The problem was more a human than a political one.

Nevertheless Goerdeler did his best to eliminate the misunderstandings which had arisen. He asked the lawyer Dr. Wirmer to get in touch with Stauffenberg in the hope that, being much of an age, the two would more quickly be able to find some confidential basis of discussion. There were several meetings between Stauffenberg and Wirmer, the first taking place on 7 April; Wirmer argued that

Goerdeler was not proposing simply to "cook up the old system afresh" but had completely "constructive new ideas" (in the words of the Gestapo report); what exactly he meant by this, however, there is now no means of knowing. After the May and June disagreements Wirmer was asked by Goerdeler to try to mediate once more;[16] Beck also took a hand in smoothing out the troubles.[17]

The Gestapo reports, from which most of this information comes, naturally lay particular emphasis on these differences of opinion in order to show up the internal weakness of the conspiracy. This stems from a complete lack of comprehension; basically these differences of opinion were a necessity, particularly when the problem was to find the right chancellor; it would have been remarkable if there had been no disagreement. The National Socialists, however, did not understand internal political differences, since the person of the Führer could not be the subject of discussion; in their eyes the conspirators' disagreements were merely a "return to party squabbles."

Little credence can be given to the Gestapo reports insofar as ideological views or differences of opinion are concerned, as shown by a report[18] of one of these talks. During the talk there was a discussion on "a suitable method of giving a Christian imprint to the state." Leber apparently opposed this and "rejected any such formula in strong terms." Leber, however, was in fact anything but an atheist. He belonged to the Roman Catholic church and at this very moment was discussing with his wife her conversion to Roman Catholicism.[19] Leber probably only opposed the "Christian imprint to the state" because in his view no label should be attached to a secular democratic state which would not be acceptable to the people as a whole.[20]

Goerdeler once more reacted with particular violence—understandably this time—when he learned that, without informing or asking him, Stauffenberg had seized an opportunity of passing a message to Churchill.

Goerdeler was "pained and surprised," considering it "undisciplined" that a section of the movement should act on its own initiative in a matter such as this. He had, he said, been faced with a number of difficult situations "stemming from the fact that Graf Stauffenberg seemed to be claiming complete independence for the military and for himself, which in practice meant for the so-called younger element or 'counts' group.' "[21] As before, Goerdeler now turned to Colonel General Beck and drew his attention to the danger and impossibility of such procedure. Beck's view, however, was that one should not try "to ride these young hotheads on too tight a rein."[22]

XIX

Foreign Policy Plans

One interpretation placed upon the clash between Goerdeler and Stauffenberg is that its primary cause was a difference of opinion on foreign policy, Goerdeler being a supporter of a West-orientated solution, Stauffenberg and his friends looking eastwards.[1] It has also been said that Stauffenberg toyed with "romantic ideas about Russo-German collaboration" once the two peoples had succeeded in throwing off the yoke of their two despots. This would have been a worthy idea on anyone's part, but to label Stauffenberg a political "easterner" simply on this score[2] is no better than tampering with the truth. In the situation as it existed at the time, Stauffenberg never even considered compromising with the Soviet Union and its system.

As early as 1943 Berthold von Stauffenberg had told Kranzfelder that the danger from Bolshevism was so great that a pact with the Soviet Union would bring about Germany's ruin. Some means must therefore be found, he said, to persuade England to negotiate, since England could not simply stand by and watch Europe being handed over to the Soviet Union.[3] In Claus von Stauffenberg's view the British were the people most likely to be ready to compromise, owing to the threatening increase of Soviet power; it was therefore, he thought, a mistake to take the official unyielding policy of the British government at its face value. The West would eventually negotiate with Germany, though not with the Nationalist Socialist government.[4]

Goerdeler was similarly hopeful. In 1943 he had heard from Jakob Wallenberg, the Swedish banker, "that the British were prepared to adopt a policy which would bring the Soviets to a halt east of the old

Polish eastern frontier and would also prevent the Baltic states falling under Soviet influence."[5]

In 1944 Adam von Trott zu Solz had an opportunity to visit Sweden from 19 June to 3 July; Stauffenberg commissioned him to find out "what the attitude of England and the U.S.A. would be if in the short term Germany found it necessary to open negotiations."[6]

This journey of Trott's was presumably both the opportunity and the occasion upon which Stauffenberg seized to send the message to Churchill referred to above.

Once in Sweden, Trott took it upon himself to try to find out what attitude the Soviet government would adopt to a new German government.[7] He obtained a copy of the "Program of the Free Germany National Committee" issued by Erich Weinert and General von Seydlitz-Kurzbach, his object being to see whether there was anyone in this committee with whom it would be possible to talk. He came to the conclusion, however, that the committee was no more than a vehicle for Soviet propaganda and that from the German point of view no positive political initiative was to be expected from that quarter. Stauffenberg also rejected these "proclamations from behind the barbed wire."[8]

Of all the men of the resistance, Stauffenberg is the only one who has been recognized by the East and who is held up as a national hero in the "German People's Republic." Even Iron Curtain research, however, has been unable to prove any leaning on his part towards Communist thinking or any contact between him and Communist cells. The Communist estimate of Stauffenberg is based primarily upon assertions by Hans-Bernd Gisevius, which will be dealt with in detail below.[9] An appreciation of Stauffenberg published in East Berlin in mid-1964 fails to produce any new evidence.[10]

After 20 July the Gestapo made considerable efforts to prove some direct connection between the conspirators and the Free Germany National Committee, since this would have given National Socialist propaganda a first-class excuse to vilify the members of the opposition. Reports submitted to Hitler were, however, forced to admit that no such contact existed: "It has so far been impossible to prove any direct connection between the Moscow National Committee and the conspirators."[11]

Trott, who claimed to be Stauffenberg's foreign policy informant,[12] summarized his views in a memorandum entitled "Europe between East and West."[13] He started from the assumption that after the war Germany's enemies would not be in a position to impose their will upon her. Soviet Russia's object would be to win Germany over to her side in order ultimately to bring the whole of Europe, to the Atlantic, under her hegemony. In this she would have the advantage that apart from the socialist working class and the radical element of German youth, she would find in Germany a state structure politically and economically similar to her own.

Russia's only European opponent would be England, the object of whose foreign policy must be to play off Germany against Russia, seeing that even after her defeat Germany would still be the second strongest power in Europe. This would only be possible, however, if England did not impose on the German people a dictated peace on the Versailles model but guaranteed them an honourable peace without loss of territory, without reparations, without political encirclement, and without economic restrictions. Cession of East Prussia to Poland might be considered as compensation for other areas being made over to Germany together with a declaration of independence for Austria.

Up to this point Trott's prognostications were more or less in line with Stauffenberg's hopes. Knowing British mentality better than Stauffenberg, however, Trott had realized that there was one overriding obstacle to a policy such as this: the British conviction that the Germans were incorrigibly aggressive and that nothing other than a harsh peace should be concluded with them. In addition, many people in England believed their country strong enough to hold the Soviet Union in check alone.

During his June trip to Sweden Trott passed on a request to influential circles in England that "should the Nazi regime fall and be replaced by a broadly based German government, the British should refrain from further air attacks on Berlin."[14] But the answer he received confirmed the impression he had gained during a trip at the end of 1943; it was a curt refusal.

Fahrner also heard of unsuccessful attempts to establish contact with England. The Western powers refused any assistance or support for a German rising against Hitler because they "preferred the complete overthrow of Germany to any contact with the German resistance fighters."[15] The coup of 20 July was therefore undertaken without prior agreement with any foreign power.[16]

Stauffenberg was unwilling to accept Trott zu Solz's pessimistic forecast. He could not imagine that England would be guided by a policy of hatred towards Germany when in the last analysis this was bound to work against Great Britain's own interests. He continued to cling to the hope that British policy would take a favourable turn. He felt that "account must be taken of the fact that, to judge from a number of Churchill's utterances, he may well under certain circumstances steer a very different course once victory has been won."[17]

Like Trott, Leber also warned against any overoptimistic estimate of the external prospects of a new German government. It was illusory, he said, to imagine that Germany could drive a wedge into the enemy coalition. Like Stauffenberg, however, he hoped that any government formed after the fall of Hitler would be recognized by the Allies as a worthy, if not equal, partner in negotiations.[18]

Stauffenberg also assumed that if it came to an occupation of Germany, "a new German government responsible for a rising against Hitler and the re-establishment of the rule of law would not simply be disregarded by the victors, even though they might not formally recognize it."[19]

Stauffenberg believed that it would be possible to bring fighting in the west to a halt at once and so to put up an all the more tenacious defense in the east. He hoped that in the first instance it would be possible to open negotiations in the west between army commanders, in other words to cut out the political authorities in the early stages and by this means to arrive at an armistice with England and the U.S.A. For this reason he made efforts in the spring of 1944 to establish contact with the Allied Supreme Command (SHAEF), either with General Eisenhower or his chief of staff, General Bedell Smith.[20]

In mid-May Stauffenberg believed that he had established such a contact. On 25 May Captain Kaiser, the go-between with Dr. Goerdeler, therefore drew up on Stauffenberg's instructions, a program outlining the German position in the event of negotiations with SHAEF. It consisted of eleven points, primarily of a military nature but including also a whole series of political prerequisites:

1. Immediate cessation of air warfare.

2. Cancellation of Allied plans for the invasion of France.

3. Avoidance of further bloodshed.

4. Preservation of a defensive capability in the east; evacuation of all occupied territories in the northwest and south.

5. No occupation of Germany.

6. A freely elected independent German government under a constitution chosen by Germany.

7. Full co-operation by Germany in fulfilling the armistice conditions and in the preparation of the peacetime European order.

8. Withdrawal to the 1914 Reich frontiers in the east; maintenance of Austria and the Sudetenland as an integral part of the Reich; autonomy for Alsace-Lorraine.

9. Energetic reconstruction in Germany, and German collaboration in the reconstruction of Europe.

10. Germany herself to deal with German criminals.

11. Re-establishment of German honour, self-respect, and standing in the world.[21]

This was undoubtedly a maximum plan; in May 1944 no German versed in politics could really have hoped that territorial demands such as those in paragraph 8 would be accepted. It remains to be seen whether it would in any case have been right to initiate negotiations on the basis of these eleven points.

Stauffenberg's thoughts on foreign policy were summarized in a six-page thesis found in his office in the Bendlerstrasse on 20 July. The memorandum had been drafted before D-day, 6 June, and there is no mention of its author, but the circumstances under which it was found and the thoughts which it contained lead to the conclusion that it was in fact drafted by Stauffenberg.

Among other things, the memorandum stresses that one of the main reasons for Germany's difficult position was the treatment of the occupied territories. "Militarily the beginning of the end was the Russian campaign; this opened with the order for execution of all commissars and continued with the starvation of prisoners of war and the practice of manhunts to obtain civil labour. . . . The most important object after a change of regime is to ensure that Germany remains a worthwhile factor in the power-politics game and that in particular the Wehrmacht remains an effective instrument in the hands of its commanders. There are various possibilities of exploiting political differences within the Allied camp. As the military position worsens, however, and in particular if the Allied invasion of northwest Europe should take place, these possibilities will become increasingly restricted."[22]

XX

D-Day

The military members of the conspiracy were in no doubt that an Allied invasion in the west was coming within the foreseeable future, and also that, should it succeed, there would be no further prospect of a negotiated peace. The time factor therefore indicated that the coup should be launched as early as possible, if for no other reason than to avoid the suspicion that Hitler had been removed only after the invasion had shown the military situation to be completely hopeless.

On the assumption that the invasion could not be prevented, Stauffenberg's thoughts turned towards methods of reducing the casualties likely to be suffered by both sides and using the invasion for the purposes of the coup d'état. For instance, he discussed with Leber whether it would not be in the best interests of Germany to lead the Allied assault troops through the German minefields, in the hope that perhaps the dreaded collapse of the eastern front might be postponed thereby. They came to the conclusion, however, that this plan was unrealistic and that the only hope lay in launching the coup d'état before the invasion took place.[1]

The pressure exerted by other civilian members of the conspiracy also forced Stauffenberg to this conclusion. Early in June Father Delp, the Jesuit member of the Kreisau Circle, visited Stauffenberg in Bamberg and expressed to him "the wish of many . . . for the earliest possible action."[2]

Goerdeler, too, was making efforts to escape from his enforced inactivity. He wrote a letter to General Zeitzler, chief of the army staff, forwarding a twenty-four page memorandum outlining the hope-lessness of the military and political situation and asking for an inter-view, in the hope that Zeitzler could arrange a personal talk with Hitler for him. This missive was handed to Stauffenberg, who was to forward it to Zeitzler via Stieff. Goerdeler had an extraordinary belief in the power of the spoken word; he had never been fully in accord with the plan for assassination and from time to time had been heard to say that he was confident that he could get the better of Hitler in any radio discussion.[3] Now he hoped that, merely by talking to him, he would be able to bring Hitler to reason. But Zeitzler never received this letter;[4] after several reminders it was returned to Goerdeler. It is more than likely that Stauffenberg, who was only too well aware that nothing could be achieved by such a conversation and that it would probably endanger everything, never forwarded the letter; it certainly never got further than Stieff.[5]

Towards the end of May 1944 the tempo of planning was stepped up; numerous emergency measures were revised once more; and the explosive, which Stieff had been holding, was returned to Berlin and put into the hands of Stauffenberg.[6] This increase of activity on the part of the conspirators was due not only to the imminent threat of invasion but also to the proposed nomination of Stauffenberg as chief of staff to commander-in-chief, replacement army.

This posting was the work of the commander-in-chief, Colonel General Fromm, who in view of Stauffenberg's widespread reputation, was bent on having him as his chief of staff and deputy.

A conversation between Himmler and Guderian is significant of the respect in which Stauffenberg was held. They were discussing the most suitable successor to Lieutenant General Heusinger, head of the army operations section. When General Guderian proposed Stauffenberg as "the best horse in the general staff stable," Himmler agreed at once.[7]

Stauffenberg was at first unwilling to join Fromm's staff, but it soon became clear that the advantages were overriding. In the first place, it meant that this important post would now be held by a member of the resistance movement, and secondly another member, Ritter Mertz von Quirnheim, was to be posted to take over from Stauffenberg. The greatest advantage, however, lay in the fact that as chief of staff Stauffenberg would also be deputy to the commander in chief of the replacement army. As such he would be able to launch the coup d'état through the "Valkyrie" plan with every outward appearance of legality and, so long as Fromm's attitude remained uncertain, act as his rightful representative. If on the great day it became necessary to eliminate Fromm, the conspirators would not be faced with the necessity of getting rid of a recalcitrant chief of staff as well, a measure likely to rouse opposition from the Wehrkreis commanders.[8]

Fromm's attitude to the resisters was ambiguous. General Olbricht, the head of the army office (AHA), had already tried to persuade him to get himself nominated commander-in-chief Home Forces; this he had done not in connection with any plans for the coup but in order to counteract the over-decentralized higher organization, which was the rule within Germany as elsewhere; alongside the commander-in-chief of the replacement army there were, for instance, base organizations of the other services and of the Waffen-SS, over which Fromm had no authority. Fromm, however, rejected Olbricht's proposal, saying that there were ways of getting round these difficulties; he then checked via Keitel that no such changes were in the air.[9]

On the other hand, Fromm was perfectly prepared to listen to laments about the gloomy military situation and statements that something must be done to bring about a change. On one occasion, however, after a conversation on these lines, Fromm had dismissed General Olbricht with the words, "That was very interesting. Heil Hitler."[10]

As soon as Stauffenberg took over, he told the general quite openly of his views. The latter listened to him calmly and in fact retorted that his own ideas were very similar—but there the matter must rest. He did nothing to help the resisters, but nothing to hinder them either.[11] He knew quite well what was going on in the office of his subordinate Olbricht, but gave forth no more than the passing remark, "For God's sake, don't forget that chap Keitel when you make your putsch."[12]

On 7 June 1944 Stauffenberg for the first time accompanied Colonel General Fromm to a briefing conference in the Führer's headquarters. Hitler had been very struck by a memorandum of Stauffenberg's and so summoned Fromm—who, after all, was the commander-in-chief of the replacement army—for the first time in two and a half years. The conference was a small one, only Himmler, Göring, and Speer being present in addition to Hitler. Stauffenberg found the whole atmosphere "rotten and degenerate." Only Speer gave him the impression of being normal; the others he characterized as "patent psychopaths."[13]

The day before, on 6 June 1944, the invasion in the west had been launched. It shattered not only Germany's last more or less stable military position but also the plans of the German opposition.

Numerous problems now faced the conspirators. In this situation would it be a responsible act to carry out the assassination? Had the coup now any purpose? Had the object of the entire plan to save Germany from chaos already gone by the board? What was the point of running the risk of civil war when the German people could be spared nothing thereby? Would not the seeds of a new "stab-in-the-back legend" be sown? Was it not better that the National Socialist system should be responsible for leading the German people to its doom?

Even Stauffenberg mulled over these questions. Basically all hope was gone. He had not thought that the invasion would take place so early, nor had he foreseen its rapid success.[14] Discussing the situation with Graf Yorck he showed himself more skeptical than ever before, saying that there seemed to be no way out.[15] He therefore asked the East Prussian Count Heinrich von Lehndorff-Steinort to get in touch with Tresckow and ask his advice as to whether there was still any point in pressing on with the coup, since it was difficult to see what practical purpose it now had. Tresckow sent back the following reply, which has since become famous: "The assassination must take place coûte que coûte. Even if it does not succeed, the Berlin action must go forward. The point now is not whether the coup has any practical purpose, but to prove to the world and before history that German resistance is ready to stake its all. Compared to this, everything else is a side issue."[16]

It was true that the only point now was to save at least some remnant of honour for Germany, and it was for this cause that the men of the resistance went to their death.

Fahrner, who was seeing a great deal of Stauffenberg at this time, wrote of this final decision: "Many questioned whether, the war situation having deteriorated so far, there was any purpose in the rising. To them it could be answered that much bloodshed and destruction on both sides would be saved by action even at this late hour. Even more important was the knowledge that this was a challenge to purge the country spiritually and to save its honour. Put in moral terms, sins of omission in this case weighed more heavily than sins of commission."[17]

On 22 June 1944 the great Soviet offensive against Army Group Center opened, and within three weeks had destroyed twenty-seven German divisions. Since the conspirators intended to hold the eastern front even after the coup, their object now became to bring fighting in the west to a halt as soon as possible—if indeed there was still any possibility of doing so. In mid-June, before the opening of the Russian offensive, Tresckow had urgently advised Stauffenberg to go at once to General Speidel, Chief of Staff Army Group B (commanded by Field Marshal Erwin Rommel), and ensure that a gap should be left in the western front to facilitate a strategic break-through by the Allies.[18]

Stauffenberg did in fact go to Paris and on 23 June met his old friend Colonel Eberhard Finckh, officer in charge of administration to C-in-C West. He went straight to the point: the situation in the east was untenable, and the break-through in the west only a matter of time. He told Finckh of Tresckow's "urgent advice" and of the plans for a coup d'état, leaving with a remark reminiscent of his comment on the senior army leaders two years before: "We have no real field marshals any more. They all shake in their shoes and stand to attention when the Führer gives an order. They are not assertive enough with their views regarding the seriousness of the situation."[19]

There was one field marshal to whom this criticism did not apply— Rommel. He had once been a disciple of Hitler's, but ever since the African campaign he and his supreme commander had not seen eye to eye; in recent months tension between them had been such as to force Rommel to the conclusion that action against Hitler involving violence was necessary. On 25 June Colonel Finckh reported to the Field Marshal that Stauffenberg was preparing an assassination attempt in Berlin. Although opposed to the assassination, Rommel gave it to be understood that in the event of a coup d'état he could be counted upon.[20]

At the end of June Tresckow intervened once more from the eastern front and sent an emissary to the newly appointed Commander-in-Chief West, Field Marshal von Kluge, imploring him simply to open the door to the allies in the west, and saying that the real enemy was neither the Americans nor the British but Hitler alone.[21]

In parallel with these events, two foreign policy initiatives were taken on the military side. Towards the end of June it became known that the opposition had taken soundings in certain highly placed British circles. Stauffenberg passed over: "(1) A list of persons who might undertake future negotiations with Britain; (2) the desire that Austria should remain part of the Reich; (3) a request that the reckoning with war criminals should be left to the future German government."[22]

The development of the situation in the meanwhile had, it will be noted, produced a radical change in the eleven-point program previously drafted by Captain Kaiser on Stauffenberg's instructions. A month earlier there had been "demands" that the 1914 frontiers should be guaranteed, that there should be no occupation, and that the eastern front should be held; now there were no more than "desires" or "requests."

In early July Colonel Stauffenberg and Georg Alexander Hansen, head of the Abwehr, dispatched Dr. Otto John, chairman of Lufthansa, to Madrid. He was to inform suitable Allied authorities that a coup in Germany was imminent and try to establish direct contact with SHAEF.

Hansen, clearly on Stauffenberg's instructions, told John, "If we could talk to General Eisenhower as soldier to soldier, we should rapidly reach an understanding."

In Madrid John was assured that all this would be immediately reported to Eisenhower, but at the same time it was indicated to him that the prerequisite for a cessation of hostilities was "unconditional surrender" to all the Allies—in other words to the Soviet Union as well.[23]

Stauffenberg's new post enabled him to travel more frequently to the Führer's headquarters to report. It would of course have been possible before this to create some occasion for him to do so on behalf of AHA but this had not been done, since his presence in Berlin had hitherto been considered essential.[24] At this point, however, Stauffenberg decided to make the assassination attempt himself. Could there, after all, be anyone equally suitable and equally determined who could take his place? It was not possible to go on searching any longer, for the situation demanded rapid and forceful action. Stauffenberg made his decision at the end of June; it was an emergency solution forced upon him only by the crisis developments of that month.

Fahrner learned that the "openings for attack have become even more problematical, and Stauffenberg is now faced with the problem of whether to make the assassination attempt himself, something which has never even been thought of, since he is indispensable for the subsequent phase."[25] Werner von Haeften, Stauffenberg's aide, in a letter written only two or three weeks before 20 July, said, "Claus-is now thinking of doing the thing himself."[26]

Berthold von Stauffenberg, Yorck, and Bernd von Haeften all stated that they learned of Stauffenberg's decision towards the end of June.[27]

XXI

July Assassination Plans

At the end of June a meeting took place between Stauffenberg and Generals Wagner (QMG of the army), Stieff (head of the organization section), and Lindemann. Technical problems were discussed once more; Wagner and General Fritz Lindemann of the OKH pressed for early action.[1] On 3 July the same three generals discussed the screening of signal communications with General Erich Fellgiebel, the Wehrmacht chief signal officer. There were then further talks in Berlin between Beck, Olbricht, Wagner, and Lindemann when plans for the coup were finally fixed. Beck meanwhile went to Berne and Goerdeler to Sweden to contact respectively the American Secret Service chief Allen Dulles and the banker Jakob Wallenberg.[2]

Just when it seemed that all was at last ready, the Gestapo unconsciously succeeded in striking at the very center of the conspiracy. On 12 June they had arrested Colonel Staehle, commander of the warwounded settlement in Berlin-Frohnau, who had worked under Oster in OKW intelligence and had been in contact with Goerdeler for years;[3] on 5 July Dr. Julius Leber was also arrested for having tried to gain contact with ex-Communists; in the process he was recognized and denounced by a police informer.[4]

It was now clearly essential to act as quickly as possible. On the very next day Stauffenberg, who had been promoted to colonel with effect from 1 July 1944, was due to appear at a conference in the Obersalzberg as the new chief of staff to the C-in-C of the replacement army.

According to the Gestapo report, he had with him on this occasion the briefcase in which he carried the bomb on 20 July, and glancing towards it, said to General Stieff, "I have got the whole bag of tricks with me."[5] This could mean either that Stauffenberg was trying to hint to Stieff that he (Stieff) was best placed to set off the bomb, or that he (Stauffenberg) intended to carry out the assassination that very day.[6]

The attack was definitely due to be made on 11 July. On that day Stauffenberg was once more ordered to the Berghof and took with him Captain Klausing, a young officer from the AHA who was party to the affair; Stauffenberg instructed him to have an HE.111 ready on Salzburg airfield and himself to wait in the car in front of the head-quarters. But nothing happened. When Stauffenberg left the Berghof he told Klausing that he had postponed the attempt, since Himmler had not been present at the conference.[7]

Under interrogation Berthold von Stauffenberg commented on his brother's decision as follows: "In order to prevent anyone from coming forward and seizing power, my brother hoped to be able to carry out the assassination at a briefing conference attended also by the Reichs-führer-SS [Himmler] and the Reichsmarschall [Göring]. Field Marshal Keitel was as a rule present at all briefing conferences."[8]

On the return journey Stauffenberg met Stieff, Fellgiebel, and Klam-roth a Lieutenant Colonel of the General Staff in the Frankenstrub barracks, north of Berchtesgaden. They discussed the screening of the repeater stations in Munich and Salzburg, and Fellgiebel was once more asked to ensure that all orders and information bulletins connected with the revolt be transmitted without a hitch and all other users cut off.[9]

At lunch in Frankenstrub Stauffenberg found himself talking to Major Percy E. Schramm, who says that he thought it "incredible in retrospect" that he noticed absolutely nothing. "The briefcase contain-ing the bomb must in fact have been lying around somewhere near. (We lunched in the open at small tables; people were coming and going as their duties allowed). I cannot now remember what we talked about, but our conversation was very intense and must have ranged far outside military matters." Schramm's impression of Stauffenberg was that he was a staff officer "who had not turned into an automaton, but had remained a man."[10]

On the evening of 11 July Lieutenant Colonel Cäsar von Hofacker, of C-in-C West's staff and one of the adherents of the plot, arrived in Berlin to talk to his cousin Stauffenberg and inform Colonel General

Beck of the catastrophic situation on the western front. His report made a shattering impression upon Beck, whose reaction was that outstanding negotiators must be dispatched to London and Moscow if tolerable conditions were to be obtained. Goerdeler, who was also taking part in this discussion, proposed that he and Beck should forthwith go to Kluge to verify the situation on the spot. Beck, however, said that Hofacker's information made it crystal clear that Kluge also considered very rapid action to be indicated.[11]

The next day someone else arrived in Berlin, a man on the fringe of the conspiracy but a close collaborator, primarily of Goerdeler—Hans-Bernd Gisevius. He was stationed in Switzerland and was responsible for keeping in touch with Dulles in the American embassy.

He met Stauffenberg during the night 12–13 July. For years the general picture has been both obscured and distorted by his subsequent accounts both of this conversation and of developments within the resistance. He is responsible for the allegation that Stauffenberg was working for an "eastern solution."

Although he had never met Stauffenberg before, Gisevius pretends that as a result of their first meeting he realized at once that "in the final analysis" Stauffenberg "was fighting for the continuation of Nazi militaristic legality," that he was "the type of man best suited . . . to purposes of assassination," "a professional soldier who was being drawn willy-nilly into the complex problems of a revolutionary era," "a swashbuckler who knew what he wanted"[12]—a series of statements which not only contradict each other but are contrary to all other reports of Stauffenberg.

Gisevius' most important statement—that Stauffenberg had "swung eastwards"—he bases upon a question by Stauffenberg: "What could I hope to gain by coming to an agreement with the Western powers? Didn't I know that Army Group Center had ceased to count for anything? The Russians would shortly be across the Vistula; . . . the decision in the east had already been reached; therefore all political activity had to be directed towards the east."

"But," Gisevius continues, "he contradicted himself in the same breath; after each statement he added that he did not want me to misunderstand him, that he had not really decided the matter in his own mind; his only object was to set out the alternatives clearly and for this reason was simply taking the role of an *advocatus diaboli*." Gisevius' conclusion is that "Stauffenberg had long since made his choice, but that he was not yet sure how he could justify his change of heart to Beck or Goerdeler."[13]

Gisevius' opinion is based not upon any actual statement by Stauffenberg, but upon supposition. He was prejudiced against Stauffenberg before he had even exchanged a word with him. A mere expression of opinion that post-war German policy could not be conducted to the exclusion of the Soviet Union—a view which did no more than take account of the facts—does not imply a "swing eastwards." Gisevius' statements are probably a malicious reflection of the prejudice and vexation which had built up in Goerdeler's mind. When, for instance, Gisevius says that since the failure at the end of 1943 Stauffenberg had made no efforts to initiate further action,[14] that is just plain untruth. In any case, what grounds could Gisevius have for such statements? He did not return to Berlin until 12 July. One can only assume that he must have obtained his information from Goerdeler, and it is a well-known fact that Stauffenberg did not tell Goerdeler of all that he was planning and trying to do. Goerdeler therefore became convinced that the Colonel promised much but did little.[15] Gisevius' judgement is in fact so distorted by prejudice that he does not perceive that other statements in his own book contradict the picture he paints of Stauffenberg. Beck, he says, told him that "after the elimination of Oster Stauffenberg's had been the only whole-hearted work to be carried on in OKW,"[16] and that "in the last six months he had come to realize that Stauffenberg was the only activist in OKW."[17]

This discussion during the night 12–13 July also touched on the problem of possible "purges." Gisevius reports that Stauffenberg put forward the view that the number of those accused should be strictly limited, although naturally SA and SS murderers must be punished.

According to Gisevius Stauffenberg wanted "the army purge restricted to the few Nazi generals, such as Reinecke and Keitel, whose crimes and lack of character were indisputable." Stauffenberg, Gisevius continues, "was opposed to proceedings being taken 'for political reasons' against senior officers as a whole—and in particular, Brauchitsch and Halder—for their attitude on the outbreak of war, or against the field marshals for their characterless attitude to Hitler's invasions."[18]

His object in this, Gisevius says, was to keep the purge within "legal" bounds. Gisevius then compares Stauffenberg's views with his own. In his opinion the myriad Nazi crimes could not be expiated "legally." "It is not possible without special courts. . . . In order to re-establish the rule of law, we must depart from legality. . . . There is no solution other than to keep in being the severe rules of the special courts and use them against their authors. Equally, certain classes of persons must be declared communally guilty—members of the Reich government and secretaries of state, Reichstatthalter and Gauleiter, field marshals and colonel generals."[19]

If Gisevius can propose a departure from legality, special courts, and collective sentences, it is paradoxical that he should reproach Stauffenberg for striving for the continuance of legality based on the Party-Wehrmacht alliance.

In these final days Stauffenberg seized every opportunity to talk to his friends. He forced himself and his friends into a merciless discussion of the political and moral justification for the use of force. His conversation with Gisevius might well have taken such a turn, but Stauffenberg liked to stimulate conversation by flat and sometimes extreme statements, and he did not find in Gisevius a man with whom he could talk in this way. The intensity with which Stauffenberg wrestled with the problem of the assassination in these last days is illustrated by the report of a conversation he had with Yorck, Lukaschek, and Dr. van Husen in the latter's house. "When Stauffenberg left for the overnight train his last remark was, 'So there is nothing for it but to kill him.' I believe that it was this conversation which finally confirmed Stauffenberg in his decision to do it himself."[20]

By mid-July all intelligent men at the front could see the collapse of the German Wehrmacht looming. In the west, although the German forces had been driven farther south, they had still contrived to maintain their cohesion, but an Allied break-through on the left flank appeared to be imminent; the German units were being rapidly worn down. Faced with this threatening situation Field Marshal Rommel, commander-in-chief of Army Group B, decided to send a "most immediate" teleprinter message to Hitler concerning the overall situation; its conclusion was as follows: "The troops are fighting heroically everywhere, but the unequal struggle is nearing its end. I must beg you to draw the political conclusions without delay. I feel it my duty as commander-in-chief of the Army Group to state this clearly."[21]

In Italy the enemy had succeeded in capturing Rome on 4 June, while the Germans withdrew slowly northwards to the "Green Line" (La Spezia–Apennines–Rimini). In the east the enemy was pouring fresh forces westwards through the yawning 220-mile gap where up to 22 June Army Group Center had been; by 13 July Vilna had been taken and the fall of Bialystok was imminent.

Such was the situation when, on 15 July, Colonel General Fromm and Colonel Graf Stauffenberg were summoned to a briefing conference in the Führer's headquarters; it was an opportunity to carry out the assassination which obviously had to be seized under all circumstances. Stauffenberg accordingly agreed with Olbricht that the latter should issue the "Valkyrie" order two hours before the estimated time of the explosion, in order to reduce the time lag before troop movements actually began.

Now for the detailed events of that day in the Führer's headquarters. Fromm and Stauffenberg were met by an officer who has stated that they landed at Rastenburg airfield about 9:35 A.M., accompanied by Klausing. They first spent some threequarters of an hour in the mess, breakfasting and discussing once more the subject they were to present —manpower replenishment for certain combat units. Stauffenberg had hardly entered the mess before he asked his commander for permission to make one or two important telephone calls. Insofar as the escorting officer remembered, these were made from "A" office to Generals Stieff and Fellgiebel, "presumably to check that all was in order for the moment."

"Colonel General Fromm and Colonel Graf Stauffenberg then went to the briefing conference together with certain other senior officers," the report continues, and on arrival at the conference room hut, "The Führer shook hands with them both." The report goes on:

> After the conference Colonel General Fromm together with certain other officers went off in the direction of HQ Area I. I myself could not accompany them, since Colonel Graf Stauffen-

berg was still in conversation in front of the briefing hut. . . . Captain Klausing was still waiting by the car, and I think I can remember that during the briefing conference he had had a talk with some other officers. Shortly thereafter Colonel Graf Stauffenberg came along, and when I told him where the Colonel General was, he told me not to worry since he still had important matters to discuss with Generals Stieff and Fellgiebel. These two, however, were already in the car park, and so the conversation could take place forthwith. Shortly before the Brunswick special train left, Colonel Graf Stauffenberg had another telephone conversation with Berlin.[22]

When the briefing conference came to an end and no explosion had taken place Generals Stieff and Fellgiebel had hurried at once to the car park to talk to Stauffenberg and find out why nothing had happened.

The reason is given in Berthold von Stauffenberg's statement to the Gestapo: "My brother told me that a conference was suddenly called in which he himself had to make the presentation, so that he had no opportunity of carrying out the attack."[23]

This was probably the news which Stauffenberg passed on in his telephone call to Berlin.

In Berlin the "Valkyrie" plan had already been set in motion, and so the conspirators were faced with the problem of regaining control of the situation. Olbricht drove straight over to the Armoured Infantry Demonstration Battalion and warned them that the issue of the code word "Valkyrie" had only been a practice alert to enable him to test the execution of the order.[24]

Meanwhile, Goerdeler was in the house of the lawyer Dr. Sprunck, waiting for the vital news—in vain. In his disappointment he exploded with wrath, saying that the officers no longer gave him any insight into their plans and were trying to ditch him.[25]

In view of the numerous previous failures and Gestapo arrests and controls, Beck and Stauffenberg in their final conversation on 16 July reached the decision that the next opportunity must under all circumstances be seized—"*coûte que coûte*," in Tresckow's words, also that the

coup d'état should be launched even if action in the Führer's headquarters had not been completely successful.[26]

As an immediate result, the same day inner-circle discussions were
held in Stauffenberg's apartment; there were present: Claus and
Berthold von Stauffenberg, Ritter Mertz von Quirnheim, Trott zu
Solz, Counts Schwerin, Schulenburg, and Yorck, together with
Hofacker and Hansen. Hofacker described the position in the west,
quoting both Rommel and Kluge as being of the opinion that in about
two weeks' time the enemy would have achieved such numerical and
material superiority that the German front could only be held for at
the most six weeks. Trott took up Stauffenberg's old idea that once the
National Socialist regime had been removed, negotiations should be
conducted between soldiers and initiated both in the west and in the
east—a clear necessity dictated by the military situation at the time. In
addition various possibilities of carrying out the coup and bringing the
war to an end were discussed once more:

> 1. The western solution, on the lines of Tresckow's June
> proposal: Stauffenberg raised the question of whether pressure
> could not be brought on the German commanders in the west to
> put a stop to the fighting on their own initiative, to withdraw
> their troops to the Siegfried line, and so prepare the way for
> combined action by the Western powers and Germany against
> the Soviet Union.
>
> 2. The Berlin solution: According to this proposal, the Wehr-
> macht signal system was to be blocked for at least twenty-four
> hours and Army Groups ordered to withdraw with such rapidity
> that the Führer's headquarters would be unable to intervene and
> cancel the orders.
>
> Both these solutions, however, contained so many imponder-
> ables that they were rejected as impracticable. As a result:
>
> 3. The central solution—the only one seriously considered:
> The assassination of Hitler was to be the signal for the coup d'état
> which was to be launched from Berlin by means of the "Valkyrie"
> plan.[27]

That same evening a remarkable rumour went round in von Bismarck's house in Potsdam. One of the guests, a young Hungarian

nobleman, told Lieutenant Commander Jessen, a friend of Berthold von Stauffenberg, that there was a rumour in Berlin that the Führer's headquarters would be blown sky-high within the next few weeks. Jessen did not feel that he could go to Hungary to nail the source of this rumour and was afraid that someone "in the know" must have been indiscreet. The next day he told the story to Berthold von Stauffenberg and another of the conspirators, Lieutenant Commander Kranzfelder. On the afternoon of 18 July the latter drove over to Claus von Stauffenberg to warn him and returned with the news that the assassination would definitely take place on 20 July. Stauffenberg had said that this would be the final attempt: "There is no other choice. The Rubicon has been crossed."[28]

The Red Army had launched its major offensive against Army Group North Ukraine in southern Poland and Galicia, aiming to reach the San and Vistula; meanwhile, the Soviet northwest front had pushed forward so far that East Prussia was now in serious danger, and the rapid constitution of fresh divisions was necessary to protect it. Stauffenberg was instructed to be prepared to speak on this subject at the briefing conference on 20 July.[29] So the day of decision was settled.

On 18 July, those of the conspirators who stood closest to Stauffenberg were informed. Stauffenberg himself visited General Wagner in Zossen. General Olbricht was told by telephone, and he passed on the news to Mertz, Bernardis, and Schulenburg. Graf Yorck was informed by Graf Schwerin.[30]

At the same time it became known that Goerdeler was threatened with arrest. Stauffenberg advised him not to use the telephone, to keep himself under cover, and to avoid contact with anybody.[31] Stauffenberg was particularly anxious regarding Leber and his wife. When he spoke to Trott, evidently in a state of considerable excitement, he said, "We need Leber; I'll get him out." On 18 July he sent a message to Frau Annedore Leber who was in the hospital: "We are aware of our duty."[32]

The day of 19 July passed like any other day. Stauffenberg was just as radiantly enthusiastic, just as calm, and working at just the same pace as before.[33] He gave not a sign of the tension under which he must have been living. But as so often before, on 19 July he wanted to be with friends, and this time went to Trott zu Solz.[34] His brother Berthold joined him and remained with him until his aircraft took off next morning.

The Stauffenberg brothers had drafted an oath to be sworn after the coup d'état. Realizing that even after the destruction of the National Socialist system, Germany would undoubtedly have to accept occupation, they were afraid that men might lose contact with each other. The oath would give them the feeling that there were still bonds between them. A few lines of this vow are still known. They are as follows:

> We wish there to be a new order of society, which will make all Germans supporters of the state, guaranteeing them justice and right, nailing the lie that all men are equal, and accepting the fact that differences of status are a natural phenomenon. We wish to see a people with its roots deep in the soil of its native country, with an affinity to the forces of nature, finding happiness and satisfaction in labouring in the status into which it has been called, and proud to overcome the base emotions of envy and ill-will. We wish to see leaders drawn from all classes of society, taking the lead on the grounds of their intelligence, breeding, and spirit of self-sacrifice.[35]

A few days prior to 20 July Stauffenberg had said to someone, "It is now time that something was done. But he who has the courage to do something must do so in the knowledge that he will go down to German history as a traitor. If he does not do it, however, then he will be a traitor to his own conscience."[36]

XXII

20 July 1944

Early on the morning of 20 July Stauffenberg, General Stieff, and Lieutenant von Haeften landed at Rastenburg airfield in East Prussia, near Wolfsschanze, the Führer's headquarters.[1] On arrival Stauffenberg breakfasted in the Wolfsschanze mess with the headquarters commandant's aide, Captain von Möllendorf. He was then called to a meeting already arranged with General Buhle, head of the OKW army staff, and his former master in the organization section. Then, together with Buhle and Lieutenant General von Thadden, chief of staff to C-in-C Wehrkreis I, he went to a meeting with Field Marshal Keitel, chief of OKW.

Up to the time of the Keitel meeting Haeften carried the briefcase containing the bomb, Stauffenberg's own briefcase being full of papers required for the meetings. After the discussion with Keitel, Stauffenberg asked Lieutenant Colonel John von Freyend, Keitel's aide, if he could have a wash and brush up and change his shirt. Freyend made his own bedroom available and Stauffenberg went in with Haeften—a perfectly normal thing to do, since he had to have help to change. The two at once set to work to repack the briefcases. The bomb was put in Stauffenberg's briefcase and the detonator pressed home with a pair of pliers.[2]

The bomb was now live and would go off in ten to fifteen minutes. Carrying it, Stauffenberg went across to the briefing hut together with Keitel and Buhle. Two officers, one of them Keitel's aide, repeatedly offered to carry the briefcase, but Stauffenberg refused, saying that he did not need help.

The conference took place in the map room, where the daily briefing conferences were always held.[3] It had already started. Keitel reported to Hitler that Stauffenberg was present to make the presentation ordered. Hitler greeted him.

Stauffenberg was given a place on the right of Lieutenant General Heusinger who was standing next to Hitler and had already begun his presentation of the situation on the eastern front. In order to place his briefcase at the right spot, Stauffenberg pushed his way forward to the table; Colonel Brandt, Heusinger's staff officer was in the way. Stauffenberg bent down and finally placed the briefcase under the right half of the map board. Then he left the room, unnoticed.

Shortly afterwards he was missed, since he was required to give some information. General Buhle left the room to look for him, but could not find him.[4]

Stauffenberg had gone straight to General Fellgiebel in Shelter 88. The two stood in front of the shelter and tried to look as unconcerned as possible, discussing the problem of fortifications on the eastern front; Lieutenant Colonel Sander, the headquarters signal officer, arrived to report that the car ordered by Lieutenant von Haeften was ready; he also reminded Stauffenberg that the headquarters commandant, Lieutenant Colonel Streve, was expecting him to lunch. Stauffenberg said that he would go but would first have to return to the conference.

In the map room Lieutenant General Heusinger was just describing the situation in Army Group North area: "The Russians are moving considerable forces northwards, west of the Düna. Their leading troops are already southwest of Dünaburg. If the Army Group does not now withdraw from Lake Peipus, a catastrophe will. . . ."[5]

Heusinger's last words were drowned by a powerful explosion. It was about 12:45. Sander, who appeared in front of Fellgiebel's shelter just at this moment, noticed that Stauffenberg started with particular violence.

"What's happening?" Fellgiebel asked. Sander, who was not taking the incident at all seriously, replied that this often occurred: someone had loosed off a round, or a mine had gone up.[6]

Immediately after the explosion Stauffenberg said that he would not now go back to the conference but would drive over to lunch with the Commandant—in fact he and Haeften set off for the airfield. He passed the briefing hut at a distance of about fifty to seventy yards. What he saw must have confirmed him in his certainty that the explosion had done its job.[7]

Stauffenberg was held up at the first checkpoint, whence the explosion in the briefing hut had been visible. He told the officer in charge that he must get to the airfield urgently, and since the officer knew him personally, he was allowed to pass. In any case, the alarm was not given until one and a half minutes later.

At the outer checkpoint, "South," Stauffenberg was held up once more. He gave the same explanation, but the sergeant on duty pointed out that in the meanwhile all entry and exit had been forbidden. Stauffenberg thereupon demanded to speak to the Commandant by telephone. He was already at the scene of the explosion, and the sergeant got his aide, Captain von Möllendorf, on the line. Stauffenberg told him curtly that he had the Commandant's permission to leave the security area, since he had to take off at 1:15. The aide, who did not yet know the reason for the alarm but did know that Stauffenberg was in Wolfsschanze on duty, said that he might proceed. Von Möllendorf confirmed this to the sergeant and Stauffenberg was allowed to pass.[8]

Stauffenberg's method of arguing his way past the guard was bold to the point of foolhardiness. If instead of the aide, the Commandant himself had come on the other end of the line, seeing that Stauffenberg had only a few minutes previously agreed to lunch with him, he would probably not have been allowed to leave HQ Area II. Stauffenberg probably relied upon the Commandant hurrying off at once to the scene of the disaster and being no longer in his room.

On the way to the airfield Haeften threw out of the car a parcel wrapped in brown paper. This was the second bomb, which would presumably have been used had the first one's detonator not functioned properly.[9]

A stop was at once placed on all news from the Führer's headquarters. Sander received from Hitler's aide the order: "No word is to be allowed to reach the outer world of an attempt at assassination." Meanwhile, Fellgiebel called his chief of staff, Colonel Hahn, in "A" telephone exchange and told him that an explosion had taken place in Wolfsschanze. He ordered: "Measures are to be taken forthwith to block outgoing signal traffic." Hahn passed this information on at once to

General Stieff. All signal traffic was stopped and General Wagner informed of the measures taken.[10]

The fact that the measures ordered by Hitler applied only to Supreme Headquarters but that Fellgiebel's had gone further and stopped traffic through the OKH exchange in Mauerwald, quickly threw suspicion on Fellgiebel, and he was arrested about midnight.

Shortly after 3 P.M. the order blocking signal traffic was first relaxed and then cancelled altogether insofar as official messages were concerned, and Fellgiebel was powerless to stop it. Had the assassination attempt succeeded, he would probably have been able to maintain the ban on signal traffic, even in the face of an order from Himmler or Göring; now he could do no more than let things take their course and do his best to warn his friends.[11]

One hour after the explosion the Reich central security office in Berlin was warned to detail a number of criminal investigators to fly to Rastenburg together with the chief of the security police, Kaltenbrunner, to undertake certain enquiries. Gisevius, who had called up Arthur Nebe, head of the central C.I.D., was told of this at 1:55 P.M. It is still incomprehensible why Nebe, a member of the conspiracy, should have failed to pass this information on to Olbricht, who was in his office in the Bendlerstrasse, itching for news.[12]

While Stauffenberg was still in the air, an order was issued to Berlin from the Führer's headquarters that a westbound HE.111 from East Prussia, the identification number of which was given, was to be shot down—probably it was suspected that Stauffenberg would attempt to make his way abroad. This order arrived on the desk of Major Friedrich Georgi of the air staff; he was Olbricht's son-in-law and, suspecting that this was in some way connected with the conspiracy, he did not pass the order on.[13]

When Stauffenberg landed at Berlin-Rangsdorf, shortly before 4 P.M., he was convinced that all in Rastenburg had gone according to plan and that action would meanwhile have been launched in Berlin. In fact, however, apart from the assassination attempt itself, the whole movement had been brought to a standstill by the decisive problem of signal communications. About 1:15 Lieutenant General Thiele, head of the Wehrmacht signal office in Berlin and a member of the conspiracy was informed that something had occurred in the Führer's headquarters.

This seemed to him a very vague piece of news and he thought it necessary to await confirmation, which, however, never arrived because of the ban on communications imposed meanwhile. It was not until about 3 P.M. that a further message arrived, giving warning of a communiqué to be issued from headquarters. This news merely complicated the issue; if the attack had been successful, it would not be possible to issue a communiqué, but if nothing had happened, why a communiqué at all? Thiele was therefore told to get further details. Between 3:45 and 3:50 he managed to obtain some firm information: "I have spoken to the headquarters but have not been able to get anything definite. All I could find out was that an explosion took place in the conference room as a result of which a large number of officers have been severely wounded."[14]

This news was enough for General Olbricht. There could be no going back now. No matter whether Hitler was dead or not, the conspirators now had their backs to the wall, for there was no possibility of concealing the fact that Stauffenberg had done the deed.

Olbricht and Mertz took the "Valkyrie" files out of the safe. Mertz was just beginning to issue the initial orders and Olbricht was about to go to Fromm when Haeften called from the airfield with the information that Hitler was dead.[15]

About 4 P.M. Colonel Hassell was summoned to the Bendlerstrasse by Mertz. Olbricht ordered him to make a signal officer available for his outer office, to get General Wagner and Field Marshal von Kluge on the telephone, and dispatch to Berlin garrison headquarters the twenty officers whom he had detained on duty, so that they might be distributed to various important points in the signal system.[16]

Olbricht thereupon went to Fromm and reported to him that Hitler was dead and that the "Valkyrie" plan must therefore be set in motion. But Fromm, who wanted to be sure of his ground, put through a telephone call to Keitel in the Führer's headquarters. The latter told him that an attempt at assassination had in fact taken place but that Hitler had only been slightly injured. Fromm thereupon refused to sign the "Valkyrie" orders.[17]

Olbricht then told his commander-in-chief that action had meanwhile been initiated without his authority. Fromm flew into a rage and demanded to know who had been responsible for this high-handed procedure. Olbricht replied that it was Colonel Ritter Mertz von Quirnheim and Fromm at once sent for Mertz and declared him under arrest. Olbricht left the room in the hope of finding Stauffenberg, who in fact arrived shortly thereafter, still convinced, as he told Olbricht, that the bomb had done its job. "I saw the whole thing from outside. I was standing outside the hut with General Fellgiebel. There was an explosion inside the hut and then I saw large numbers of medical personnel come running up and cars being brought along. The explosion was as if the hut had been hit by a six-inch shell. It is hardly possible that anyone could still be alive."[18]

Olbricht then urged that this information be passed to Fromm. Stauffenberg reported back to his commander, told him what he had seen and informed him quite openly that he himself had placed the bomb. Fromm replied acidly, "Graf Stauffenberg, the plot has misfired; you must shoot yourself forthwith." Stauffenberg countered with, "No, I shall do no such thing."[19]

Olbricht made one more attempt to convince Fromm of the necessity for action—but in vain. When it eventually came to fisticuffs between the two men, Stauffenberg and Mertz intervened. Colonel General Fromm was arrested and incarcerated in his room. He was not, however, placed under too strict a guard, and when, shortly thereafter, he asked that the officer on guard be removed from his room, Colonel General Hoepner, who had taken over Fromm's appointment, agreed. Later he even allowed Fromm to go to his private apartment, Fromm having stated that he would do nothing and make no telephone calls without prior agreement with Hoepner.[20]

A full hour had now gone by. The signal center had dispatched the "Valkyrie" orders to the various addressees. Although they had no troops under their command, which, under the circumstances, they clearly could not have, the conspirators were confident that their instructions would be obeyed, provided no counterorders were issued.

At this point, however, it became necessary to issue the supplementary orders complementary to the "Valkyrie" plan mobilization instructions and dealing solely with the coup d'état. By "Teleprinter Message No. 1" the new "Supreme Commander" of the Wehrmacht, Field Marshal von Witzleben, invested theatre commanders-in-chief

and certain Army Group commanders with "full powers". At the same
time, he nominated—with the same powers—the former commander-
in-chief of the replacement army as "Supreme Commander" in the
home forces area. Within their territorial areas all the above were
given authority over Wehrmacht headquarters and units, the Waffen-
SS, the Reich labour service, and the Todt organization; equally, all
"public authorities"—"Nationalist Socialist party functionaries,
organizations, and formations connected therewith"—were subordinated to them and charged with the preservation of law, order, and
public security. Since Colonel General Fromm was no longer exercising
his functions, the orders "signed" by him were authenticated by his chief
of staff, "Graf Stauffenberg." The first documents to bear the signature
of Colonel General Hoepner, the new "Supreme Commander" for
the home forces area, were the further "Regulations for Martial Law,
Nos. 1–5."

The main provisions of these regulations were prohibition of all
demonstrations, meetings, or assemblies; continuation of normal
traffic and economic activity under the supervision of the Wehrkreis
commanders: suspension of all party functionaries: confiscation of all
Nazi party property and of the property of the Reichsleiter, Gauleiter,
and all party functionaries down to Kreisleiter; anyone attempting to
destroy, make away with, or falsify party documents or files to be
punishable by martial law. Other martial law regulations were directed
against crimes committed against defenseless citizens through the
misuse of power and authority or for purposes of personal gain.[21]

Between 4 and 5 P.M. Colonel General Beck appeared. Olbricht
reported to him that the difficulties with Fromm had been dealt
with, and Hoepner had now been nominated "Supreme Commander
Home Forces Area." Stauffenberg had meanwhile summoned the
section heads within the office, and Hoepner gave them a short address:
"Gentlemen, the Führer is dead. Field Marshal von Witzleben has taken
over supreme command of the Wehrmacht and has appointed me here
in place of Colonel General Fromm, who is no longer carrying out his
functions. I would ask you to continue to work as loyally and reliably
as hitherto."[22]

Beck also spoke: "We are at a fateful turning point. On all fronts
the military situation is to all intents and purposes hopeless, and with

every day which passes we suffer new defeats, further losses, and additional destruction of our Reich. This cannot now be averted by military measures. It is the duty of all those who really love their country to do their utmost to achieve this end. If we do not succeed, we shall at least have done our duty."[23]

An officer asked Hoepner whether Hitler was really dead. The answer he was given was: "I have received numerous reports to that effect. There is still doubt in some quarters, however."[24] This may have been an honest answer, but at this particular moment it could be calculated only to spread uncertainty. When Beck was faced with a similar question from the inner circle of the conspirators, he took a different line: "For me this man is dead. That is the basis of my further activity. We must adhere to this line, otherwise we shall merely sow confusion within our own ranks. Indisputable proof that Hitler—and not his double—is still alive cannot possibly come from headquarters for hours. By then the action in Berlin must be completed."[25]

Shortly before this, the officer detailed to occupy the Deutschland and Nauen radio transmitting stations with a group of radio operators and propaganda personnel and to broadcast the declaration of the new government had reported to Stauffenberg and Olbricht. He did not, however, get his marching orders. Olbricht said that it was too soon and the situation still too unclear.[26]

Meanwhile the Führer's headquarters had learned that, contrary to expectations, Stauffenberg had landed at Rangsdorf. SS Obergruppen-führer Piffrader in Berlin was therefore ordered by telephone to go to the Bendlerstrasse and quietly arrest the Colonel. When the security official arrived, Stauffenberg invited him genially into his office, dis-armed him and put him under arrest.[27] While this was going on, the Berlin guard battalion had moved in accordance with the "Valkyrie" orders and started to throw a cordon round the government quarter. So far, all seemed to be going according to plan, but at this point came a serious hitch in the Bendlerstrasse signal center. The number of teleprinter messages was so great that the signal traffic officer found all his own circuits blocked. The necessity for speed having been im-pressed upon him, he now made use of the OKW circuits, which passed via Wolfsschanze. So the orders for the coup d'état arrived direct in the Führer's headquarters. This was the first indication that headquarters had that the assassination attempt was not the work merely of one man but was intended as the signal for a coup d'état initiated from Berlin.

OKW instructed the signal officer to hold up forthwith all tele-printer messages, adding that Hitler was not dead and that this was a treasonable coup by officers under the command of the commander-in-chief of the replacement army. The signal traffic officer thereupon returned the orders to Lieutenant Colonel Sadrozinski, a section head in OKH whom Stauffenberg had ordered to pass them on to the signal center. Sadrozinski was not in good health. Under the pressure of events an old chest wound had started to give trouble that very day. He lay on the sofa with a compress over his heart, quite incapable of issuing the orders. In this state he was visited by his predecessor, Colonel Rudolf Langhaeuser, who was on his way to Munich, knew nothing of what was going on, and was paying a purely chance visit to OKH. Sadrozinski asked him to deliver the teleprinter messages to the signal center. On arrival there, the signal traffic officer told Colonel Lang-haeuser what was happening and refused to dispatch the orders. Langhaeuser returned to Sadrozinski with the teleprinter messages still unprocessed; whereupon Sadrozinski lost his head completely.[28]

Evidently some other officer must have succeeded, for when Klausing appeared in the signal center about 5:50 P.M. with the second teleprinter message, the priority of which he had changed from "operations immediate" to "Führer priority," both it and a number of the follow-up orders were dispatched, although the signal officer, not now know-ing whom to obey, was no longer working at the speed ordered.[29] He must, however, have been so pressured either by Klausing or someone else that he did not completely block the issue of the orders.

After 6 P.M. the officer who was to occupy the radio stations appeared once more; the answer he received showed that the leaders of the coup were already becoming unsure of themselves. Olbricht said that no one who was not already in the secret should be brought into the business. This applied to the radio and propaganda personnel. In Olbricht's view to put them into the radio stations at this moment would mean their certain death, since it was to be assumed that the SS would have also realized the importance of the stations. When the officer asked whether he would be alone there with his radio and propaganda personnel, Olbricht gave him the distinctly vague answer: "Some combat troops will come presently."[30]

Shortly thereafter, at about 6:20 P.M., General Fellgiebel from the Führer's headquarters called Colonel Hassell in the Bendlerstrasse to give his friend a warning: "What are you up to over there? Are you all crazy? The Führer is now with the Duce in the tea-room. What's more, there will shortly be a radio communiqué."[31]

Meanwhile it became evident that the conspirators' generous treatment of Fromm was working out to their disadvantage. The dispossessed commander-in-chief of the replacement army had not the smallest intention of keeping his promise not to telephone or do anything without Hoepner's knowledge. About 6:20 P.M. Colonel Langhaeuser met Fromm in the passage and asked him what was going on. Fromm drew him into the first empty office he could find, and told him the story. "From him I learned that he had himself spoken by telephone from his apartment both to Hitler and Keitel, that the claim that Hitler was dead was therefore untrue, and that in OKW suspicion was directed at Stauffenberg as the perpetrator of the assassination attempt. Fromm went on that this was clearly a coup d'état, which, moreover, had already miscarried. He advised me to be sure to get out of here as quickly as possible if I did not wish to risk my neck."[32]

At 6:45 the first special announcement was broadcast over the main German radio: "A bomb attack was made upon the Führer today. The following of his entourage were severely wounded as a result: Lieutenant General Schmundt, Colonel Brandt, and Herr Berger of his staff. The following were slightly wounded: Colonel General Jodl, Generals Korten, Buhle, Bodenschatz, Heusinger, Scherff, Admirals Voss, von Puttkammer, Captain (navy) Assmann, and Lieutenant Colonel Borgmann. The Führer was unhurt apart from minor burns and contusions. He continued with his work forthwith and, as arranged, received the Duce for a lengthy discussion. Shortly after the attack the Reichsmarschall waited on the Führer."[33]

Calls from Wehrkreis headquarters were now coming in continually, demanding confirmation from the commander-in-chief of the replacement army of the validity of the orders issued. When General Schaal called from Prague at 7 P.M. he was put through to Stauffenberg, who told him, "The Führer is dead; the radio news is false. The essential now is to use all means to keep full power in your hands and to guarantee law and order. The measures ordered against the SD should be carried out urgently."[34]

Vienna asked for Colonel General Fromm in person. Once again Stauffenberg took the call and pressed for the orders issued to be carried out, emphasizing their validity.

To Kassel he stated that all Keitel's statements were lies. In the majority of Wehrkreis, however, the code word "Valkyrie" produced no action, since the Wolfsschanze counterorders were either already on the table when the Berlin teleprinter messages arrived or came in shortly afterwards.[35]

Meanwhile the guard battalion had completely cordoned off the government quarter. Its commander, Major Remer, however, was persuaded by Lieutenant Hagen, an officer of his unit and in civil life an official in the propaganda ministry, to seek out Goebbels, the Reich propaganda minister, to get some explanation of the situation. Goebbels put through a call to the Führer's headquarters; Hitler himself came on the line and spoke to Remer. He invested Remer with "full powers" in Berlin—an incredible delegation of authority to a battalion commander and one which made him temporarily the superior even of a general. Hitler ordered him to suppress the Berlin coup d'état. Remer did as he was told. He withdrew the cordon from the government quarter and also the guard which the battalion had placed on the Bendlerstrasse office. He then sent detachments to meet units moving into the city to inform their officers of the situation and call on them to halt.[36]

From this point onwards the measures taken by the conspirators encountered increasing opposition. At 7:15 further teleprinter messages were handed in to the Bendlerstrasse signal centre, but the signal traffic officer was now obviously adopting delaying tactics and had already reported to his superiors. When AHA began to ask with increasing impatience why the teleprinter messages had in many cases not yet arrived with their addressees, the signal officer made technical difficulties the excuse. Nevertheless further orders continued to be sent to the signal office up to 9 P.M. At about this time, however (8:35 to be exact), the counterorder from the Führer's headquarters arrived in the Bendlerstrasse itself and was routed to General Olbricht with an "immediate action" label. The order ran: "The Führer has nominated

the Reichsführer SS, Himmler, as commander-in-chief of the replace-
ment army with immediate effect, and has invested him with all
necessary plenary powers over members of the replacement army.
Orders are only to be accepted from the Reichsführer SS and from me.
Any orders which may be received from Fromm, von Witzleben, or
Hoepner are invalid."[37]

Keitel, the signatory of this message, did not yet know that General
Olbricht himself had had a major hand in events. The latter decided
that the message should be given no further distribution. But the signal
center was no longer obeying his orders and, starting at 9:15 P.M.,
distributed Keitel's message over all circuits to the twenty addressees
of the conspirators' original message, at the same time blocking further
transmission of previous orders or declaring them invalid.[38]

One of the tragic features of this day was the fact that the very men
who passed on the counterorder to the Bendlerstrasse signal center for
transmission were members of the conspiracy. Major General Stieff,
for instance, ordered the signal distribution center not to process any
further messages signed by von Witzleben and Fromm. In the Bendlerstrasse General Thiele, the man who had given the news that an
explosion had taken place in Wolfsschanze and so had triggered off the
entire "Valkyrie" action, together with Colonel Hahn in the Führer's
headquarters, seemed now only to be concerned to prevent further
orders from the conspirators from reaching the field army.[39]

People were in fact now trying to cover up their own tracks, and so
immediately after the special radio announcement Graf Helldorf, the
Berlin police president, and Arthur Nebe, the head of the CID,
defected.[40]

Eventually, the only men left making no attempt to escape were
those in a small group in the Bendlerstrasse: Generals Beck, Hoepner,
and Olbricht, Colonels Stauffenberg and Mertz von Quirnheim,
Lieutenant von Haeften, and some of their close friends. Even Field
Marshal von Witzleben, who had just been appointed "Supreme
Commander of the Wehrmacht," left OKH in short order after a
raging quarrel with Beck at the very moment (8 P.M.) when Colonel
Mertz was comforting Paris: "Our armour is on the move; carry on
as before."[41]

Late in the evening, things seemed to take a favourable turn once

more. About 9 P.M. Colonel Müller, head of a division in the infantry
school, Döberitz, and privy to the coup, returned to his unit, having
had most unfortunately to be absent all day on a duty trip. Throughout
the afternoon the men in the Bendlerstrasse had been waiting in vain
for the infantry school demonstration battalion to report completion
of their mission, which was to occupy the radio stations of Nauen and
Tegel and the concentration camp at Oranienburg. Since, in addition
to Colonel Müller, the commanding officer of the school was also
absent and the officers were unclear as to what they were supposed to
do, and seeing that in the meanwhile the special announcement had
been broadcast over the radio, the troops, though standing by, had
remained in their barracks. On his return Colonel Müller immediately
assumed command and drove to the Bendlerstrasse to request special
powers of command, primarily in order to take action against the SS.
This special authority, signed by Olbricht, was delivered to him by
Mertz von Quirnheim. On his return to Döberitz at 10:45, however,
he heard of the collapse of the coup; the men refused to obey him.[42]

In spite of previous failures, the conspirators continued to the end
trying to mobilize some troops to support them. In this final and
increasingly hopeless phase it was primarily Stauffenberg and Mertz
von Quirnheim who continued to make every effort to save the
situation, using the argument that Hitler was dead and that the radio
announcement could do nothing but sow general confusion.[43]

Stauffenberg took all incoming telephone calls: "Stauffenberg here.
Yes, all orders from the home army. . . . Yes, of course. . . . That is
so. . . . All orders to be carried out immediately. You must occupy all
radio stations and signal offices. All resistance must be crushed. . . . It
is probable that counterorders will be issued from the Führer's headquarters . . . they should not be believed. . . . No. The Wehrmacht has
taken over full powers; no one other than C-in-C, home army is
authorized to give orders. . . . Do you understand? . . . Yes, the Reich
is in danger, and as always happens in the hour of danger, the soldiers
are taking over command. . . . Yes, Witzleben has been appointed
Supreme Commander. . . . It is a mere formality; you are to occupy
all signal offices. . . . Do you understand? Heil."[44]

At 10 P.M. General Olbricht summoned all officers present and told
them that the situation was serious and that they themselves must take

over the protection of the building.[45] This made the failure of the coup only too clear. The officers allowed themselves to be divided up into watches, but one of the staff officers remained behind in Olbricht's office and asked him what game was being played here and against whom these weapons were to be used. Olbricht replied, "Gentlemen, we have for a long time been watching the development of the situation with the greatest anxiety; there can be no doubt that catastrophe is on the horizon. Measures must be taken to forestall this situation. These measures are now in train. I beg you to support me."[46]

Opinions were divided. Some stood by their chief; others—the members of the AHA arms sections, Colonel Herber, Major Fliessbach, and Lieutenant Colonels von der Heyde and Pridun—went into a neighbouring room, where they armed themselves. They then charged into the conspirators' room, demanded an explanation from General Olbricht, and speech with Colonel General Fromm. Olbricht led them to Colonel General Hoepner. Stauffenberg, who had so far been in Olbricht's office, wished to warn Hoepner, or at least let him know of these developments. As he ran down the passage he was shot at from behind and hit in the arm.

In his deposition before the People's Court Hoepner described this moment as follows:

> Suddenly shooting started. I heard Stauffenberg come into the next-door office and say to Haeften, "Go out and put things in order." Shortly after, several officers with sub-machine-guns appeared and a lieutenant colonel came up to me and said, "Colonel General, we would like to know what game is being played here. May I speak to Colonel General Fromm?" I then said, "Of course; please do." I then dispatched the lieutenant colonel to Fromm's apartment, and shortly thereafter he reappeared with Fromm and a number of officers, all armed. They appeared in my room and Fromm said, "Now, gentlemen, I am going to treat you as you treated me this morning."[47]

It would still have been possible to give the conspirators a method of escape; in fact Major Georgi, Olbricht's son-in-law, had agreed with the Luftwaffe target towing wing that they should be flown abroad.

But General Olbricht refused, saying, "We are fighting with our backs to the wall."[48]

Fromm then demanded that the conspirators lay down their arms. Lieutenant von Haeften raised his revolver to shoot Fromm down, but Stauffenberg signalled to him not to attempt any further resistance.

Beck asked Fromm to be allowed to keep his revolver, saying, "I shall myself draw the necessary consequences from this unfortunate situation." Olbricht was allowed to write one more letter.

Fromm left the room, but came back shortly afterwards, accompanied by officers of the guard battalion, which had meanwhile surrounded the building. He declared that he had convened a summary court martial which had condemned four officers to death: "Colonel Mertz, General Olbricht, this colonel whose name I no longer know, and this lieutenant [Haeften]."

The four were led out into the courtyard, Haeften supporting the wounded Stauffenberg. They were lined up against the center of the southern wall. Lorries were driven up to light the execution scene with their headlights. Each went to the appointed place in turn. Stauffenberg died with a call to Germany on his lips.[49]

So ended the life of Claus Schenk Graf von Stauffenberg, chief of staff to the C-in-C of the replacement army and colonel on the General Staff. He was in his thirty-seventh year.

His persecutors thought that his name could be effaced from all memory, but they were wrong. The name of Stauffenberg has its place in German history as that of a man who perceived that his duty as a soldier and General Staff officer lay not within the strict confines of military matters, but who was conscious of his "supreme responsibility to the German people as a whole."[50] He will go down in history as a man who worked on the principle formulated by Helmuth von Moltke for command of troops and enshrined in every army regulation: "Neglect and inactivity . . . are more serious faults than misjudgment in the choice of methods."[51]

Stauffenberg acted in response to obligations: the responsibility laid upon him by his profession; love of his country; conscience born of his Christian convictions. As his epitaph may well stand the sentence he himself wrote[52] of a friend killed in action: "I believe that heaven will be merciful to those who make the supreme sacrifice in fulfillment of their duty."

APPENDICES

I. Extracts from Lecture "Thoughts on Home Defense against Enemy Parachute Troops" by Captain Schenk Graf von Stauffenberg [1]

. . . After this short survey of possible and probable targets for enemy raids in the interior of the country, I now turn to the modern means of executing such raids—in other words to the parachute troops themselves.

There is an important point to observe here: part of the parachute troops' job can be done without fighting, but for the rest, fighting is unavoidable.

In the first category are all those tasks which can be done by agents, together with such demolitions as can be carried out by a single man or a small number of men and require little material or time. I propose to call parachute units designed for this category of task parachute detachments.

In contrast to these parachute detachments, I propose to call parachute units designed for fighting, or which can only fulfill their mission after fighting, parachute combat troops. [2]

Both the conditions and methods of employment of these two types of parachute units differ fundamentally. The problem of defense against them therefore also differs in the two cases.

The characteristic of the parachute detachments is that they neither can nor should fight. The aircraft and the parachutes are simply means of getting them into enemy territory unobserved. The important point is that both the approach of the aircraft and the parachute jump should be completely concealed; otherwise it is impossible for them to carry out their task. . . .

I now turn to consideration of the parachute combat troops.

They must be in a position to fight. This will determine both their strength and their equipment. Their organization will be similar to that of a normal force of all arms. Strength will depend upon the task in hand. It must, however, invariably be so adjusted that the unit is capable of *independent* fighting. It can, therefore, seldom be less than battalion strength and will frequently be greater.

Such units, whether composed entirely of parachute troops or partially of parachutists and partially of airborne infantry, will require a large number of transport aircraft. It is not possible, therefore, to count upon their approach being undetected by the enemy defenses. The possibility of the approach flight must, therefore, also be fought for. . . .

Both the speed and radius of action of parachute combat troops open up the possibility of their use in a surprise attack at the outbreak of war. At a moment when the enemy concentration will not be complete and his defense preparedness therefore small, use of these troops may be highly effective and carry with it comparatively little risk. At this period rapid offensive action in the frontier area may be able to create most favourable conditions for subsequent operations.[3] Tasks which hitherto required the use of cavalry and specially mobile formations of all arms, can today be allotted to parachute troops and airborne infantry.

Although such operations do not affect the home area in the true sense of the word but only the future operations zone, they should, nevertheless, be mentioned. In the event of a surprise attack without declaration of war, circumstances will be very similar to those in our own home area.

Just as parachute combat troops may be used in the frontier zone, they can, of course, also be employed in landing operations on the coast. . . .[4]

In broad terms the defense must aim to fulfill three objects: the first and most obvious is to prevent the parachute units approaching and landing at all. This would be the ideal solution if it could be achieved with any certainty. Under war conditions, however, it is hardly worth consideration.

The next objective of the defense must be to increase the risk run by the enemy. The greater the risk he runs and the smaller his prospect of success the less will the enemy be willing to undertake such operations, since they will no longer be a paying proposition. The third objective must be to minimize damage. Under this heading I include all those measures designed to remove vulnerable t⌐rgets from the danger of enemy attack, to afford direct protection to these targets, and to minimize the adverse effect of a successful attack upon the conduct of the war. In short, the effect of any successful landing should be reduced to a minimum. . . .

I would now like to put forward my thoughts on the problem of the danger to the home area presented by parachute units and on the defense against them. I am only too conscious of the fact—and would wish to stress this once more in conclusion—that what I say is based upon purely theoretical considerations, from which, however, I have tried to draw logical conclusions. Today we are not only justified but it is our duty to give consideration to such problems; if we do not, the realities of war may well teach us a bitter lesson.

There may well be many who consider that the danger of parachute attack is small; in particular there may be many who consider the use of parachute combat troops deep in the interior of a country a fanciful idea. Nevertheless, so long as there has been no war to show us the real possibilities of the use of parachute troops, our national defense must prepare for all eventualities. In the worst case excessive preparation can always be quickly and easily adjusted in war, but conversely, defense cannot be so quickly and easily improvised.

II. *Letter to Field Marshal Friedrich Paulus*[1]

HQ, OKH

12 June 1942

Dear General,

Army Group South has informed me that I should not visit their headquarters, since they will have no time for me, owing to a visit by the Führer on the day in question. For this reason, I decided to return at once on the OKW aircraft, since by this means I could gain a whole day.

As a result, it was not possible for me to take leave of you, General, nor to express to you my most respectful thanks for my pleasant reception in your headquarters. I hasten to repair the error in writing, and in particular, to send you my most respectful thanks for the invitation I was fortunate enough to receive to be your personal guest.

It was a great pleasure to me to spend these few days in and around Kharkov and gain contact with all the divisions I visited; it was a real stimulus. It made one realize forcibly how much one misses by being away from troops. There can be no more pleasant duty than to expend oneself on the immediate care of the troops. Nevertheless, any satisfaction which naturally is to be found in some degree in my present duties can be no more than a second-rate substitute. This is all the more true in that with some experience—which I think I can claim to have, after two years in this job—one is forced to realize from the outset that there are strict limits to any possibilities of action, whatever the subject may be, limits which all too often lack any sound basis. I realize only too clearly that, nevertheless, the fighting must go on, and I continue to make every effort to impress this on all those who are in the game with me. But it is not always easy to keep up one's enthusiasm. You will no doubt realize, General, how refreshing such a visit can be when it brings one into an atmosphere where the troops are staking their all, where men are ready to sacrifice their lives without demur, while the commanders, who should set an example, squabble about prestige and are unable to pluck up the courage to put forward their views or indeed their convictions even though thousands of lives may depend on them.

To tell the truth, life here is not easy when one sees things going that way. As soon as one ceases to see it, however, one should take steps to get out of this office as quickly as possible.

You will shortly be engaged in another operation, General, and we shall follow every development with intense interest. May good fortune attend this and all your future ventures.

With respect and gratitude I remain, General, your obedient servant,

[Signed] Stauffenberg

SOURCES

I. *Persons Consulted*

The following list contains the names of those persons who contributed to the assembly of the material for this biography either in writing or by interviews, of which notes were kept. I have not included the names of all those others who knew Stauffenberg but could give no pertinent information.

BLOMBERG, Ruth von   *Letter, 24 July 1962*

BRÄUTIGAM, Dr. Otto (Consul-General—retd.)   *Letter, end 1963*

BREMME, Beate   *Letter, 3 October 1962*

BREMME, Dr. Hans   *Letter, 28 October 1962*

BROICH, Friedrich Freiherr von (Lieutenant General—retd.)   *Letters, 14, 20, 25 June 1962*

BÜRKLIN, Wilhelm (Colonel—retd.)   *Letters, 15 June and 15 July 1962*

BUSSE, Theodor (General—retd.)   *Letter, 29 November 1962*

CRAMER, Hans (General—retd.)   *Letter, 20 February 1963*

EISMANN, Georg (Colonel)   *Letter, 9 October 1963*

FAHRNER, Prof. Dr. Rudolf (professor of literature, Karlsruhe Technical High School)   *Letter, 15 July 1963*

FRITSCH, Dr. Georg Freiherr von (Foreign Service)   *Letters, 26 November and 7 December 1963*

GEORGI, Friedrich (Major—retd.; publisher)   *Interviews, 1962 and 1963*

GERSDORFF, Rudolf-Christof, Freiherr von (General—retd.)   *Letter, 9 June 1962*

GÖTZ, Waltraud von   *Letters, 5 September and 24 November 1962*

GREINER, Heinz (Lieutenant General—retd.)   *Letters, 6 and 15 May 1964*

HALDER, Franz (Colonel General—retd.)   *Letters, 4 and 26 January, 23 March, and 18 May 1962*

HARDENBERG, Margarete Gräfin von (nee von Oven)   *Interview, 26 November 1961*

HERWARTH VON BITTENFELD, Hans-Heinrich (Ambassador)   *Interview, 3 February 1963*

HUSEN, Dr. Paulus van (late President of the North Rhine–Westphalia Constitutional Court)   *Letter, 2 July 1963*

JESSEN, Käthe   *Interview, June 1962*

KEMPF, Werner (General—retd.)   *Letters, 14 April 1962 and 7 January 1963*

KLEIKAMP, Helmut (General—retd.)   *Letters, 18 December 1962; 15 and 21 January 1963*

*K—— R—— (Colonel—retd.)   *Interview, 25 July 1963*
KÜCHLER, Georg von, Field Marshal   *Letter, 17 December 1962*
LANGHAEUSER, Rudolf (Major General—retd.)   *Letters, 26 February and 28 March 1963*
LEBER, Annedore   *Interviews, 1964*
LIST, Wilhelm, Field Marshal   *Letter, 17 December 1962*
LOEPER, Friedrich-Wilhelm, Freiherr von (Lieutenant General—retd.)   *Letters, 19 June and 18 November 1962; interview 2 October 1962*
MAIZIERE, Ulrich de (Lieutenant General, Army Inspector General)   *Interview, 20 January 1963*
MANSTEIN, Erich von, Field Marshal   *Letters, 20 August and 15 November 1962*
MANTEUFFEL, Hasso von (General—retd.)   *Letter, 20 June 1964*
MENDE, Prof. Dr. Gerhard von (head of East European Research Service, Düsseldorf)   *Letters, 19 and 26 July 1963*
MÜLLER-HILLEBRAND, Burkhart (Lieutenant General)   *Letters, 30 April and 15 July 1962*
PERFALL, Gustav Freiherr von (Lieutenant General—retd.)   *Letter, 17 July 1962*
PEZOLD, Bernd von (Colonel—retd.)   *Interview, 17 May 1963*
REERINK, Werner (Lieutenant Colonel—retd.; chemist)   *Report, June 1963*
REIMANN, Hans (Colonel—retd.)   *Letter, 17 July 1962*
*R—— J—— (Colonel—retd.)   *Interview, 5 October 1962*
SACHENBACHER VON SCHROTTENBERG, Alfred (Colonel—retd.)   *Letter, 21 March 1963*
SAUCKEN, Olga von (nee Gräfin Üxküll)   *Letter, 29 March 1965*
SAUERBRUCH, Peter (Lieutenant Colonel—retd.; merchant)   *Interview, 12 February 1963*
SCHMID, Heinz (Colonel—retd.; engineer)   *Letter, 23 September 1963*
SCHMÖLDERS, Prof. Dr. G.   *Letters, 1 and 5 July 1963*
SCHÖNE, Volkmar (Colonel—retd.; civil servant—retd.)   *Letters, 17 September and 17 December 1962*
SCHRAMM, Prof. Dr. Percy Ernst (history professor—emer.)   *Letter, 19 November 1963*
SCHULENBURG, Charlotte Gräfin von der   *Letter, 12 August 1963*
SMOLKA, Prof. Dr. Georg (professor of modern political history, Speyer School of Administrative Science)   *Letter, 23 September 1963*
STAEDKE, Helmut (Lieutenant General—retd.)   *Letter, 13 January 1963*
STAUFFENBERG, Nina Schenk Gräfin von   *Letters, 22 October and 13 December 1961; 17 March, 23 May, 16 November 1962; 22 April and 1 July 1964; interview, 10 October 1962*
STRIK-STRIKFELDT, Wilfried (Captain—retd.; engineer)   *Letters, 1 and 11 August 1963*
THÜNGEN, Dietz Freiherr von (Major—retd.)   *Report, 25 January 1946*
TROTT ZU SOLZ, Dr. Clarita von   *Letter, 8 October 1961*

* Names not given by request.

WALZER, Hans (Lieutenant Colonel—retd.)   *Report, 9 March 1964; Letters,*
19 May and 27 June 1964
WEDEMEYER, A. C. (General U.S. Army—retd.)   *Letters, 6 March, 9 May,*
22 June, and 6 September 1962
YORCK VON WARTENBURG, Dr. Marion Gräfin   *Interview, 5 September 1963*
ZEITZLER, Kurt (Colonel General—retd.)   *Letters, 3 and 26 July 1962*
ZIPFEL, Dr. Friedrich (scientific adviser)   *Report, 18 January 1964*

II. *Unpublished Sources*

First Light Division war diary, 5 September–19 October 1938; in the possession of Werner Reerink

Army general staff organization section war diary, 1 January–31 December 1942; in the National Archives, Alexandria, Virginia; German files on microfilm, Series 385, Roll 417

Army order 8000/42 (ref. no. GenStH/Org/Abt/II); in Military History Research Office, Freiburg im Breisgau

Basic Order No. 1 (Annex 504 to war diary) issued by the Army High Command, Chief of Staff (ref. no. Org/Abt/II, No. 9900/42) in National Archives, Alexandria, Series 382, Roll 414

Field Army Order of Battle issued by Army High Command (ref. no. GenStH/Org/Abt/II, No. 7850/42) in National Archives, Series 382, Roll 414

School-leaving certificate for Claus Schenk Graf von Stauffenberg from Eberhard-Ludwigs-Gymnasium, Stuttgart, dated 5 March 1926

Record of service for Claus Schenk Graf von Stauffenberg, in the German Federal Archives, Central Section, Kornelimünster, 21 June 1961

Two reports of the visit of Colonel Graf von Stauffenberg to the Führer's headquarters on 15 July 1944; in the National Archives, Series 39, Rolls 19–21, connected with the Kaltenbrunner report

"Army Cavalry—A Study" by Claus Schenk Graf von Stauffenberg; in the possession of Nina Gräfin von Stauffenberg

Letter to Prof. Pfau from London, dated 4 September 1936; in the possession of Gerda Pfau

Letter to Wilhelm Bürklin from Munich, dated 9 June 1943; in the possession of Wilhelm Bürklin

Postcard to Wilhelm Bürklin from Lautlingen, dated June 1943; in the possession of Wilhelm Bürklin

Letter to Ruth von Blomberg, undated (?1942) and without address; in the possession of Ruth von Blomberg

Stauffenberg, Alexander Schenk Graf von, "Erinnerung an Stefan George," address given in Berlin on 4 December 1958 (cyclostyled)

III. *Bibliography*

BAUM, Walter, "Marine, Nationalsozialismus und Widerstand," in *Aus Politik und Zeitgeschichte*, supplement to the weekly *Das Parlament*, published by the Bundeszentrale für Heimatdienst, Bonn, 15 July 1963

BAUMONT, Maurice, *La grande conjuration contre Hitler*, Editions Mondiales, Paris, 1963

BESGEN, Achim, *Der stille Befehl: Medizinalrat Kersten, Himmler und das 3 Reich*, Nymphenburger Verlagsanstalt, Munich, 1960

BOEHRINGER, Robert, *Mein Bild von Stefan George*, Küpper, Düsseldorf, 1951

BOVERI, Margret, *Der Verrat im XX Jahrhundert*, Vol. II; *Für und gegen die Nation, Rowohlt's German Encyclopaedia*, No. 24, Hamburg, 1956

BRAUBACH, Max, *Der Weg zum 20 Juli: Ein Forschungsbericht*, Opladen, Cologne, 1953

BUDDE, Eugen, and LÜTSCHES, Peter, *Die Wahrheit über den 20 Juli: Auszüge aus den Vernehmungsprotokollen des Volksgerichthofes gegen v. Witzleben und Genossen am 7 und 8 August 1944*, Raven, Düsseldorf, 1952 (referred to as "record of hearings")

BULLOCK, Alan, *Hitler: A Study in Tyranny*, Odhams Press, London, 1952

Bundeszentrale für Heimatdienst, 20 Juli 1944, 3rd ed. (1st and 2nd eds. compiled by Hans Royce), revised and amplified by Erich Zimmermann and Hans-Adolf Jacobsen, Berto, Bonn, 1960

BUSSMANN, Walter, "Betrachtungen zum militärischen Widerstand," in *Aus Politik und Zeitgeschichte*, supplement to the weekly *Das Parlament*, published by the Bundeszentrale für politische Bildung, Bonn, 15 July 1964

DAHMS, Helmuth Günther, *Der zweite Weltkrieg*, Wunderlich, Tübingen, 1960

DALLIN, Alexander, *Deutsche Herrschaft in Russland*, Droste, Düsseldorf, 1958

DEMETER, Karl, *Das deutsche Offizierkorps in Gesellschaft und Staat 1650–1945*, Bernard and Graefe, Frankfurt, 1962; *The German Officer Corps*, translated by Angus Malcolm, Weidenfeld and Nicolson, London, 1965

DULLES, Allen Welsh, *Germany's Underground*, Macmillan, New York, 1947

EHLERS, Dieter, *Technik und Moral einer Verschwörung: 20 Juli 1944*, Athenäum Verlag, Frankfurt, 1964

ERFURTH, Waldemar, *Die Geschichte des deutschen Generalstabes von 1918 bis 1945*, 2nd revised ed., Musterschmidt, Göttingen, 1960 (also published as *Studien und Dokumente zur Geschichte des Zweiten Weltkrieges*, issued by the Arbeitskreis für Wehrforschung, Stuttgart, Vol. I)

FAHRNER, Rudolf, *Gneisenau*, Delfin, Munich, 1942

Festschrift zur Neubaueinweihung des Eberhard-Ludwigs-Gymnasium in Stuttgart 1957, edited by Dr. Paul Ludwig, Klett, Stuttgart, 1957

FITZGIBBON, Constantine, *The Shirt of Nessus*, Cassell, London, 1956

FOERSTER, Wolfgang, *Generaloberst Ludwig Beck: Sein Kampf gegen den Krieg*, 2nd ed., Isar-Verlag, Munich, 1953

FOERTSCH, Hermann, *Schuld und Verhangnis: Die Fritsch-Krise im Frühjahr 1938 als Wendepunkt in der Geschichte der NS-Zeit*, Deutsche Verlagsanstalt, Stuttgart, 1951

FRAENKEL, Heinrich, and MANVELL, Roger, *Der 20 Juli*, Ullstein, Berlin and Frankfurt, 1964

Genealogisches Handbuch des Adels, Gräfliche Häuser, A/II, C. A. Starke, Limburg, 1955

GISEVIUS, Hans-Bernd, *Bis zum bitteren Ende*, Fretz and Wasmuth, Zurich, 1946; *To the Bitter End*, translated by Richard and Clara Winston, Jonathan Cape, London, 1948

GÖRLITZ, Walter, *Der deutsche Generalstab*, Verlag der Frankfurter Hefte, Frankfurt, 1950

GRIMM, Gerhard, *Das Dritte Reich in Quellen und Darstellungen II*, in *Politische Studien*, 16, 1965, No. 161

HAGEN, Hans W., *Zwischen Eid und Befehl, Tatzeugenbericht von den Ereignissen am 20 Juli 1944*, 2nd ed., Munich, 1959

HALDER, Franz, *Hitler als Feldherr*, Dom-Verlag, Munich, 1949; *Kriegstagebuch* (Diary) *1931–1942*, published in three volumes by the Arbeitskreis für Wehrforschung Stuttgart, Kohlhammer, Stuttgart, 1964

HASSELL, Ulrich von, *Vom anderen Deutschland*, from his diaries 1938–*1944*, Atlantis, Zurich, 1946

HERWARTH VON BITTENFELD, Hans-Heinrich, "Dem Andenken des Generals der Kavallerie Ernst Köstring," in *Geopolitik, Weltwirtschaft, Weltpolitik und Auslandswissen*, XXV, 1954, No. 12

HEUSINGER, Adolf, *Befehl im Widerstreit*, Wunderlich Verlag, Tübingen and Stuttgart, 1950

HIMMLER, Heinrich, speech in Posen on 3 August 1944, in *Vierteljahrshefte für Zeitgeschichte*, 1953, p. 382

Hitler's Weisungen für die Kriegführung 1939–1945 edited by Walther Hubatsch, Bernard and Graefe, Frankfurt, 1962; *Hitler's War Directives*, edited by H. R. Trevor-Roper, translated by Anthony Rhodes, Sidgwick and Jackson, London, 1964

HOFER, Walther, *Der Nationalsozialismus: Dokumente 1933–1945*, Fischer-Bücherei, Frankfurt and Hamburg, 1957 (No. 172); "Offiziere mit politischem Verantwortungsbewusstsein," in *Aus Politik und Zeitgeschichte*, supplement to the weekly *Das Parlament*, issued by the Bundeszentrale für politische Bildung, Bonn, 15 July 1964

HOFFMANN, Peter, "Zum Ablauf des Staatsstreichversuches des 20 Juli 1944 in den Wehrkreisen," *Wehrwissenschaftliche Rundschau*, July 1964; "Zum Attentat im Führerhauptquartier," "Wolfsschanze am 20 Juli 1944", *Vierteljahrshefte für Zeitgecshichte*, XII, 1964, No. 3

International Military Tribunal, *The Nuremberg Trial*, English version 1947–1949

JACOBSEN, Hans-Adolf, *1939–1945: Der Zweite Weltkrieg in Chronik und Dokumenten*, 5th revised ed., Verlag Wehr und Wissen, Darmstadt, 1961

JASPER, Gotthard, *Der Schutz der Republik. Studien zur staatlichen Sicherung der Demokratie in der Weimarer Republik 1922–1930*, Mohr, Tübingen, 1963

JOST, Dominik, *Stefan George und Seine Elite*, Speer-Verlag, Zurich, 1949

KALTENBRUNNER-BERICHTE, *Spiegelbild einer Verschwörung* (the Kaltennbruner report), issued by Archiv Peter für historische und zeitgeschichtliche Dokumentation, Seewald, Stuttgart, 1961

KRAMARZ, Joachim, "Oberst Claus Schenk Graf von Stauffenberg," in *Der Tagesspiegel*, Berlin, 1963, No. 5428 (29 July)

KREBS, Albert, *Fritz-Dietlof Graf von der Schulenburg, Zwischen Staatsraison und Hochverrat*, Leibniz, Hamburg, 1964

Kriegstagebuch des Oberkommandos der Wehrmacht (Wehrmachtführungsstab) 1940–1945 (OKW operations staff war diary), edited by Percy Ernst Schramm together with Andreas Hillgruber, Walther Hubatsch, and Hans-Adolf Jacobsen (4 vols.), Bernard and Graefe, Frankfurt, 1961–1964

LEBER, Annedore, *Das Gewissen steht auf. 64 Lebensbilder aud dem deutschen Widerstand 1933–1945*, Mosaik-Verlag, Berlin and Frankfurt, 1954

LEBER, Annedore, and Moltke, Freya Gräfin von, *Für und wieder, Entscheidungen in Deutschland 1918–1945*, Mosaik-Verlag, Berlin and Frankfurt, 1962

LEBER, Julius, *Ein Mann geht sein Weg* (writings, speeches, and letters), edited by his friends, Mosaik-Verlag, Berlin and Frankfurt, 1952

MCCLOY, John J., II, *Conspiracy against Hitler*

MELNIKOW, Daniel, *Der 20 Juli in Deutschland—Legende und Wirklichkeit*, VEB Deutscher Verlag der Wissenschaften, East Berlin, 1964; "Der Kreisauer Kreis und die Gruppe Stauffenberg." *Zeitschrift für Geopolitik*, XIII, 1965, Nos. 7/8 and 9/10; "Der 'Kreisuaer Kreis' und die Gruppe Stauffenberg," *Blätter für deutsche und internationale Politik*, VIII, 1965, No. 7

MENDE, Gerhard von, *Erfahrungen mit Ostfreiwilligen in der deutschen Wehrmacht während des Zweiten Weltkrieges—Vielvölker-Heere und Koalitionskriege*, Leske, Darmstadt, 1952

MÜLLER, Wolfgang, *Gegen eine neue Dolchstosslegende: Ein Erlebnisbericht zum 20 Juli 1944*, 2nd ed., Verlag Das andere Deutschland, Hannover, 1947

OSAS, Veit, *Walküre: 20 Juli 1944*, Deutschland-Verlag, Hamburg, 1953

PARTSCH, K. J., "Stauffenberg. Das Bild des Täters," *Europa-Archiv*, V, 1950 (20 July)

PFIZER, Theodor, "Die Brüder Stauffenberg"—contribution to *Freundesgabe Für Robert Boehringer*, Mohr, Tübingen, 1957

PHILIPPI, Alfred, and HEIM, Ferdinand, *Der Feldzug gegen Sowjetrussland 1941–1945: Ein operative Überblick*, issued by the Arbeitskreis für Wehrforschung, Kohlhammer, Stuttgart, 1962

RITTER, Gerhard, *Carl Goerdeler und die deutsche Widerstandsbewegung*, Deutsche Verlagsanstalt, Stuttgart, 1955

RÖNNEFARTH, Helmuth K. G., *Die Sudetenkrise in der internationalen Politik* (2 vols.), Steiner, Wiesbaden, 1961

ROMMEL, Erwin, *Kreig ohne Hass*, edited by Lucie-Marie Rommel and Fritz Bayerlein, Heidenheimer Verlagsanstalt, 1950; *The Rommel Papers*, edited by Captain B. H. Liddell Hart, translated by Paul Findlay, Collins, London, 1953

ROTHFELS, Hans, "Die deutsche Opposition gegen Hitler: Eine Würdigung," *Fischer-Bücherei*, No. 198, Frankfurt and Hamburg, 1960

SALIN, Edgar, *Um Stefan George*, Küpper, Düsseldorf, 1954

SCHEIBERT, Horst, *Bildband der 6 Panzerdivision 1939–1945*, Podzun, Bad Nauheim, 1958

SCHEURIG, Bodo, *Claus Graf Schenk von Stauffenberg*, Colloquium, Berlin, 1964 (also in *Köpfe des XX Jahrhunderts*, Vol. XXXIII)

SCHLABRENDORFF, Fabian von, "Offiziere gegen Hitler," *Fischer-Bücherei*, No. 305, Frankfurt and Hamburg, 1959

SCHRAMM, Percy Ernst, *Hitler als militärische Führer*, Athenäum, Frankfurt, 1962

SCHRAMM, Wilhelm Ritter von, *Der 20 Juli in Paris*, Wörishofen, 1953

SCHWERIN-KROSIGK, Lutz Graf von, *Es geschah in Deutschland*, Wunderlich, Tübingen, 1952

SHIRER, W. L., *The Rise and Fall of the Third Reich*, Secker and Warburg, London, 1960, Simon & Schuster, New York.

SOERGEL, Albert, and HOHOFF, Curt, *Dichtung und Dichter der Zeit*, Vol. I, Bagel, Düsseldorf, 1961

SPEIDEL, Hans, *Invasion 1944*, Wunderlich, Tübingen, 1949; *We Defended Normandy*, translated by Ian Colvin, Herbert Jenkins, London, 1951

STAUFFENBERG, Alexander Schenk Graf von, "Claus Graf Schenk von Stauffenberg," in *Lebensbilder aus dem Bayerischen Schwaben*, edited by Götz Freiherr von Pölnitz, Munich, 1954
Denkmal, edited by Rudolf Fahrner, Küpper (Stefan George Foundation), Düsseldorf and Munich, 1964

STAUFFENBERG, Claus Schenk Graf von, "Gedanken zur Abrochr feindliches Fallschirmeinheiten im Heimatgebiet", in *Wissen und Wehr*, No. 7, 1938

TESKE, Hermann, *Die silbernen Spiegel*, Vowinckel, Heidelberg, 1952

THORMAEHLEN, Ludwig, *Erinnerungen an Stefan George*, Hauswedell, Hamburg, 1962

TOPF, Erwin, "Claus Graf Stauffenberg"—article in *Die Zeit*, Hamburg, 18 July 1946

TROTT ZU SOLZ, Adam von, "Trott und die Aussenpolitik des Widerstandes," *Vierteljahrshefte für Zeitgeschichte*, XI, 1963, No. 3

Die Vollmacht des Gewissens, issued by Europäischen Publikation, Rinn, Munich, 1956

WAGNER, Elisabeth, *Der Generalquartiermeister, Eduard Wagner*, Olzog, Munich, 1964

WHEELER-BENNETT, Sir J. W., *The Nemesis of Power*, Macmillan, London, 1953

WEISENBORN, Günther, *Der lautlose Aufstand*, 1962

ZELLER, Eberhard, *Geist der Freiheit: Der 20 Juli*, 4th and fully revised ed., Müller, Munich, 1963

NOTES

INTRODUCTION

1. From *20 Juli 1944*, issued by the Bundeszentrale für Heimatdienst and published by Berto, Bonn, 1960 (for Hitler see p. 178, Bormann p. 183, Ribbentrop p. 188, Göring pp. 179 *et seq.*). Himmler's speech was made in Posen on 3 August 1944 and is given in *Vierteljahrshefte für Zeitgeschichte*, 1953, p. 382.

2. For Himmler's recommendation of Stauffenberg as head of the operations section see p. 170 below. The phrase "remarkable gift of oratory" is to be found in *Spiegelbild einer Verschwörung*, Kaltenbrunner's report to Bormann and Himmler on the 20 July 1944 plot (p. 305), published by Seewald, Stuttgart, 1961, hereafter referred to as Kaltenbrunner report.

3. Years before, Himmler and Goebbels had said that at the end of the war there should be a mass execution of the aristocracy in the Lustgarten in Berlin. Himmler told his masseur, Felix Kersten, "The lords are no better than the Jews." See Achim Besgen, *Der stille Befehl*, and Kersten, *Himmler und das 3 Reich*, Nymphenburger Verlagsanstalt, Munich, 1960, p. 110.

4. This letter was found in the files concerning the plot (which also contained the Kaltenbrunner report). The files were taken over by the Americans and have been preserved on microfilm in the National Archives, Alexandria, Virginia (ref. T84, Roll 21).

5. Kaltenbrunner report, pp. 477 *et seq.*

CHAPTER I

1. See Gerhard Grimm, *Das Dritte Reich in Quellen und Darstellungen*. Vol. II. In *Politische Studien*, 16, 1965, No. 161 it is stated that Berthold was two years younger than Claus. This is not so. For the question of title see p. 249.

2. Information from Nina Gräfin von Stauffenberg (letter 22 April 1964). See also *Genealogisches Handbuch des Adels*.

3. The story handed down in the Stauffenberg family is that the reason for the King's dislike of Franz Ludwig von Stauffenberg was that in 1871, during the debate in the Bavarian parliament on adherence to the German Reich, he had obtained the agreement of the two houses by underhand means; he told the lower house that the upper house would vote for unification, at the same time telling the upper house that the lower house was voting for the Reich (from Nina Gräfin von Stauffenberg—interview 10 October 1962).

4. Duke Philipp of Württemberg was the son of Duke Albrecht; he became pretender to the throne, since the King had no direct male descendant.

5. In the 20 July 1944 interrogation files (see Introduction, note 4) there is a statement by Princess Wied, daughter of the last King of Württemberg, accusing Count Alfred von Stauffenberg of having falsified her father's will to her disadvantage after her father's death. This statement was shown to Duke Philipp of Württemberg, who categorically contradicted it. The passage quoted is taken from his rebuttal. Duke Philipp also says of the accusation against Count von Stauffenberg "I know that Princess Wied did not like Count Alfred von Stauffenberg and was neither fair nor impartial as far as he was concerned. She is, however, in my view too intelligent to have made the accusations quoted in the report, since she must know as well as I do that they are untrue and that such a thing was impossible, if only from the point of view of time. I think it more likely that Rauschnabel [the official carrying out the interrogations] cooked up the statement in typical National Socialist fashion, in order to produce evidence damaging to the Stauffenberg family."

6. Theodor Pfizer, "Die Brüder Stauffenberg," in *Freundesgabe für Robert Boehringer*, Mohr, Tübingen, 1957, p. 491.

7. Nina Gräfin von Stauffenberg—interview 10 October 1962.

8. Friedrich-Wilhelm, Freiherr von Loeper—interview 2 October 1962; Dietz Freiherr von Thüngen.

9. Theodor Pfizer, *op. cit.*, pp. 491 *et seq.*

10. Nina Gräfin von Stauffenberg—letter dated 22 October 1961.

11. For a history of the school see *Festschrift zur Neubaueinweihung des Eberhard-Ludwigs-Gymnasium*, Klett, Stuttgart, 1957.

12. Nina Gräfin von Stauffenberg—letter dated 16 November 1962.

13. Bernd von Pezold.

14. Wilhelm Bürklin—letter dated 15 July 1962.

15. Pfizer, *op. cit.*, p. 496.

16. The *Neupfadfinder* (lit: "Pathfinders") later combined with other groups to form the *Deutsche Freischar* (lit: "German Volunteers"), which was responsible for organizing the first volunteer labour service for young men and girls. Graf Moltke's Kreisau Circle, one of the most important groups in the subsequent opposition to Hitler, was an offshoot of the *Deutsche Freischar*.

17. Pfizer, *op. cit.*, p. 498.

18. Nina Gräfin von Stauffenberg—interview 10 October 1962.

19. Pfizer, *op. cit.*, p. 498.

20. Pfizer, *op. cit.,* p. 499.

21. Nina Gräfin von Stauffenberg—interview 10 October 1962.

22. Nina Gräfin von Stauffenberg—letter dated 17 March 1962. The Gestapo reports pay a great deal of attention to Stauffenberg's religious convictions, partly in their search for a motive, and then as a form of vilification. The report (Kaltenbrunner, p. 435) quotes Berthold von Stauffenberg as follows: "*We were not in fact faithful Catholics in the strict sense of the word. We seldom went to church and never to confession.* My brother and I felt that nothing creative was likely to come out of Christianity."
    The last sentence was clearly inspired by the poet Stefan George (see p. 33). The interrogating officials, however, obviously thought the content of the third sentence less important than the information in the first two (that the Stauffenbergs seldom went to church), since the first two sentences are under-lined. In addition, they drew from Berthold von Stauffenberg's interrogation the conclusion that for the Stauffenbergs the church in Lautlingen was merely a place for family flag-showing. The purpose behind this report is obvious— to show up the Stauffenberg attitude to the church as hypocrisy and so demon-strate their moral degradation. The interrogating officials were not interested in conducting an impartial examination. In any case, only a short extract from the record of Berthold von Stauffenberg's interrogation is available; we know nothing of what he said on the subject of religion in general.

23. Franz Halder—letter dated 26 January 1962; Dietz Freiherr von Thüngen unpublished memorandum 1946; Ulrich de Maiziere.

24. Nina Gräfin von Stauffenberg—letter dated 17 March 1962.

CHAPTER II

1. Nina Gräfin von Stauffenberg—letter dated 22 April 1964.

2. Edgar Salin, *Um Stefan George,* Küpper, Düsseldorf, 1954, p. 62.

3. Margarete Gräfin von Hardenberg.

4. Information from Peter Sauerbruch.

5. Edgar Salin, *op. cit.,* p. 324, footnote.

6. From a cyclostyle of a lecture given by Prof. Alexander Schenk Graf von Stauffenberg in Berlin on 4 December 1958. Elsewhere in his lecture Alexander von Stauffenberg said: "I think therefore that, like me, you will now see in a new light George's dictum that the inmost destiny of a people is revealed in its poetry; in other words, classic poetry can indeed determine the destiny of a people, of the Germans in particular; poetry can be the driving force behind the men who determine and fulfill our fate; poetry can inspire the activists to act and, in the event of failure, to sacrifice themselves."

7. Albert Soergel and Curt Hohoff, *Dichtung und Dichter der Zeit*, Vol. I, Bagel, Düsseldorf, 1961, p. 414.

8. Soergel and Hohoff, *op. cit.*, pp. 414 *et seq.*; Robert Boehringer, *Mein Bild von Stefan George*, 1951, pp. 173 *et seq.*

9. From the lecture referred to in note 6 above.

10. Salin, *op. cit.*, p. 95.

11. Dominik Jost, *Stefan George und Seine Elite*, Speer, Zurich, 1949, pp. 72 *et seq.* George named the following as the hallmarks of this hollow utilitarianism—traffic, technical progress, social services, emancipation of women, professional training, universal education, permanent peace, religious yearnings. (Wolters, *Jahrbuch für die geistige Bewegung*, 1910, pp. 385 *et seq.*)

12. Robert Boehringer, *op. cit.*, p. 149.

13. Salin, *op. cit.*, p. 216.

14. Boehringer, *op. cit.*, p. 150.

15. Alfred Schuler, George's "comrade" in the Munich circle, discovered the swastika in Johann Bachofer's book published in 1861 *Das Mutterrecht*. The matriarchal system was here described as the source of all culture. Schuler regarded this book as a new revelation, holding out thrilling prospects of a nobler way of life, compared to which Jewish culture, Christendom, and the classical humanist period would seem no better than eras of decadence. In 1922, long after he had broken with George, Schuler gave a lecture in Elsa Bruckmann's drawing room in Munich, when he peddled his strange ideas. In the audience was Adolf Hitler. See also Soergel and Hohoff, *op. cit.*, pp. 384 *et seq.*

16. Salin, *op. cit.*, pp. 271 and 248.

17. Boehringer, *op. cit.*, p. 149.

18. Jost, *op. cit.*, pp. 48 *et seq.*

19. From his anthology *Der Teppich der Seele*.

20. Jost, *op. cit.*, pp. 71 and 44.

21. Ludwig Thormaehlen, "Die Grafen Stauffenberg, Freunde von Stefan George," in collection in honour of Robert Boehringer, Mohr, Tübingen, 1957, p. 693. Thormaehlen reverts to the theme of this article in his book *Erinnerungen an Stefan George*, Hamburg, 1962. Unless otherwise stated, however, quotations are from the article in the collection in honour of Boehringer.

22. *Blätter für die Kunst*, 1910, p. 2.

23. Salin, *op. cit.*, pp. 31 and 54.

24. Thormaehlen, *op. cit.*, p. 693.

25. *Ibid.*

26. Theodor Pfizer, *op. cit.,* p. 492.

27. Alexander Schenk Graf von Stauffenberg, *op. cit.*; Thormaehlen, *Erinnerungen an Stefan George,* p. 241.

CHAPTER III

1. The certificate of examination results was issued by the Eberhard-Ludwigs school.

2. Theodor Pfizer (*op. cit.,* p. 490) says that the decision was a sudden one taken after the examination. Under the heading "Intended Profession," however, the certificate shows "Officer," so the decision must have been made beforehand.

3. This speculation is based on information from Gräfin Nina von Stauffenberg (interview on 10 October 1962).

4. The Seventeenth Cavalry Regiment was in fact a newly constituted Reichswehr unit. But since it was formed by merging all the old Bavarian cavalry regiments, it carried on their traditions.

5. After a year in Dresden, training was continued in the special-to-arm schools, infantry remaining in Dresden, artillery going to Jüterbog, and cavalry to Hannover.

6. Information from Friedrich-Wilhelm, Freiherr von Loeper—interview 2 October 1962.

7. From Bernd von Pezold.

8. On this course he met Captain Burkhart Müller-Hillebrand, later to be his section head in the General Staff and now a lieutenant general (retd.) in the Bundeswehr. He says the following of Stauffenberg: "The impression I took away with me at the time was of a very good fellow, whom I found naturally attractive. He was head and shoulders above the general run of officers in personality, intelligence, and general education. He was a cheerful soul but never superficial or over-boisterous therewith, as was often the case with young officers at the time." (Letter dated 30 April 1962.)

9. There were five children of the marriage: Berthold, born 3 July 1934, now a captain in the Bundeswehr; Heimeran, born 9 July 1936, now in industry; Franz Ludwig, born 4 May 1938, now a barrister; Valerie, born 15 November 1940; Konstanze, born 27 January 1945.

10. From Nina Gräfin von Stauffenberg—interview 10 October 1962 and letter dated 22 April 1964. After he had been so badly wounded in 1943 Stauffenberg gave up riding altogether, since he could no longer have the necessary light touch of the hands. When told about a fellow officer who was riding again in

spite of having two artificial arms, he said that he would never be able to do any good with it again. He did once allow himself to be persuaded onto a horse again. In July 1944 he visited the cavalry school in Krampnitz where the CO, Colonel Harold Momm, was a personal friend. Momm tried to persuade Stauffenberg to start riding again and eventually had a horse led out in front of the mess. Stauffenberg got the horse to do a piaffe and was overjoyed to find that in spite of his disabilities he could still manage so difficult a movement.

11. Regarding the military district examination and the principles of selection for the Staff College see Waldemar Erfurth, *Geschichte des deutschen Generalstabes von 1918 bis 1945*, Musterschmidt Verlag, Göttingen, 1960, pp. 138 *et seq.*; also Hermann Teske, *Die silbernen Spiegel*, Vowinckel, Heidelberg, 1952, pp. 36 *et seq.*

12. Nina Gräfin von Stauffenberg—letter dated 16 November 1962.

13. Bernd von Pezold.

14. Heinz Greiner—letter dated 15 May 1964.

15. Bernd von Pezold gives a somewhat similar description: "However many people there might be present, it was impossible not to take notice of Stauffenberg. Almost involuntarily he would become the focus of any gathering; people found him attractive, convincing, and a man they could trust. He could give cohesion to any group of men, even if thrown together by chance; he would raise the level of any discussion."

16. Wilhelm Bürklin—letter dated 15 July 1962.

17. Bernd von Pezold. The following appreciation of Stauffenberg, written by one who worked with him at a later period, may sound somewhat overdrawn today but nevertheless gives an indication of the fascination Stauffenberg exerted on members of his own circle: "One felt that he possessed an unassailable strength amounting to genius; the result was to make one feel that it would be a joy to work for and with him. If you looked at Stauffenberg, the present-day notion that only the coarse, violent type of character can achieve anything seemed completely out of place. You had merely to look at him to realize that extreme forcefulness of character can perfectly well be combined with all the best natural qualities of a gentleman" (Eberhard Zeller in *Festschrift zur Neubaueinweihung des Eberhard-Ludwigs-Gymnasium*—see Chapter I, note 11).

18. The Court of Honour was an organization stemming from the imperial era. It was elected by the corps of officers and would be charged by the commanding officer to enquire into matters involving the honour of an officer. It would express an opinion to the commanding officer which he was not bound to accept but which in most cases formed the basis of his decision.

19. Bernd von Pezold.

20. *Ibid.*

21. Nina Gräfin von Stauffenberg—interview 10 October 1962. Information confirmed by Hans Cramer.

22. Bernd von Pezold.

23. Erfurth, *op. cit.,* pp. 108 and 110.

24. Bernd von Pezold.

25. Heinz Greiner—letter dated 15 May 1964.

26. Nina Gräfin von Stauffenberg—interview 10 October 1962.

CHAPTER IV

1. Hermann Foertsch, *Schuld und Verhangnis: Die Fritsch-Krise im Frühjahr 1938,* Deutsche Verlagsanstalt, Stuttgart, 1951, p. 22.

2. After the publication of the book Sauerbruch protested that Foertsch had included this information in a context which he (Sauerbruch) had not anticipated. Foertsch agreed that in future editions the contentious passage should be dropped. But Foertsch died, and no further edition of the book appeared.

3. From notes of interview with Sauerbruch on 12 February 1963.

4. No. 25, 31 January 1933, Stoppress "Latest Local News."

5. Based on Bodo Scheurig's monograph *Claus Graf Schenk von Stauffenberg* (Colloquium Verlag, Berlin, 1964), rumours have recently appeared to the effect that there were eye-witnesses of the incident prepared to testify that Stauffenberg did take part in the demonstration. Proof was said to be available in the Institut für Zeitgeschichte, Munich, but a secrecy ban had been imposed by the Stauffenberg family.
In answer to this: On 15 June 1961 the Institut für Zeitgeschichte assured me that, apart from material which I already knew, they possessed no further background evidence of any importance. Secondly, Gräfin von Stauffenberg told me in a letter dated 8 March 1964 that neither she nor her sons had imposed any secrecy ban.

6. Municipal police office, Bamberg, Criminal Police K VII. The statement is signed "Hofmann, Inspector."

7. Letter dated 17 July 1962.

8. Report by Hans Walzer.

9. This is the date given by Manteuffel; Hans Walzer puts the incident at 6 March 1933, the day after the Reichstag elections.

10. Information from Manteuffel. He would have it that Stauffenberg was also present on this occasion. He cannot, however, give any reason why Stauffenberg

should have attached himself to the Fifth Squadron on this particular day. Walzer, Stauffenberg's squadron leader, thinks it quite out of the question, merely on technical grounds, that Stauffenberg could have attached himself to another unit; the First Squadron and the Fifth Squadron used entirely different training areas.

11. Report by Hans Walzer.

12. *Reichgesetzblatt*, I, 1935, No. 100.

13. Bund Deutscher Mädchen (lit: German Girls' League), the National Socialist young women's organization.

14. Information from Bernd von Pezold.

15. From Heinz Greiner—letter dated 15 May 1964.

16. From Hans Walzer—letter dated 9 March 1964.

17. Prof. Rudolf Fahrner, quoted by Eberhard Zeller in *Geist der Freiheit*, Müller, Munich, 1963, pp. 240 *et seq.* Throughout this book quotations from Prof. Fahrner originate either from information which he gave to me personally or from information given to Dr. Zeller, which the latter then quoted in his book.

18. Prof. Rudolf Fahrner, quoted by E. Zeller, *op. cit.*, p. 241.

19. *Ibid.*

20. Information from Bernd von Pezold.

21. From Nina Gräfin von Stauffenberg—interview 10 October 1962.

22. *Ibid.*

23. *Reichsgesetzblatt*, I, 1934, No. 71.

24. From Hans Walzer—letter dated 19 May 1964.

25. Hermann Teske, *op. cit.*, p. 31.

26. Prof. Rudolf Fahrner, quoted by E. Zeller. *op. cit.*, p. 240.

CHAPTER V

1. This letter is in the possession of Frau Gerda Pfau, Prof. Pfau's daughter, who lives in Berlin.

2. See Hermann Teske, *op. cit.*, p. 41.

Under interrogation subsequent to 20 July 1944 Finckh stated that even during the course Stauffenberg had been the moving spirit of his study hall and had played the preponderant role (Kaltenbrunner report, p. 305).

3. Eberhard Zeller, *op. cit.,* p. 227.

4. "Gedanken zur Abwehr feindlicher Fallschirmeinheiten im Heimatgebiet," in *Wissen und Wehr,* the monthly bulletin of the Deutsche Gesellschaft für Wehrpolitik und Wehrwissenschaften, No. 7, 1938, pp. 459 *et seq.* See Appendix 1.

5. Letter dated 29 October 1964.

6. In the possession of Nina Gräfin von Stauffenberg.

7. The Russian campaign proved Stauffenberg right on this point. When the Russian "mud glue-pot" period immobilized motor vehicles and tanks, cavalry units were used in many areas.

8. Waldemar Erfurth, *op. cit.,* pp. 189 *et seq.*

9. Information from Nina Gräfin von Stauffenberg—interview 10 October 1962.

10. Letter from Wedemeyer dated 22 June 1962.

11. *Ibid.*

12. Letter from Wedemeyer dated 9 May 1962.

13. *Ibid.*

14. *Ibid.*

15. See p. 39 above.

16. For instance, in the essay on cavalry mentioned above there is a page with corrections by Mehnert on it.

17. Rudolf Fahrner, *Gneisenau,* Delfin, Munich, 1942, p. 42.

18. Information from Prof. Fahrner.

19. From Nina Gräfin von Stauffenberg—letter dated 22 April 1964; see also Zeller, *op. cit.,* p. 227.

20. The exercise lasted from 15 to 24 June 1938. It dealt with the problem of the defense of Germany west of the Rhine in face of a French invasion, while major German forces were pursuing a beaten enemy in the east. The exercise therefore anticipated the situation which the German army feared might arise on the outbreak of the Second World War.

21. Teske, *op. cit.,* p. 41.

CHAPTER VI

1. Bernd von Pezold, on information from General Buhle.

2. Erwin Topf, "Claus Graf Stauffenberg," in *Die Zeit,* 18 July 1946.

3. Bernd von Pezold.

4. See Alan Bullock, *Hitler: A Study in Tyranny*, Odhams Press, London, 1952, p. 471.

5. See Horst Scheibert, *Bildband der 6 Panzerdivision 1939–1945*, Podzun, Bad Nauheim, 1958, p. 6.

6. It is in Werner Reerink's possession. It is evidently Stauffenberg's own copy as it carries "Gf St" on the outside, and there are a number of notes in his handwriting.

7. War diary of First Light Division, 30 September (p. 6).

8. *Ibid.*, 4 October (p. 8).

9. *Ibid.*, 9 October (p. 15).

10. *Ibid.*, 13–14 October (pp. 21 *et seq.*).

11. *Ibid.*, 13 October (p. 21).

12. *Ibid.*, 4 October (p. 10).

13. *Ibid.*, 6 October (p. 13).

14. *Ibid.*, 7 October (p. 14).

15. *Ibid.*, 12 October (p. 21).

16. *Ibid.*, 8 October (p. 15).

17. *Ibid.*, 12 October (p. 21).

18. *Ibid.*, 9 October (p. 16).

19. *Ibid.*, 10 October (p. 21).

20. *Ibid.*, 10–11 October (pp. 18 *et seq.*).

21. *Ibid.*, 11 October (p. 19).

22. *Ibid.*, 16 October (p. 26).

23. Eberhard Zeller, *op. cit.*, p. 232; also Nina Gräfin von Stauffenberg.

24. Friedrich-Wilhelm, Freiherr von Loeper—letter dated 18 November 1962.

25. Volkmar Schöne—letter dated 17 December 1962.

26. Werner Reerink.

27. It was probably due to the fact that the personnel section had already planned Stauffenberg's move to the organization section of the General Staff. This took place in May 1940.

28. From Ruth von Blomberg and Werner Reerink.

29. Ruth von Blomberg.

30. Werner Reerink.

31. *Ibid.*

32. See Helmuth Günther Dahms, *Der zweite Weltkrieg*, Wunderlich Verlag, Tübingen, 1960, pp. 53 *et seq.*; also Waldemar Erfurth, *op. cit.*, pp. 242 *et seq.*, and many others. For the history of the Sixth Panzer division see Horst Scheibert, *op. cit.*, p. 6.

33. Werner Reerink.

CHAPTER VII

1. Rudolf Fahrner, quoted by Eberhard Zeller, *op. cit.*, p. 232.

2. From Concordia records. Information from Fritz Weddigen, now president of the club.

3. From Beate Bremme—Freiherr von Loeper thinks he can remember that the talk dealt primarily with National Socialist ideology and that Stauffenberg was trying to convert the industrialists, who were dragging their feet, to the new ideas. This seems pretty improbable, particularly since the talk was given just after *Kristallnacht*. Others, for instance, remember definitely that *Kristallnacht* produced a marked change in Stauffenberg's attitude to the regime. Freiherr von Loeper did not himself hear Stauffenberg's talk, and his memory of it is not therefore very clear. Merely from its subject, the talk could hardly have been concerned with National Socialist ideology. The fact remains, however, that the audience got no impression that their speaker was an opponent of National Socialism.

4. Nina Gräfin von Stauffenberg—interview 10 October 1962.

5. The crack SS formation, unquestionably loyal to Hitler.

6. Werner Reerink.

7. Prof. Rudolf Fahrner.

8. Helmut Staedke.

9. Werner Reerink.

10. Friedrich-Wilhelm, Freiherr von Loeper—interview 2 October 1962.

11. Rudolf Fahrner, quoted by Zeller, *op. cit.*, p. 242.

12. Zeller, *op. cit.*, pp. 242 *et seq.*

13. *Ibid.*, p. 242.

CHAPTER VIII

1. See U. Liss, *Westfront 1939-40*, Vowinckel, Neckargemünd, 1959, pp. 132 *et seq.*

2. Bernd von Pezold.

3. This section is based on information from Franz Halder—letter dated 26 January 1962.

4. Ulrich de Maiziere.

5. The copy of this letter still in existence is one made by the Gräfin von Stauffenberg for her mother and her in-laws, her husband not having time to write to them all.

6. Burkhart Müller-Hillebrand and Ulrich de Maiziere.

7. Eberhard Zeller, *op. cit.*, p. 243.

8. Bernd von Pezold.

9. Nina Gräfin von Stauffenberg—interview 10 October 1962.

10. See organization section war diary 1942, 10 January (p. 22), 1-5 June (p. 204), 8-13 March (p. 106), 11-20 September (pp. 324 *et seq.*), 4 December (p. 386).

11. Dietz Freiherr von Thüngen.

12. "Basic Order" No. 1, displayed in all offices during the war. It laid down that no one, however senior in rank, was to know one word of any important military or political matter over and above that strictly necessary for the fulfillment of his duty in connection with that matter.

13. Ulrich de Maiziere.

14. Dr. Georg Freiherr von Fritsch.

15. Ulrich de Maiziere.

16. Kurt Zeitzler—letter dated 3 July 1962; see also report by Major Heinz Hoppe, a staff officer on the eastern front in 1942, given in *Conspiracy against Hitler* by John McCloy II

17. Helmut Kleikamp—letter dated 18 December 1962.

18. Franz Halder—letter dated 23 March 1962.

19. Franz Halder—letter dated 26 January 1962.

20. Franz Halder—letter dated 23 March 1962. Stauffenberg on his side had the highest possible respect for Halder. Freiherr von Thüngen says: "There

were some men—not many—of whom Claus would speak with veneration and respect. There was one who occupied a special place in his estimation—Colonel General Halder. 'A man of incredible ability,' he would say, 'a splendid person.' It was like a son talking of his father or favourite schoolmaster. The 'father's' opinion of the 'son' was no doubt similar."

21. See p. 70 above.

22. See Waldemar Erfurth, *op. cit.*, pp. 217 *et seq.*, and elsewhere—*e.g.*, *Die Vollmacht des Gewissens*, Europäischer Publikation, Rinn, Munich, 1956, pp. 332 *et seq.*; Helmuth K. G. Rönnefarth, *Die Sudetenkrise in der internationalen Politik*, Steiner, Wiesbaden, 1961.

23. *Die Vollmacht des Gewissens*, pp. 408 *et seq.*

24. *Ibid.*, pp. 436 *et seq.*

25. Zeller, *op. cit.*, p. 234.

26. Franz Halder—letter dated 23 March 1962.

27. *Ibid.*

28. Letter dated 19 June 1940; see also note 5, above.

29. Letter dated 21 June 1940; see also note 5, above.

30. Franz Halder—letter dated 23 March 1962.

31. Franz Halder—letter dated 26 January 1962.

32. Franz Halder—letter dated 23 March 1962.

33. Hans-Bernd Gisevius, *To the Bitter End*, Jonathan Cape, London, 1948, p. 479.

34. Franz Halder—letter dated 23 March 1962. Stauffenberg and Halder lost touch after the latter's dismissal. Apart from one visit by Stauffenberg to Halder in Berlin (referred to on p. 111), they never met again. Some form of contact was maintained through a friend of Halder's who worked in the army office. At the end of 1943 Halder sent Stauffenberg a message: "The aim remains the same." Early in 1943, shortly before leaving for Africa, Stauffenberg visited his friend Peter Sauerbruch in a hospital in Berlin and asked him to pass on a letter Halder visited Sauerbruch the next day and so received the letter. (Information from Peter Sauerbruch.)

CHAPTER IX

1. Werner Reerink.

2. Waldemar Erfurth, *op. cit.*, p. 231.

3. Franz Halder, *Kriegstagebuch* (Diary), Vol. III, Kohlhammer Verlag, Stuttgart, 1964.

4. Erfurth, *op. cit.*, p. 289.

5. Wilhelm Bürklin—letter dated 15 July 1962.

6. Halder's diary—entry for 21 August 1941.

7. Hans von Herwarth.

8. Alfred Philippi and Ferdinand Heim, *Der Feldzug gegen Sowjetrussland 1941-1945*, Kohlhammer Verlag, Stuttgart, 1962, and other sources.

9. Friedrich-Wilhelm, Freiherr von Loeper—interview 2 October 1962.

10. *Reichsgesetzblatt*, 1942, I, p. 247.

11. Von Loeper—interview 2 October 1962.

12. *International Military Tribunal (IMT) Nuremberg*, Vol. XXVI, pp. 403–408; Vol. XXXIV, pp. 249 *et seq.*; Vol. XLIII, pp. 231 *et seq.*; Vol. II, p. 454 Vol. XX, p. 609; Vol. XXXIX, pp. 128–29; Vol. XXVI, Document 498.

13. Werner Reerink; see also p. 87.

14. Information from Werner Reerink.

15. *KTB Org Abt* (organization section war diary) 1942. (Up to October, entries cover a period of five to ten days; from 25 October they were as a rule made daily.) See entries for 21–31 July (p. 260), 1–10 August (p. 268), 4 November (p. 383).

16. War diary, 21 December, p. 402.

17. *Ibid.*, 21–31 July, pp. 260 and 266; 29 November, p. 383.

18. *Ibid.*, 25 October, p. 355.

19. *Ibid.*, 21–30 September, p. 331; 11–20 October, pp. 348 *et seq.*; 25 October, p. 355.

20. *Ibid.*, 16–20 January, p. 27.

21. *Ibid.*, 16–21 February, p. 83.

22. *Ibid.*, 16–22 June, p. 217.

23. *Ibid.*, 11–20 September, p. 319.

24. *Ibid.*, 11–20 September, p. 320; 11–20 October, p. 347.

25. *Ibid.*, 1–5 February, p. 59; 1–7 March, p. 98.

26. *Ibid.*, 19–25 March, p. 118.

27. *Ibid.*, 1–10 August, p. 269.

28. *Ibid.*, 1–14 April, p. 144; 19–25 March, p. 126; 1–10 September, p. 305.

29. *Ibid.*, 16–22 June, p. 217; 15 November, p. 370.

30. *Ibid.*, 21–31 July, p. 258; 1 November, p. 361.

31. *Ibid.*, 15–21 April, p. 150; 26–30 June, p. 237; 26 November, p. 380.

32. *Ibid.*, 4 December, p. 386.

33. *Ibid.*, 21–25 January, p. 35.

34. *Ibid.*, 16–21 February, p. 83.

35. *Ibid.*, 1–7 April, p. 133; 8–14 April, p. 144.

36. *Ibid.*, 16–21 February, pp. 81 *et seq.*

37. *Ibid.*, 26–31 May, p. 193.

38. *Ibid.*, 21–30 June, p. 235.

39. *Ibid.*, 11–20 October, p. 350.

40. *Ibid.*, p. 352.

CHAPTER X

1. Gerhard von Mende, *Erfahrungen mit Ostfreiwilligen in der deutschen Wehrmacht während des Zweiten Weltkrieges* (Studien zur Auslandskunde, No. 1), Leske, Darmstadt, 1952, p. 24.

2. War diary, 1–5 January, p. 3.

3. Wilfried Strik-Strikfeldt—letter dated 1 August 1963. See also Alexander Dallin, *Deutsche Herrschaft in Russland*, Droste, Düsseldorf, 1958, p. 557.

4. Gerhard von Mende, *op. cit.*, p. 25.

5. Dr. Otto Bräutigam, Hans von Heewarth.

6. War diary, 6–10 February, p. 66.

7. Hans von Herwarth.

8. War diary, 6–10 February, p. 66.

9. Alexander Dallin, *op. cit.*, p. 555, note 2. The reference of the order was OKH/Gen StdH/Org Abt (II).

10. Dallin, *op. cit.*, p. 555.

11. War diary, p. 228.

12. Others were present at this meeting whom Prof. von Mende cannot now remember.

13. Prof. Gerhard von Mende—letter dated 19 July 1963.

14. From Hans von Herwarth.

15. *Ibid.*

16. See Dallin, *op. cit.,* p. 556, note 3.

17. The reference number of the instruction was Gen StdH/Org (II) No. 8000/42.

18. War diary, 8–20 August, pp. 286 *et seq.*

19. *Ibid.,* 5 November, p. 363.

20. *Ibid.,* 13 November, p. 368.

21. He left the headquarters saying, "The Russian bear has only just woken from its winter sleep and is still somewhat bemused. After the first blows it will rise on its hind legs and hit back hard, and don't forget that it is cold in Russia in winter." (Hans von Herwarth, "Dem Andenken des Generals der Kavallerie Ernst Köstring," in *Zeitschrift für Geopolitik,* XXV, 1954, No. 12, p. 767.)

22. Hans von Herwarth, *op. cit.,* p. 767.

23. War diary, 8–31 August, pp. 292 *et seq.*

24. Dallin, *op. cit.,* pp. 250 *et seq.*

25. Prof. G. von Mende—letter dated 19 July 1963; Wilfried Strik-Strikfeldt—letter dated 11 August 1963.

26. *Die Tat,* Zurich, 25 November 1946; E. Zeller, *op. cit.,* p. 236.

27. Eberhard Zeller, *op. cit.,* p. 246.

28. Dallin, *op. cit.,* p. 557.

29. Wilfried Strik-Strikfeldt—letter dated 11 August 1963.

30. War diary, 19 December, p. 401.

31. Dallin, *op. cit.,* pp. 163, 371, 561.

32. *Ibid.,* p. 164.

33. Quoted in Dallin, *op. cit.,* p. 562 (reference—OKH/Gen StdH/Gen Qu/Abt, Kr–Verw, Aufzeichnungen über die Ostfragen, 3 January 1943).

34. Dallin, *op. cit.,* pp. 562 *et seq.*

35. Hans von Herwarth. A memorandum from Rosenberg to Hitler dated January 1943 produces ideas similar to those of Stauffenberg, Tresckow, and Gehlen: "These people are all asking the same question—if we are now to risk

our lives fighting against the slavery of Bolshevism, we must know what we are fighting for; the prospect of exchanging Russian for German slavery can never produce an enduring will to fight" (Dallin, *op. cit.*, p. 575).

The idea that Stauffenberg intended to use the volunteers against Hitler is a pure figment of the imagination (confirmed by Hans von Herwarth and Gerhard von Mende). Moreover, on 20 July 1944 there was no plan envisaging the use of these troops. According to Dallin (*op. cit.*, p. 606, footnote) one of those intimately involved stated that "the idea had been mooted but we all agreed that this business must be carried through by Germans."

CHAPTER XI

1. Quoted from H. A. Jacobsen, *1939–1945*, Verlag Wehr und Wissen, Darmstadt, 1961, p. 383.

2. Ulrich de Maiziere.

3. Hans von Herwarth; Prof. Gerhard von Mende—letter dated 19 July 1963.

4. Ulrich de Maiziere.

5. Burkhart Müller-Hillebrand—letter dated 30 April 1962.

6. Walter Bussmann, "Betrachtungen zum militärischen Widerstand," in *Aus Politik und Zeitgeschichte* (supplement to the periodical *Das Parlament*), 15 July 1964, p. 13.

7. Helmut Staedke, Ulrich de Maiziere.

8. Friedrich Freiherr von Broich—letter dated 20 June 1962.

9. Eberhard Zeller, *op. cit.*, pp. 247 *et seq.*

10. Letter dated 12 June 1942, given *in extenso* in Appendix II. The original was in the possession of Ernst Alexander Paulus.

11. Information from Küchler and List.

12. Erich von Manstein—letters dated 20 August 1962 and 15 November 1962; confirmed by Theodor Busse, Chief of Staff Army Group South.

13. From Nina Gräfin von Stauffenberg—interview 10 October 1962.

14. Theodor Busse.

15. Hans von Herwarth.

16. Franz Halder, *Hitler als Feldherr*, Dom-Verlag, Munich, 1949, pp. 52 *et seq.*

17. Freiherr von Thüngen gives a graphic account of the increasingly unwholesome atmosphere of the headquarters: "Many first-class brains, an immeasurable amount of hard work, but little, very little influence even on the

part of those who could lay some claim to it. We had no influence because he considered the General Staff at best as drudges—unheroic, conceited, pedantic little men, lacking the sweep of his genius, men in whom he had no confidence. The more difficult the situation, the less credence was given to factual reports, the more powerful became those prepared to tell him what he wished to hear and the fewer became the able and responsible men ready to tell him the truth and warn him. The enemy's production figures, strengths, reserves, and actual achievements were all written off as untrue as soon as they topped our own potential. Then they would be compared with reports from other 'sources' available to the Führer and adjusted accordingly."

18. Franz Halder—letter dated 26 January, 1962.

19. See A. Philippi and F. Heim, *op. cit.*, pp. 182 *et seq.*

20. Nina Gräfin von Stauffenberg—interview 10 October 1962.

21. Helmut Kleikamp—letter dated 15 January 1963.

CHAPTER XII

1. Nina Gräfin von Stauffenberg—interview 10 October 1962.

2. Wilhelm Bürklin—letter dated 15 July 1962.

3. Friedrich Freiherr von Broich—letter dated 14 June 1962.

4. Heinz Schmid—letter dated 23 September 1963.

5. *The Rommel Papers*, edited by B. H. Liddell Hart, translated by Paul Findlay, Collins, London, 1953, pp. 406, 409, 421.

6. Hans Reimann.

7. Friedrich Freiherr von Broich—letter dated 14 June 1962.

8. Heinz Schmid.

9. Hans Reimann.

10. Dr. Friedrich Zipfel.

11. Friedrich Freiherr von Broich—letter dated 14 June 1962.

12. *Ibid.*

13. There is an error here—Stauffenberg was only one of the section heads in the organization section. Friedrich Freiherr von Broich— letter 25 June 1962.

14. Friedrich Freiherr von Broich—letter dated 25 June 1962. Stauffenberg did not keep his political views solely for his divisional commander but was quite ready to air them to more junior officers. When asked by Freisler, president of

the People's Court, whether Stauffenberg had already been giving vent to any "striking criticisms" while still in Africa, Lieutenant von Hagen, who was later executed in connection with 20 July 1944, replied that Stauffenberg had often said to him quite openly: "The shortcomings which we think we see here are not the fault of commanders in Africa, either at corps or army headquarters; the trouble lies far higher up." (Extracts from the record of hearing in the People's Court on 7 and 8 August 1944 in the case against "von Witzleben and others," published by Eugen Budde and Peter Lütsches in *20 July 1944* [Raven, Düsseldorf, 1952]—hereafter referred to as Budde and Lütsches, record of hearings.)

15. Friedrich Freiherr von Broich—letter dated 14 June 1962.

CHAPTER XIII

1. Letter dated 9 June 1943. Wilhelm Bürklin has the original.

2. Kaltenbrunner report, p. 305.

3. Dr. Georg Freiherr von Fritsch.

4. Dr. Paulus van Husen.

5. Wilhelm Bürklin—letter dated 15 July 1962.

6. Kurt Zeitzler—letter dated 3 July 1962. The significance of this visit should not, however, be overrated. Zeitzler says: "Had I had the opportunity, as Chief of Staff I would have visited all severely wounded officers in hospital, just as I did Graf Stauffenberg."

7. Nina Gräfin von Stauffenberg—interview 10 October 1962.

8. Helmut Kleikamp—letter dated 21 January 1963.

9. Nina Gräfin von Stauffenberg—interview 10 October 1962.

10. Wilhelm Bürklin—letter dated 15 July 1962.

11. Kurt Zeitzler—letter dated 3 July 1962: confirmed by Helmut Kleikamp—letter dated 21 January 1963: "Graf Stauffenberg's request to be re-posted to the front was no doubt made with the best intentions. At that time and in the existing situation the majority of staff officers felt similarly."

12. *Ibid.*

13. Nina Gräfin von Stauffenberg—interview 10 October 1962.

14. Ferdinand Sauerbruch, *Das War mein Leben*, Kindler, Munich, 1951, pp. 550 *et seq.*

15. Peter Sauerbruch.

16. Nina Gräfin von Stauffenberg—interview 10 October 1962.

17. Peter Sauerbruch.

18. Prof. Rudolf Fahrner quoted by Eberhard Zeller, *op. cit.*, pp. 253 *et seq.*

19. Nina Gräfin von Stauffenberg—interview 10 October 1962.

CHAPTER XIV

1. Kaltenbrunner report, p. 145; Veit Osas, *Walküre*, Deutschland-Verlag, Hamburg, 1953 (record of the case against Goerdeler and others).

2. Albert Krebs, *Fritz-Dietlof Graf von der Schulenburg, Zwischen Staatsraison und Hochverrat*, Leibniz, Hamburg, 1964, pp. 237 *et seq.*

3. Goerdeler stated to the Gestapo that he had been responsible for introducing Stauffenberg to Leber (Kaltenbrunner report, p. 210). According to information from Frau Annedore Leber this is incorrect; the contact was arranged by Schulenburg.

4. See pp. 122 *et seq.*, above.

5. See pp. 157 *et seq.*, below.

6. From Dr. Marion Gräfin Yorck von Wartenburg.

7. From Dr. Paulus van Husen.

8. See Annedore Leber and Freya Gräfin von Moltke, *Für und wieder, Entscheidungen in Deutschland 1918–1945*, Mosaik-Verlag, Berlin, 1962, pp. 106 *et seq.* In his defense Graf Schwerin von Schwanenfeld told the Gestapo that he had only been recruited into the coup d'état plans in September 1943—and by Stauffenberg.

9. From Dr. Marion Gräfin Yorck von Wartenburg.

10. From Waltraud von Götz—letter dated 5 September 1962.

11. From Dr. Marion Gräfin Yorck von Wartenburg.

12. From Olga von Saucken.

13. From Dr. Marion Gräfin Yorck von Wartenburg and Dr. Paulus van Husen.

14. From a paper by Gräfin Yorck von Wartenburg.

15. Draft in the possession of Gräfin Yorck von Wartenburg. A study of the Kreisau Circle is being made by the Dutch historian Ger van Roon and will be issued by the Institut für Zeitgeschichte, Munich.

During a conversation in which Stauffenberg took part, a thesis by Prof. Schmölders on "Labour Service Duty" was discussed. On the copy given to van Roon by Schmölders there is a marginal note, "Discussed with Graf Stauffenberg."

16. Draft in the possession of Gräfin Yorck von Wartenburg.

17. This so-called Wednesday Club originated in 1860; it included a number of men of letters, diplomats, and officers who expounded their special subjects to each other at fortnightly meetings. (Information from Käthe Jessen.)

18. From Käthe Jessen.

19. Ulrich von Hassell, *Vom anderen Deutschland*, from his diaries 1938–1944. Atlantis, Zurich, 1946. Hassell unfortunately does not say why he wished to meet Stauffenberg alone.

20. Kaltenbrunner report, p. 205. Although this information comes from the Gestapo report, it checks with Stauffenberg's views as reported elsewhere and so may be taken as correct.

21. Kaltenbrunner report, pp. 100 and 360.

22. Kaltenbrunner report, p. 360.

23. Henning von Tresckow had been designated to succeed Helldorf as chief of police.

CHAPTER XV

1. See Veit Osas, *op. cit.*, pp. 70 *et seq.* The conspirators were connected primarily with the army. Berthold von Stauffenberg was, it is true, a legal adviser and judge advocate to the navy and in Lieutenant Commander Kranzfelder he found a kindred spirit. Two other naval officers were won over, but no great efforts were made to enlarge the circle, since the navy could make little direct contribution to a coup d'état. The only connection between army and navy opposition circles was via Berthold von Stauffenberg, and since the navy was inevitably somewhat on the sidelines, only the most essential information was passed on to it. (See Walter Baum's article: "Marine, Nationalsozialismus und Widerstand," in *Politik und Zeitgeschichte* (supplement to the weekly *Das Parlament*), 15 July 1963.

2. There is no certainty that this was in fact the first meeting between Beck and Stauffenberg. Prof. Rudolf Fahrner believes that they had been in touch long before this: "Stauffenberg had long before referred to Beck in terms which were as unmistakable as was his discretion in regard to other people."

3. Osas, *op. cit.*, pp. 70 *et seq.*; Kaltenbrunner report, pp. 532 *et seq.*

4. Kaltenbrunner report, p. 410 (statement by Goerdeler).

5. *Ibid.*

6. See Fabian von Schlabrendorff, *Offiziere gegen Hitler*, Fischer, Frankfurt, 1959, pp. 128 *et seq.*; also Wheeler-Bennett, *The Nemesis of Power*, p. 588. The statements in both these books that action was planned for September are incorrect, as the present account shows. The plans were only worked out in September.

7. From Fabian von Schlabrendorff, *op. cit.*, p. 131; Budde and Lütsches, record of hearings (interrogation of Stieff); Kaltenbrunner report, p. 88.

8. *Hitler's Table Talk*, introductory Essay by Professor H. R. Trevor-Roper. Translated by Norman Cameron and R. H. Stevens. Wiedenfeld & Nicolson, London, 1953, p. 452.

9. Kaltenbrunner report, p. 42.

10. Von Schlabrendorff, *op. cit.*, p. 103.

11. Friedrich Georgi.

12. Kaltenbrunner report, p. 157.

13. Eberhard Zeller, *op. cit.*, p. 255.

14. Kaltenbrunner report, p. 368.

15. Margarethe von Oven, now Gräfin von Hardenberg.

16. Gräfin von Hardenberg remembers that the orders utilized on 20 July 1944 were already on paper at this time.

17. From Charlotte Gräfin von der Schulenburg.

18. Kaltenbrunner report, pp. 157 *et seq.*; see also article by Peter Hoffmann, "Zum Ablauf des Staatsstreichversuches des 20 Juli 1944 in den Wehrkreisen," in *Wehrwissenschaftliche Rundschau*, July 1964, pp. 379 *et seq.*

19. Kaltenbrunner report, p. 158.

20. Kaltenbrunner report, p. 67.

21. Letter from Prof. Rudolf Fahrner.

22. From Colonel (retd.) R—— K——.

23. *Ibid.*

24. Under interrogation the members of the conspiracy arrested subsequent to 20 July must have made much of the evils of the higher organization as one of their primary motives for participation, since the Gestapo report devotes a great deal of space to this point (see Kaltenbrunner report, pp. 292 *et seq.*).

25. Kaltenbrunner report, p. 31.

26. Kaltenbrunner report, p. 292.

27. Kaltenbrunner report, pp. 145 and 334.

28. Kaltenbrunner report, p. 145; see also Osas, *op. cit.*, case against Dr. Goerdeler.

29. Hofacker was initiated into the conspiracy on 25 October 1943, when he visited Berlin for a family wedding (from Nina Gräfin von Stauffenberg— letter dated 1 July 1964).

CHAPTER XVI

1. From Dr. Marion Gräfin Yorck von Wartenburg.

2. Budde and Lütsches, record of hearings, examination of Stieff.

3. Fabian von Schlabrendorff, *op. cit.*, p. 132. Under interrogation Stieff stated that he had refused to make the attempt. This must have been an attempt to protect himself from the Gestapo.

4. Axel von dem Bussche, information on gramophone records *Der stille Befehl*, side II, Fonoverlagsgesellschaft; see also von Schlabrendorff, *op. cit.*, p. 132, and Eberhard Zeller, *op. cit.*, p. 333.

5. Kaltenbrunner report, pp. 54, 258, and 262.

6. Kaltenbrunner report, p. 533. J. W. Wheeler-Bennett (*op. cit.*, p. 591) says that Stauffenberg himself made this attempt, but unfortunately does not give his source. I have therefore not quoted the passage concerned. It says that Olbricht was ordered to supreme headquarters on 26 December for a conference on manpower reserves, but on the pretext of being sick, sent Stauffenberg to represent him. When, however, Stauffenberg arrived in Rastenburg, the assembled company was told that the conference had been cancelled.

William L. Shirer in *The Rise and Fall of the Third Reich* (Secker and Warburg, London, 1960), pp. 1027–1028, repeats Wheeler-Bennett's story, but again with no mention of source.

7. Veit Osas, *op. cit.*, p. 71.

CHAPTER XVII

1. Fabian von Schlabrendorff, *op. cit.*, pp. 133 and 126 *et seq.*

2. *Ibid.*, p. 136.

3. See p. 134, above.

4. From Prof. G. Schmölders—letter dated 5 July 1963.

5. Kaltenbrunner report, p. 435 (deposition by Colonel Meichssner).

6. From an address by Prof. Alexander Schenk Graf von Stauffenberg.

7. Kaltenbrunner report, p. 435.

8. Information from Colonel (retd.) R—— K——.

9. From an address by Prof. Alexander Schenk Graf von Stauffenberg.

10. Kaltenbrunner report, p. 167.

11. From Rudolf Freiherr von Gersdorff.

12. Von Schlabrendorff, *op. cit.*, p. 134.

13. Eberhard Zeller, *op. cit.*, p. 338; based on a personal report.

14. *Ibid.*; also von Schlabrendorff, *op. cit.*, p. 137.

15. Von Schlabrendorff, *op. cit.*, p. 135.

16. J. W. Wheeler-Bennett, *op. cit.*, p. 596.

17. Kaltenbrunner report, p. 225.

18. Von Schlabrendorff, *op. cit.*, p. 135.

19. Veit Osas, *op. cit.*, pp. 71 *et seq.*

20. From Dr. Paulus van Husen.

21. From Peter Sauerbruch.

22. *Ibid.*

23. *Ibid.*

24. Kaltenbrunner report, pp. 20 and 295.

25. *Ibid.*, pp. 373 *et seq.*

26. *Ibid.*, pp. 305, 306, and 312 *et seq.* Statements concerning Stauffenberg by Finckh and others almost invariably show one clearly defined tendency: it almost seems as if Stauffenberg was a hypnotizer, capable of draining all will power from a man to whom he was talking; he is referred to, for instance, as "not quite normal" (Kaltenbrunner report, p. 305), as having "ridden roughshod" over his partner (p. 306), as having spoken in such a way that "any questioning or counterargument" was impossible (p. 306), and as someone in whose presence "it was hardly possible . . . even to think" (p. 306). Those concerned clearly wished to give the impression that, when committing themselves to Stauffenberg, they were acting under pressure and not of their own free will.

27. From Peter Sauerbruch.

28. Budde and Lütsches, record of hearings, interrogation of Bernardis.

29. Kaltenbrunner report, pp. 523 *et seq.*

30. Lieutenant Urban Thiersch, quoted by Zeller, *op. cit.*, p. 361.

31. Kaltenbrunner report, p. 521.

32. *Ibid.*, p. 522.

33. *Ibid.*, pp. 96, 296, and 297.

34. *Ibid.*, p. 297.

35. From Margarete Gräfin von Hardenberg. See also p. 29.

36. From Peter Sauerbruch. See also p. 29.

37. From Charlotte Gräfin von der Schulenburg.

CHAPTER XVIII

1. Kaltenbrunner report, pp. 206 *et seq.*

2. Albert Krebs, *op. cit.*, p. 265.

3. *Ibid.*, pp. 265 *et seq.*; Kaltenbrunner report, p. 207. On these problems Schulenburg had already worked out far-reaching plans, including the re-organization of the Reich. In addition, by January 1944 he had drawn up an almost complete appointments scheme; it has not survived but is said to have contained the names of some thousand persons from section heads in the ministry of the interior down to district presidents (*Landräte*) and nominated mayors of major cities (Krebs, *op. cit.*, p. 239).

4. See p. 169, below.

5. Kaltenbrunner report, p. 393.

6. From Dr. Marion Gräfin Yorck von Wartenburg; see also Veit Osas, *op. cit.*, p. 16.

7. Kaltenbrunner report, p. 257.

8. See *Ein Mann geht sein Weg*, Julius Leber's writings, speeches, and letters, published by his friends, Mosaik-Verlag, Berlin and Frankfurt, 1952, pp. 280 and 284.

9. *Ibid.*, p. 84.

10. Kaltenbrunner report, p. 352.

11. Osas, *op. cit.*, p. 75.

12. *Ein Mann geht sein Weg*, pp. 290 *et seq.*

13. Kaltenbrunner report, p. 118. The Gestapo report states that Goerdeler said as much in a letter. This seems doubtful, since in the dangerous position in which these people were, expressions of opinion were only committed to paper on the rarest occasions.

14. Kaltenbrunner report, pp. 212, 118, and 179.

15. See p. 167, below.

16. Kaltenbrunner report, p. 212.

17. *Ibid.*, pp. 118, 179, and 212.

18. *Ibid.*, p. 234.

19. Information from Frau Annedore Leber.

20. In this and other instances the juxtaposition in the Gestapo report of information given in the various statements is designed to present the most unfavourable picture possible.

21. Kaltenbrunner report, pp. 247 *et seq.*

22. Osas, *op. cit.*, p. 68. On p. 385 of his *Carl Goerdeler und die deutsche Widerstandsbewegung* (Deutsche Verlagsanstalt, Stuttgart, 1955) Gerhard Ritter says, "The problem was, Whose was the final and ultimate decision regarding the timing and execution of the coup d'état—his [Goerderler's] or Stauffenberg's?" By overemphasizing this question, Ritter presents the Goerdeler-Stauffenberg problem in a false light, for on this particular issue there was in fact no question of any prerogative of decision on which there could be argument. Timing and execution were so dependent on circumstances that there could not be freedom of decision.

The assassination question was another matter. In this case Stauffenberg had refused to be influenced by Goerdeler's objections.

CHAPTER XIX

1. Hans-Bernd Gisevius, *To the Bitter End.* Led by Gisevius, J. W. Wheeler-Bennett and many others have followed the same line.

2. J. W. Wheeler-Bennett, *op. cit.*, p. 618.
Gisevius, *op. cit.*, p. 478: "Stauffenberg, who looked towards reconciliation with Russia. . . ."

3. Kaltenbrunner report, p. 116.

4. *Ibid.*, pp. 111 and 175.

5. *Ibid.*, p. 247.

6. *Ibid.*, pp. 174 *et seq.*

7. See article "Trott und die Aussenpolitik des Widerstandes, in *Vierteljahrshefte für Zeitgeschichte*, No. 3, 1964, p. 309. Trott also proposed to speak to Madame Kollontay, the Soviet ambassador in Stockholm, but in fact they never met.

8. Kaltenbrunner report, pp. 174 *et seq.*

9. See below, p. 178 *et seq.*

10. "Entwurf einer Konzeption zur Verschwörung vom 20 Juli 1944," issued (cyclostyled) by the Institut für Geschichte der Deutsche Akademie der Wissenschaften für Marxismus-Leninismus und Deutsche Militärgeschichte, Potsdam.

11. Kaltenbrunner report, p. 190.

12. *Ibid.*, p. 174: "My work enabled me to obtain an overall view of the foreign policy situation. I had access to the necessary telegrams from German representatives abroad and passed on to Stauffenberg the information I obtained from them."

13. On 20 July the Gestapo found a copy in the possession of Graf Schwerin (see Kaltenbrunner report, pp. 34 *et seq.*). The summary of it given here is based upon the Gestapo report, since the memorandum has not survived in any other form. (Information from Dr. Clarita von Trott zu Solz.)

14. "Trott und die Aussenpolitik des Widerstandes," *op. cit.*, p. 322.

15. Letter from Prof. Rudolf Fahrner.

16. Kaltenbrunner report, p. 502.

17. Letter from Prof. Rudolf Fahrner.

18. *Ein Mann geht sein Weg*, pp. 285 *et seq.*

19. Letter from Prof. Rudolf Fahrner.

20. Kaltenbrunner report, p. 174. This mentions General Marshall as Eisenhower's Chief of Staff—an obvious error; Marshall was, of course, U.S. Chief of Staff.

21. Kaltenbrunner report, pp. 126 *et seq.* An article by Wilhelm Ritter von Schramm, "Zur aussenpolitischen Konzeption Becks und Goerdelers," in *Aus Politik und Zeitgeschichte* (supplement to the weekly *Das Parlament*) of 15 July 1964, pp. 36 *et seq.*, shows that there was considerable similarity between these eleven points and a plan of action agreed on by Rommel and Stülpnagel on 15 May 1944.

22. Kaltenbrunner report, p. 34.

CHAPTER XX

1. *Ein Mann geht sein Weg*, p. 286.

2. From Prof. Georg Smolka. As far as Gräfin von Stauffenberg remembers

(letter dated 1 July 1964) this was the last, or last but one, time when Stauffenberg saw his family. Delp sent a message during the afternoon announcing his arrival, came late in the evening, and stayed until about 11 P.M.

3. Kaltenbrunner report, p. 178.

4. I had written to Colonel General Zeitzler on this subject, but he died before he could answer. Immediately after receiving my letter, however, Zeitzler had commented on it to his wife. I am particularly grateful to Frau Zeitzler for passing this information on to me after her husband's death.

5. Kaltenbrunner report, p. 112.

6. *Ibid.*, pp. 55 and 94; Budde and Lütsches, record of hearings, interrogation of Hagen. This was some German explosive which in the end was not utilized, Colonel Freiherr von Freytag-Lofinghoven, head of the army personal services section, having obtained a mixed British-German charge via the Abwehr (Kaltenbrunner report, p. 129).

7. Graf von Schwerin-Krosigk, *Es geschah in Deutschland*, Wunderlich Verlag, Tübingen, 1952, p. 346.

8. From Friedrich Georgi.

9. Kaltenbrunner report, p. 340.

10. From Colonel (retd.) R——J——.

11. *Ibid.*; Fabian von Schlabrendorff, *op. cit.*, p. 145.

12. J. W. Wheeler-Bennett, *op. cit.*, p. 585.

13. From Nina Gräfin von Stauffenberg (interview 10 October 1962) and Frau Annedore Leber.

14. Wheeler-Bennett, *op. cit.*, p. 627, based on an account by Dr. Otto John. This document has meanwhile been reproduced by Fraenkel and Manvell in *Der 20 Juli Berlin*, Ullstein, Berlin and Frankfurt, 1964, pp. 227 *et seq.*

15. Veit Osas, *op. cit.*, p. 23.

16. Von Schlabrendorff, *op. cit.*, p. 138.

17. Letter from Prof. Rudolf Fahrner.

18. Von Schlabrendorff, *op. cit.*, p. 138.

19. Kaltenbrunner report, pp. 306 and 313.

20. Eberhard Zeller, *op. cit.*, pp. 355 *et seq.*

21. Von Schlabrendorff, *op. cit.*, p. 140.

22. Kaltenbrunner report, p. 127.

23. Account by Dr. Otto John (see note 14).

24. From Friedrich Georgi.

25. Letter from Prof. Rudolf Fahrner.

26. From Peter Sauerbruch.

27. Kaltenbrunner report, pp. 19, 110, and 195.

CHAPTER XXI

1. Budde and Lütsches, record of hearings, interrogation of Stieff.

2. Kaltenbrunner report, p. 91.

3. *Ibid.*, p. 363.

4. *Ein Mann geht sein Weg*, p. 287.

5. Kaltenbrunner report, p. 130.

6. *Ibid.*, p. 119.

7. Budde and Lütsches, record of hearings, interrogation of Klausing; Kaltenbrunner report, pp. 44, 49, and 130.

8. Kaltenbrunner report, p. 21.

9. *Ibid.*, p. 146.

10. From Prof. Dr. Percy Ernst Schramm.

11. Kaltenbrunner report, pp. 136 and 409.

12. Hans-Bernd Gisevius, *op. cit.*, pp. 505, 502, 503.

13. *Ibid.*, p. 504.

14. *Ibid.*, p. 481; Gerhard Ritter (*op. cit.*, pp. 382 *et seq.*) also takes issue with this statement.

15. See p. 150, above.

16. Gisevius, *op. cit.*, p. 495; "In OKW" is in fact an error. Stauffenberg was never in OKW; the army office (AHA/BdE) was subordinate to OKH (army headquarters).

17. Gisevius, *op. cit.*, (German original), p. 338.

18. *Ibid.*, p. 505.

19. *Ibid.* (German original), p. 349.

20. From Dr. Paulus van Husen. There is some lapse of memory here. Stauffen-berg went to Rastenburg on 15 July by air. Either Dr. van Husen is mixing up two incidents, or Stauffenberg in fact left to catch a tram or underground.

21. Hans Speidel, *We Defended Normandy*, Herbert Jenkins, London, 1951, p. 127.

22. National Archives, Alexandria, Virginia, U.S.A. Miscellaneous German Records collection, Microfilm T84, Roll 21.

23. Kaltenbrunner report, p. 21. In all earlier accounts the statement appears that Stauffenberg did not set off the bomb on 15 July because neither Himmler nor Göring was present. This stems from Gisevius (p. 352). He makes out that he was present when Stauffenberg telephoned from the Führer's headquarters, asking whether he should carry on even though Himmler and Göring were not there. Haeften is supposed to have relayed to him "instructions" to do so, but when Stauffenberg got back to the conference room Hitler had already brought the meeting to an end and left.
   This statement does not hold water. After the failure of the 11 July attempt Beck had given express instructions that the attempt was to be made on the very next occasion; moreover on 15 July "Valkyrie" had already been set in motion. It seems completely incredible therefore that Stauffenberg could have been so unsure of himself. Berthold von Stauffenberg's statement convincingly refutes that of Gisevius and there seems no reason to suppose that he was not speaking the truth.

24. Kaltenbrunner report, p. 45.

25. *Ibid.*, p. 362.

26. J. W. Wheeler-Bennett, *op. cit.*, p. 634.

27. Kaltenbrunner report, pp. 101 and 175.

28. *Ibid.*, p. 117.

29. Budde and Lütsches, record of hearings, interrogation of Bernardis.

30. *Ibid.*, interrogations of Bernardis and Graf Yorck von Wartenburg; Kaltenbrunner report, pp. 21 and 146.

31. Gisevius, *op. cit.*, pp. 361 *et seq.* (German original).

32. *Ein Mann geht sein Weg*, p. 292.

33. Eberhard Zeller, *op. cit.*, pp. 375 *et seq.*

34. Waltraud von Götz—letter dated 5 September 1962. Trott spoke to her on 21 July and told her of this conversation.

35. Zeller, *op. cit.*, pp. 489 *et seq.* Zeller does not give his source. I first learned of this oath from Prof. Rudolf Fahrner, and Zeller's version of it comes from him.

Prof. Alexander Schenk Graf von Stauffenberg, who died in 1964, turned this oath into a poem in his book entitled *Vigil*; he connects the oath with a conversation between Berthold and Claus (Alexander Schenk Graf von Stauffenberg, *Denkmal*, edited by Rudolf Fahrner, Küpper, Düsseldorf and Munich, 1964, pp. 21 *et seq.*).

36. From Bernd von Pezold; Stauffenberg made this remark in conversation with Pezold's wife.

CHAPTER XXII

1. My account of the events of 20 July is confined to the important points. The manifold repercussions of the happenings of this day are to be found in detail in Eberhard Zeller, *op. cit.*

2. See Peter Hoffmann, "Zum Attentat in Führerhauptquartier 'Wolfsschanze' am 20 Juli 1944," in *Vierteljahrshefte für Zeitgeschichte*, 1964, No. 3, p. 268—account based on information from John von Freyend; also Kaltenbrunner report, p. 85.

3. The location of the briefing conference was the same as usual, not, as has often been stated, some flimsy hut used only on this particular day. The Security Service report, the technical side of which is summarized in the Kaltenbrunner report, states unequivocally: "The actual scene of the attack was the map room where the daily briefing conferences were held" (Kaltenbrunner report, p. 83). This gives the lie to the statement that Stauffenberg was forced by circumstances to make the attack on a particularly unsuitable day. The attempt planned for 15 July would also have had to be carried out in the same place.

4. Hoffmann, *op. cit.*, pp. 270 *et seq.*

5. Adolf Heusinger, *Befehl im Widerstreit*, Wunderlich, Tübingen, 1950, pp. 354 *et seq.*

6. Kaltenbrunner report, p. 86.

7. Leber and Moltke, *op. cit.*, p. 205 (Lieutenant Colonel Sander's report).

8. Kaltenbrunner report, p. 86.

9. *Ibid.*, p. 84. On the subject of the purpose of the second bomb see also Hoffmann, *op. cit.*, pp. 283 *et seq.*

10. Kaltenbrunner report, p. 330.

11. See p. 195, below.

12. Hans-Bernd Gisevius, *op. cit.*, p. 532.

13. From Friedrich Georgi.

14. Budde and Lütsches, record of hearings, interrogation of Hoepner; also Kaltenbrunner report, p. 377.

15. Budde and Lütsches, record of hearings, interrogation of Hoepner; Leber and Moltke, *op. cit.*, p. 114, where Friedrich Georgi confirms the statement made by General Hoepner to the People's Court that General Olbricht had not set the "Valkyrie" plan in motion only after Stauffenberg's telephone call from Rangsdorf.

16. Kaltenbrunner report, p. 377.

17. Fabian von Schlabrendorff, *op. cit.*, p. 149; Budde and Lütsches, record of hearings, interrogation of Hoepner.

18. Budde and Lütsches, record of hearings, interrogation of Hoepner.

19. Von Schlabrendorff, *op. cit.*, p. 150. Schlabrendorff's account is based on information given by Fromm himself while under arrest.

20. Budde and Lütsches, record of hearings, interrogation of Hoepner.

21. Kaltenbrunner report, pp. 65 *et seq.*

22. Budde and Lütsches, record of hearings, interrogation of Hoepner.

23. Kaltenbrunner report, p. 191.

24. Veit Osas, *op. cit.*, p. 82.

25. Gisevius, *op. cit.*, p. 536.

26. From R—— K——.

27. Kaltenbrunner report, p. 22.

28. Rudolf Langhaeuser—letters dated 26 February and 28 March 1963.

29. Kaltenbrunner report, p. 63.

30. From R—— K——.

31. Kaltenbrunner report, p. 377.

32. Rudolf Langhaeuser—letter dated 26 February 1963.

33. From *20 Juli 1944*, published by the Bundeszentrale für Heimatdienst, Bonn, 1960, p. 157.

34. Kaltenbrunner report, pp. 105 *et seq.*

35. Peter Hoffmann, article entitled "Zum Ablauf des Staatsstreichversuches des 20 Juli 1944 in den Wehrkreisen," in *Vierteljahrshefte für Zeitgeschichte*, No. 3, 1964, p. 390.

36. Eberhard Zeller, *op. cit.*, pp. 441 *et seq.*

37. Kaltenbrunner report, p. 75.

38. *Ibid.*, p. 64.

39. *Ibid.*, p. 330.

40. Osas, *op. cit.*, p. 42.

41. Kaltenbrunner report, p. 46.

42. Wolfgang Müller, *Gegen eine neue Dolchstosslegende: Ein Erlebnisbericht zum 20 Juli 1944*, Verlag Das andere Deutschland, Hannover, 1947.

43. Kaltenbrunner report, p. 336.

44. Dr. Otto John's account—see Chap. 20, note 14.

45. Kaltenbrunner report, p. 23.

46. Budde and Lütsches, record of hearings, interrogation of Bernardis.

47. *Ibid.*, interrogation of Hoepner.

48. From Friedrich Georgi; he did not finally stand the squadron down until the night of 20–21 July.

49. Zeller, *op. cit.*, p. 399. Stauffenberg's last cry has generally been given as "Long live our sacred Germany," but this cannot be accepted as certain. Wolfgang Müller, *op. cit.*, p. 90, and Hans Hagen in *Zurischen Eid und Befehl*, Munich, 1959, p. 48, give "Long live a free Germany." Edgar Salin, *op. cit.*, p. 324 supports "Long live our secret Germany," a phrase current in the George circle. There is a further though not altogether reliable report that the cry was simply "Long live Germany."

50. Wolfgang Foerster, *Generaloberst Ludwig Beck*, Isar-Verlag Munich, 1953, p. 122 (words of Beck's on 16 July 1938).

51. Army instruction 300/1 "command" dated 17 October 1933, p. 5, para. 15.

52. Letter to Ruth von Blomberg.

APPENDIX I

1. Published in *Wissen und Wehr*, No. 7, 1938 (pp. 459 *et seq.*). See also p. 53 of this book.

2. Parachute detachments are commando-type units. Parachute troops are parachute formations as used in the last war.

3. An example was the employment of a parachute division at Moerdijk, Maastricht, in 1940.

4. An example was the use of parachute troops on D-Day in June 1944.

APPENDIX II

1. The original is in the possession of Ernst Alexander Paulus.

INDEX

Note: According to Article 109, para. 2, of the Weimar Constitution "titles" were to be considered "merely as part of the name." Prior to 1919 the designation "Graf" (Count), being a title, stood before the christian name; subsequently, in accordance with the provisions of the Constitution, it was placed immediately before the surname. The full family name invariably includes "Schenk"; since this indicated an official position dating from the Middle Ages, the title "Graf" still came immediately before the surname. In the case of the parents, who spent the greater part of their life under the monarchy, I have used the old order of title and name, *i.e.,* "Graf Alfred Schenk von Stauffenberg." In the case of the sons, however, I have followed the Weimar Constitution and put the name as follows: "Claus Schenk Graf von Stauffenberg." Stauffenberg himself cut down his signature to the bare name—"Claus Graf Stauffenberg."